FROM EXCLUSION TO INCLUSION

FROM EXCLUSION TO INCLUSION

The Long Struggle for African American Political Power

Ralph C. Gomes
AND
Linda Faye Williams

CONTRIBUTIONS IN AFRO-AMERICAN
AND AFRICAN STUDIES,
NUMBER 148

GREENWOOD PRESS
New York • Westport, Connecticut • London

Library of Congress Cataloging-in-Publication Data

From exclusion to inclusion : the long struggle for African American
    political power / edited by Ralph C. Gomes and Linda Faye Williams.
        p.   cm.—(Contributions in Afro-American and African
    studies, ISSN 0069-9624 ; no. 148)
    Includes bibliographical references and index.
    ISBN 0-313-27968-3 (alk. paper)
    1. Afro-Americans—Politics and government.   I. Gomes, Ralph C.
II. Williams, Linda F.   III. Series.
E185.615.F76   1992
323.1'196073—dc20   91-20041

British Library Cataloguing in Publication Data is available.

Library of Congress Catalog Card Number: 91-20041
ISBN: 0-313-27968-3
ISSN: 0069-9624

First published in 1992

Greenwood Press, 88 Post Road West, Westport, CT 06881
An imprint of Greenwood Publishing Group, Inc.

Printed in the United States of America

The paper used in this book complies with the
Permanent Paper Standard issued by the National
Information Standards Organization (Z39.48–1984).

10 9 8 7 6 5 4 3 2 1

To our family: Lionel and Lena Gomes,
   W.C. and Wilma Williams, and Chris,
   Alex, and Sha-sha.

Contents

Tables

Preface

This book is an outgrowth of a conference sponsored by Howard University in Washington, D.C., in November 1989. That conference was titled "One Third of a Nation"—the name drawn from census projections that blacks, Latinos, and Asians would compose one-third of the population of the United States by the year 2000. The conference covered thirteen issue areas that this soon-to-be one-third of the nation needs to explore in order to improve its status in the United States and to aid the nation in a changing world. These issue areas were:

(1) voting and political participation;
(2) substance abuse—causes, prevention, and treatment;
(3) immigration, migration, and United States foreign policy;
(4) employment and labor;
(5) education, finance, innovation, and effectiveness;
(6) the role of religion in the black community;
(7) economic development and empowerment;
(8) science and technology;
(9) black family life;
(10) housing—equity availability and affordability;
(11) health—status, service delivery, prevention, and care;
(12) media, communication, and culture; and
(13) historically black colleges and universities.

The papers herein were developed for a series of panels in the first issue area—

voting and political participation—and represent the first publication stemming from the conference.

The goals for the three-day conference were to address issues related to the conditions of black Americans as well as other racial/linguistic minorities in the twenty-first century. To do so, conference participants were charged with assessing the past, analyzing the present, and designing guidelines for the future that could be carried out in the public and private sectors in each of the issue areas. The chapters in this book generally follow this format and organization.

The contributors to this volume, while generally accepting the premise that blacks have made considerable political progress, particularly in the last twenty-five years since passage of the Voting Rights Act, come together around a common perception that many obstacles and constraints to black political progress remain. A thread that unites this collection is that new forms of political methods (including protest and interest group activity), coalition politics, and lures for greater black political participation must be developed to make further progress. The spirit of this volume accepts as an initial premise that much remains to be done before racial and linguistic minorities in the United States are fully part of the United States and beneficiaries of its largesse. We hope that this book makes at least a modest contribution to identifying ways in which a better America, replete with full inclusion of all its citizens, can be built.

We would like to thank Howard University's task force for the "One-third of a Nation" conference (Lorenzo Morris, Ura Jean Oyemade, Leroy Wells, and Gloria Smith) and the officers of the Howard University Senate (James E. Cheek, then president of the university; Taft Broome; Robert Murray; and Beatrice Adderley-Kelly) for their scholarly and financial support. We are also grateful to the political participation committee of the conference. Committee members were Betty Bennett, Victor Dates, Ralph Gomes, William Lewis, Lorenzo Morris, Frances Murphy, and Linda Faye Williams. The charge of the committee was to identify the pressing problems in the area of political participation and to recommend solutions for these problems.

Lorenzo Morris, in particular, was one of the driving forces of this section. His advice, always witty criticism, and geniality have been invaluable. We appreciate, as well, conversations over the years on the merits and limits of black political participation with Carol Page, Ronald Walters, Lani Guinier, William Ellis, Lezli Baskerville, Thomas Cavanagh, Emmett Carson, Peyton McCrary, Eddie Williams, Jewel Prestage, Joseph McCormick, Sheila Harmon, William Nelson, Georgia Persons, Chandler Davidson, Adolph Reed, Paul Peterson, Joyce Ladner, Willie Smith, Mack Jones, and Katherine Tate.

We also gratefully acknowledge Odette Davis for getting us through the mysteries of word processing and being a real sport about working at odd times and hours.

As is customary, we unfortunately realize that all mistakes are those of the editors and contributors.

FROM EXCLUSION TO INCLUSION

Introduction

Ralph C. Gomes and Linda Faye Williams

As the United States approaches the twenty-first century, the long struggle for African American political power and the fight for inclusion take on new meaning.[1] No longer can African Americans afford to see their fight for political power as simply the fight for the vote within a political and economic system that is increasingly exclusionary and crisis-ridden. Rather, the question of electoral participation is prelude to and preparation for the next stage of the historical struggle for equality not only of the races, but of the classes. C. L. R. James understood this complexity of race and class, and of economics and politics, when he wrote: "The race question is subsidiary to the class question in politics, and to think of imperialism in terms of race is disastrous. But to neglect the racial factor as merely incidental is an error only less grave than to make it fundamental."[2]

Mindful of the inextricable link between politics and economics and the role of class in the American political economy, this book focuses on the racial factor. By providing a balanced account, the book assesses the historical and current position of African Americans in politics throughout the nation. By assessing the impact of the Voting Rights Act of 1965, this book clarifies the significance of the struggle for voting rights and how extensively equitable voting rights have been achieved. By focusing on the economic and legal contexts of African American politics, the book evaluates both the potential for success and the built-in limitations in U.S. society for improving black status and everyday life-chances through the electoral arena. By subjecting the possibilities for coalition politics to careful analysis, the book provides useful insights into the pitfalls and opportunities of coalition-building among minorities and between minorities and various classes of whites. By providing recommendations for increasing and benefiting from African American political participation in both domestic and foreign policy arenas, the book's goal is to provide a strategy for the new politics that takes into consideration racial and class factors.

Throughout the chapters, evidence is presented that demonstrates that the history of American voter participation and its impact are strewn with frustrating twists and turns. Denied basic citizenship rights under slavery, African Americans first gained access to the ballot after the Civil War when ratification of the Fifteenth Amendment forbade states from denying the right to vote on the basis of race. For about two decades during Reconstruction in the late nineteenth century, African Americans actively participated in state and local politics, voting regularly and electing some African Americans to public office.

In the mid-1880s through the 1890s, however, southern white Democrats, with northern white Republicans' acquiescence, systematically removed African Americans from electoral politics through voting regulations such as the "grandfather clause," poll taxes, and literacy tests, through electoral procedures, such as the white primary, and all too often through acts of white terrorism perpetrated against African American voters. Indeed, there is perhaps no better indicator of the importance of voter participation than the lengths to which whites throughout the nation went to keep African Americans from voting. The strong resistance of whites to African Americans' voting belies the idea that there is no power to be gained by means of electoral participation.

The central questions of this book are: What has the Voting Rights Act of 1965 wrought? To what extent have African Americans gained access to the ballot? Does access mean the ability to cast an "effective" or "meaningful" ballot? What was and is the role of African American organizations in mobilizing African American voters? To what extent has progress in African American voter participation resulted in the election of more African American officials? What barriers or electoral structures still hamper African American political progress? What economic constraints impinge upon the relevance of black electoral participation? Is African American electoral participation enough to improve African American life-chances in the social and economic spheres? Can African American elected officials produce "policy payoffs" for the African American poor in general or the so-called "underclass" in particular? What other kinds of action might be necessary? Is multiracial/multiethnic coalition politics the frontier for a new politics of race and class? If so, which groups are likely to be the most reliable coalition partners for the African American masses? How might the development of successful coalitions affect the 1990s redistricting process? How might African Americans have more influence in not only domestic politics but also foreign policy?

To answer these questions, part one of the book focuses on the historic struggle for securing and expanding African American voting rights; part two focuses on the economic, legal, and cultural context that often constrains the impact of African American politics; and part three focuses on prospects and directions for African American politics in the immediate future.

The chapters of the book are written by a diverse group of scholars and practitioners. Most are political scientists and sociologists; others are voting rights
litigators and voter mobilization practitioners. An overview of each chapter is
provided below.

PART I: THE ELECTORAL ARENA: FROM EXCLUSION
TO ACCESS

This part contains three chapters. In chapter 1, Sonia Jarvis provides a historical overview of the long struggle for voting rights for blacks and other excluded Americans from the Declaration of Independence and the Articles of
Confederation to the modern Civil Rights Movement and the ensuing Voting
Rights Act of 1965.

Jarvis points out that securing black voting rights in the South was one of the
principal goals of the Civil Rights Movement of the 1950s and 1960s. Through
mass protests, voter registration drives, congressional lobbying, and suits in
federal courts, civil rights activists fought a fight costly in both jail sentences
served and people maimed and killed, to eliminate discriminatory electoral
practices that obstructed black political participation and to secure federal
protection of black political rights. The crowning achievement of the campaign, according to Jarvis, was the Voting Rights Act, which outlawed unfair
electoral procedures and required the Justice Department to supervise southern elections.

With passage of the Voting Rights Act, many blacks registered and voted.
Yet, analyzing data collected by the United States Census Bureau, Jarvis finds
that even by 1968, growth in the proportion of blacks voting in presidential
elections stagnated, and in later years, the proportion declined. This should be
hardly surprising, because blacks were subject to the same forces that generated declining turnout among whites and other groups (for example, reduction
in the age of the electorate as the first baby boomers reached voting age, the potentially negative influence of Vietnam and Watergate on governmental trust
and voter participation, and so forth). What is notable, however, is that the gap
between black and white voter participation rates narrowed considerably in the
last twenty years. The narrowing of the gap between black and white voter participation is an important sign of blacks' increasing access to the ballot.

In chapter 2, Dianne Pinderhughes discusses the role of black organizations
in producing the black political progress documented by Jarvis. Pinderhughes
examines not only those organizations specifically devoted to securing voting
rights and mobilizing the black vote, but more general civil rights organizations
such as the National Association for the Advancement of Colored People
(NAACP) and the National Urban League (NUL), and especially historic and
current black women's organizations. Pinderhughes shows that the oft-ignored
efforts of black women have been key—inside the better-known civil rights
groups and especially within those groups specifically devoted to voting rights.

For example, practically all of the key voter mobilization groups (for example the Voter Education Project, Operation Big Vote/National Coalition of Black Voter Participation, and so forth) from the 1960s to today have been or are headed by black women. These black women are following the footsteps of earlier black women's civic organizations and sororities at least since the days of Ida B. Wells Barnett. Not only in the electoral sphere, but in protest politics as well, black women have been key players in the effort to improve the access of all blacks to the ballot, Pinderhughes concludes.

Theresa Chambliss demonstrates in chapter 3 that as more blacks voted, more blacks were elected to public office. The number of black elected officials grew from fewer than 500 in 1965 to 7,370 in January 1970. The South, where most blacks remained disenfranchised until 1965, has been the region of greatest progress. In January 1990, there were sixty-four times more black elected officials in the South than there were in 1965 (4,955 compared to 78). Since approximately two out of every three black elected officials represent a majority black jurisdiction, the increase in the number of black elected officials is an important measure of black voting strength.

Chambliss points out that blacks have also made gains in party politics. Although the Republican party remains basically a white people's bastion, the adoption in the mid-1960s of proportionality principles required Democratic state party organizations to ensure the selection of convention delegations that reflected as nearly as possible the racial and gender composition of the Democrats' electorate. This led to sharp increases in the number of black delegates to the Democratic National Conventions. Between 1964, when the last convention under the old order took place, and 1988, the proportion of black delegates grew from 2.8 percent to 23.1 percent. Perhaps the best evidence of black access to influence in the Democratic party is that Ronald Brown, a black man, was elected chairman of the Democratic National Committee after the 1988 presidential election, and Representative William Gray of Pennsylvania became the majority whip in the United States House of Representatives in 1989.

Chambliss concludes that the Voting Rights Act was not only a central accomplishment of the Civil Rights Movement, but also a milestone in blacks' struggle for political representation. The act has gone a long way toward reducing the gap between black and white electoral participation, and it has improved black representation in the political arena. By 1990, blacks had held elective office in almost every category except president and vice president.

Chambliss cautions, however, that blacks remain severely underrepresented in every kind of office and at every level of government. Still, her basic point is that blacks would not have achieved even the present level of progress without the Voting Rights Act.

In sum, part I provides strong evidence demonstrating that the Voting Rights Act of 1965 is probably the most effective piece of the civil rights legislation passed in the mid- to late-1960s. Still, has the Voting Rights Act achieved as much as was expected, or are there still continuing barriers impeding black political progress? Moreover, what has been the impact of the securing of voting rights and the election of black officials on the everyday lives of the masses of African Americans? These questions are taken up in part II.

PART II: THE PRESENT LEGAL, ECONOMIC, AND CULTURAL CONTEXT OF AFRICAN AMERICAN POLITICS

This section focuses on continuing constraints on black political participation and the limits of political participation to date in producing change for black Americans in the social and economic spheres.

While Frank Parker agrees with Jarvis, Pinderhughes, and Chambliss that the Voting Rights Act has done much to re-enfranchise blacks, he emphasizes in chapter 4 that other electoral practices or barriers still stand in the way of blacks casting a "meaningful ballot." Such barriers include: (1) minority vote dilution through sophisticated legal and administrative barriers such as at-large electoral systems, racial gerrymandering, unfair candidate slating procedures, and runoff requirements; (2) class barriers to participation, such as poverty and lack of education; (3) psychological barriers, such as the lack of a habit of voting derived from years of exclusion from voting, fear, deference to whites, and apathy; and (4) institutional obstacles, such as the problem of inadequate information concerning voter registration procedures, the often-inconvenient time and place of registration, and the scarcity of black registration officials, especially in the South.

This latter factor (that is, cumbersome, diverse, and complex registration requirements) is the most important remaining ballot *access* issue, according to Parker. He points out that some social scientists argue that difficult registration procedures are in fact the chief barrier to increasing electoral participation among all groups, but especially poor and minority groups.

To be sure, most Americans who are registered to vote, do so. According to the United States Census Bureau, more than 80 percent of both blacks and whites who were registered to vote in November 1988 voted in the presidential election that year. As Parker points out, these findings have led many voting rights advocates to champion making registration easier. Parker discusses legislation currently before Congress that would mandate simplified and more convenient registration procedures (such as registration by mail, registration in government agencies including those extensively used by the poor, registration on the same day of voting, fairer purge systems, and so forth). In addition, he points out, many voting rights activists are seeking to institute these same changes in state and local elections, either through lawsuits or by lobbying state legislatures.

These actions could increase ballot access, but Parker concludes that other barriers lie at the heart of the thrust for a "meaningful ballot" because they reduce the impact of black voting. Parker points out that it has been relatively well-established, for instance, that at-large or multimember districts tend to dilute the impact of minority votes. For example, cities with high black populations that use district elections are more than twice as likely to have a high proportion of blacks in their city council as similarly populated cities that use at-large elections.

Parker adds that there is some evidence that at-large election systems are declining. The decline is somewhat predictable, because at-large systems have been embroiled in controversy and legal challenge in light of the Voting Rights Act amendments in 1982 and subsequent broad interpretation of these amendments by the Supreme Court in *Thornburgh v. Gingles*. The amendments to Section two of the Voting Rights Act make it clear that laws that have the effect of diluting minority votes are just as impermissible as those that are accompanied by discriminatory intent. In *Gingles,* the Supreme Court—in light of changes in the law—struck down several multimember state legislative districts in North Carolina based upon their discriminatory voting results. Factors considered by the Court included the pattern of historical discrimination, racial appeals in campaigns, racially polarized bloc voting, responsiveness on the part of present public officials to minority group interests, and the proportion of minorities elected to public office.

Subsequent decisions in the lower federal courts have supported the ruling in *Gingles*. For example, in *Dillard v. Crenshaw County,* the United States District Court in Central Alabama ordered several Alabama counties to elect all their county commissioners from single-member districts. As a result of other settlements surrounding *Crenshaw,* 180 counties and cities throughout the state were required to eliminate discriminatory at-large voting and to adopt single-member districts. This change figured heavily in the election of more than 250 new black county commissioners and city council members.

The shift from the right to vote to the right to cast a meaningful vote expands the issues of minority voting rights beyond southern politics and beyond places with large black populations, according to Parker. For example, in *McNeal v. Springfield,* the central Illinois United States District Court ruled that Springfield had to change its election system to a district plan and expand the size of the council in order to create a black majority district in the city. Springfield is only about 10 percent black. A similar decision was reached in *Derickson v. City of Danville*. The central Illinois United States District Court ordered the city of Danville to elect its council members by district and expand its legislative body. The change in Danville's election system from at-large to district resulted in the election of the first two black council members in the city's history.

Parker concludes that these developments indicate that as late as 1990 structural barriers continue to play a major role in impeding progress in black political empowerment. Once these barriers are removed, black voters will have new opportunities to gain black representation at all levels of government and in all regions of the nation.

Walda Fishman, Ralph Gomes, Nelson Peery, and Jerome Scott argue that the more important barriers to meaningful black political progress, however, are not predominantly political but rather economic ones. In chapter 5, they point out that even as more and more blacks have been elected to public office, more and more blacks have fallen into poverty. Using the framework of dialectical materialism, politics is viewed as the concentrated expression of economics by Fishman, Gomes, Peery, and Scott. Thus, the Civil Rights Movement and the election of African Americans to office was possible during the stage of the expansion of the United States and world capitalist economy in the post-WW II period. Similarly, the recent roll-back of civil and constitutional rights and the genocidal attack on the African American people is the necessary expression of the current stage of contraction of that economy and is the leading edge of the general fascist attack on the entire United States working class, according to the authors of chapter 5. In this period of economic contraction, they add, African American elected officials and African American corporate and professional elites are especially constrained and limited in their ability to deliver to the masses the goods and services the masses need by the very dynamics of the capitalist economy. The position of African American workers, conditioned by the legacy of slavery, places them at the heart of the United States working class as the most exploited and oppressed section, but also as the most revolutionary section.

At this stage in history, participation in electoral politics is mainly important for providing an invaluable learning experience about "what is possible" through this form of political activity. At the same time, the mobilization of the masses through the electoral arena sets the stage for their political organization for other forms of activity, including the actual revolutionary transformation of society.

The authors contend that new conditions of contraction of the United States and the world capitalist economy both demand and make possible the politics of social transformation. The African American workers cannot tolerate politics as usual, nor can the working class as a whole. Today the revolution in the forces of production—that is, electronically based production replacing machine-based production—is the foundation of the social, economic, and political upheaval that is shaking up society in the United States and the world. The capitalist organization of society around machine production, the private ownership of the productive forces, and the distribution of the necessities of life based on wages and the market system is no longer viable. The workers have lower and lower wages and the capitalists can circulate fewer and fewer of their goods and services.

Fishman, Gomes, Peery, and Scott conclude that society has entered the epoch of an objective and historically necessary social revolution. The social relations of production and the organization of society must be brought into line with the new productive forces. The African American masses, more and more of whom are superfluous workers within the contracting capitalist world economy, face genocide within capitalism. They must prepare for the attainment of power in society. The working class, organized around the urgent lead of the black worker, must plan and carry out the transformation of society necessary for human survival and human development.

In chapter 6, Robert Smith also argues that politics as routinely practiced in the United States by black Americans is not enough to alter the "terrible conditions of the American underclass." As a result, the life-chances and conditions of the bottom third of black America have grown worse by almost any measure of well-being. This situation persists, according to Smith, because despite black progress in winning electoral office, blacks have been unable to obtain sufficient resources to pressure the system to yield substantive policies for the poor.

Meanwhile, Smith argues, the primary agenda of black Americans has not changed much since the early 1900s when the Niagara Movement was formed. From those days through the formation of the NAACP and its successors, the black agenda has centered around not only freedom and social justice, but also substantive equality. At the heart of the demand for equality is the demand for a full employment economy. Although numerous black conferences have been held to define the agenda of blacks, this demand has always been central.

Smith points out, however, that demand has been softened as black leaders and would-be leaders become so thoroughly integrated into institutional structures and processes that they become removed both physically and psychologically from the mass base of the black community. Rather than being leaders for the black poor, the black institutional elite today, according to Smith, act in the classic tradition of middle-class liberal reformers, pursuing a top-down hierarchical model of social change.

This is hardly a result of innocence or naivety, Smith adds. Most black leaders know that the conditions of the black poor cannot be effectively addressed without changes in the structure of the national economy. But in order to maintain their status among white leadership, they act as if fundamental changes can come about as a result of playing routine power games in Washington or in city politics.

Smith points out that he is not arguing that routine institutional politics is not necessary, but simply that it is not enough. What is needed, he says—following the view of Ronald Walters—is a "balanced strategy" of politics and protest.

In sum, part II provides dismal testimony regarding the weakness of black political progress in producing benefits for most blacks—especially the black poor. Part of the problem is continuing electoral barriers weakening the chances for blacks to elect those candidates of their choice, but another part of the problem (and a larger one, according to the chapters in this section) is the very nature of the American political economy and the practice of politics as usual. How can blacks overcome these constraints and barriers? This is the subject of part III.

PART III: CHALLENGES AND PROSPECTS FOR THE FUTURE

The chapters in this section look at some possible opportunities (and pit-falls) for blacks in the political arena in the immediate future.

In chapter 7, Ralph Gomes and Linda Faye Williams argue that the new frontier of black politics, given the economic, cultural, and practical constraints discussed in part II, is coalition politics. The historical and current record of African Americans in coalition politics and the implications of this record for the future are discussed. Second, to provide a perspective for the following analysis, theoretical and methodological issues of coalition formation and maintenance are presented. Third, two *historical* examples of coalition politics involving African Americans are examined. Fourth, two *current* examples of coalitions involving African Americans are examined. Fifth, based on a study of these four examples of African American involvement in coalition politics, an analysis of what worked, what did not work, and why is presented. Lessons are derived and recommendations made for building more successful "winning coalitions" involving African Americans in the future.

In general, Gomes and Williams argue that future advances in electing blacks to public office and in struggling for black demands for equality are increasingly dependent on a coalition of working-class members of all races; but they point to many practical difficulties in building such a coalition. Working-class members have rarely united across the races in this country; and when they have, as behind agrarian populists in the late nineteenth century, coalitions have been difficult to maintain and are short-lived.

Gomes and Williams point out, however, that coalition politics per se is nothing new for blacks, and the kinds of groups likely to join coalitions with blacks are also not new. From the formation of the NAACP to the elections of 1989, the non-African Americans who have supported African American causes have been liberal, relatively affluent, well-educated white professionals, according to Gomes and Williams.

Thus, Gomes and Williams conclude that although emphasis on a class-based lower income coalition touches the heart of objective needs of the great bulk of African Americans, other minority Americans, and white working-class Americans, the history of interracial coalition-building in the United States demonstrates the continuing difficulty of forming such a coalition. There is not only the problem of producing an alliance between African Americans and working class whites. Even among ethnic and racial minorities, there is a general pattern of conflict and competition rather than cooperation. Thus, African Americans often worry about ceasing to be the largest minority; Latinos often view African Americans as keeping them from getting their just due; in cities such as Philadelphia and Detroit, Arab-Americans and African Americans often oppose each other; in the District of Columbia and New York, Koreans and other Asians sometimes find themselves in violent conflict with African Americans; and much attention has been given to the conflict between Jews and Af-rican Americans.

Hence, Gomes and Williams state, just as in 1909 when the NAACP was founded, upwardly mobile whites are more likely than their more unfortunate brothers to support or join issues-oriented coalitions and electoral coalitions with African American partners today. A minority-based coalition between Latinos, Asians, other minorities, and African Americans has not materialized in an effective way. The means by which to build a class-based coalition in this nation remain to be discovered, they conclude. In addition, as long as middle- and upper-status African Americans suffer from vestiges of racial discrimina-tion, race-based coalitions remain the order of the day. Meanwhile, Gomes and Williams point out, coalitions of African Americans with upwardly mobile whites have the potential for having high entry prices and consequences. Those who benefit from the economic status quo are hardly eager to support calls for the kind of fundamental restructuring of the economy that the vast majority of African Americans might need to move forward. The more that economic is-sues dominate the political agenda, the more coalitions of African Americans and upwardly mobile whites have the potential for falling apart. In short, a coa-lition with either class of whites and some minorities remains fragile and diffi-cult to maintain.

Gomes and Williams argue that in attempts to build such coalitions, then, African American groups and candidates are often likely to downplay racial and economic issues. From the standpoint of poor African Americans, the question is whether what such coalitions win, when they win, is worth the effort.

To be sure, Gomes and Williams point out, there have been significant pay-offs flowing from African American involvement in past coalitions. The struc-ture of legal segregation of the races has been mostly dismantled. A multitude of public accommodations from schools to washrooms have been integrated or at least desegregated. In most places, blacks can now vote. The number of African American elected officials has grown. Important changes in the social structure of African American communities have resulted from higher education and skills levels, rising incomes, and better occupations for a substantial minority of Afri-can Americans. Yet, they stress, it is important to thoroughly consider that as higher-status African Americans have moved upward in American society and sometimes out of African American communities, there has been increased class bifurcation among African Americans. While a substantial and influential minor-ity of African Americans have benefited from the payoffs of past coalitions, then, a large majority of African Americans have fallen farther and farther behind. Ac-cording to Gomes and Williams, it is this bifurcation that accounts for much of the lack of progress revealed in important overall African American/white socio-economic indicators such as the median-income gap between whites and African Americans, residential segregation, and so forth.

Thus Gomes and Williams conclude, it remains to be seen whether a win-ning coalition of African Americans, other minorities, and whites can be mobilized in the interests of the poor. Since African Americans remain disproportionately poor, this has strong implications for the interests of African Americans viewed as a whole.

Yet, only the emergence of a genuine coalition on the left with strong roots in working class communities of all racial and ethnic groups could improve the chances for the bulk of African America. Finally, Gomes and Williams argue that the potential components of this new and larger coalition capable of determining rewards in American society are still in the free political marketplace. Blacks, other minorities, and progressive whites are not being coopted by the increasingly restrictive major parties. Given the strong prospect of continued political and economic retrenchment, the growing divisions between housed and homeless, employed and structurally unemployed, rich and poor, the coming fights over redistricting, presidential politics, and a host of other issues, the response to a coalition invitation might be stronger in the near future. Much, according to Gomes and Williams, depends on whether the friends of coalition politics have the courage, will, and skill to organize.

Walter Hill, in chapter 8, points out that the redistricting battles of the 1990s provide an opportunity for developing such coalitions. Hill begins by discussing the new technology developed by the Census Bureau both for counting the population and disseminating the results of the count. He argues that the new ability to use census tapes on personal computers will open the process of political cartography to far more players than ever before. Minority groups armed with the census, political data, and the new and more inexpensive software and personal computers will be able to draw sophisticated maps representing their interests; they also will be more easily able to see the effects of maps drawn by state legislatures that include racial gerrymanders.

Hill cautions that population figures demonstrate few places where blacks will be able to pick up new congressional districts. Indeed, he points out that some of the congressional districts presently represented by blacks are among the nation's top population loses. In short, blacks must be politically organized to protect the districts currently represented by blacks. Opportunities for expanding the number of districts represented by blacks depend on the successful participation of blacks in coalitions—especially coalitions with Latinos in states such as Texas and Florida.

Chapter 10 by Elliott Skinner turns attention from the domestic to the international context. Skinner argues that one task for African Americans in the immediate future is to develop mechanisms and build institutions with which to play a larger role in the foreign policy of the United States. We points out that African Americans have had a long tradition of interest in international affairs but that interest has been largely ignored by the larger society. Even the centuries-long interest of blacks in Africa was generally overlooked by most white Americans. Instead, Skinner points out, foreign policy has been under the control of a small, ingrown elite of white men clustered in Washington and New York.

The danger of leaving foreign policy formulation and execution to the present actors, Skinner writes, is due to the rapid changes taking place in the global system that make past notions clearly inadequate for the United States' future. Vietnam and other recent American foreign policy initiatives suggest that those responsible for United States foreign policy were not the brightest and the best. The fact that African Americans, Latinos, and Asians are a larger proportion of the total American population presents the United States with an opportunity. Many of these people, Skinner concludes, understand other cultures and peoples better than the present set of decision makers do. The inclusion of their voices in making U.S. foreign policy could help the United States deal better in the new world of multiple power centers.

Using the Free South Africa Movement as an example of the merits of African American influence in international affairs, Skinner calls for African Americans to assert boldly their perspective on foreign policy; by doing so they will help the United States deal with the problems of a new century that will affect the entire nation.

The final chapter provides several specific recommendations for producing fuller inclusion of African Americans in the polity of the nation. These recommendations are preceded by a brief discussion of general conclusions derived from the preceding chapters and are made in the context of these general conclusions. Just how to proceed to build the political will in order to realize these recommendations is also explored.

CONCLUSION

By the year 2000, African Americans, Latinos, and Asians will compose one-third of the nation's population. They will have an unprecedented opportunity to influence domestic and foreign policy if they are organized and if they heavily participate in the nation's politics. Expanding the full range of political participation and influence of these soon-to-be one-third-of-the-nation Americans in domestic and international decision-making must continue to be a number-one priority for black Americans, other minority groups, and all those committed to a fair, equitable, and just society.

The goal of this book is to encourage discussion and debate about past, present, and future roles of the electoral process and its relation to the larger political forces that shape the contours of the racial and linguistic "minority" experience in the United States. Here, the focus is on black Americans, but many of the findings have some applicability to other groups. Thus, the following chapters are offered as a modest toehold for the struggle for greater inclusion of African Americans and other racial/linguistic minorities in the power bases of this society.

NOTES

1. The terms "black," "African American," and "Afro-American" are used interchangeably throughout this work. At this writing, there is no clearly preferred term. In September 1990, however, the Joint Center for Political Studies/Gallup Organization Survey found that slightly more than seven of every ten African Americans preferred the term "black." There are at least two theoretical reasons for preferring the term "black." First, it succinctly describes a racial identity and status based on color that is shared to some degree by other people of color with different ancestral lineage as opposed to an ethnic identity and status based on nationality. Blacks struggled in the 1960s to *not* be considered as just one more ethnic group among many, because that had not been their real experience. Unlike ethnic whites, they had been oppressed and separated on the basis of color from all whites. Although "they came before the Mayflower," skin color stigmatization had kept them from moving up any so-called ethnic ladder. Second, reference to the black community is a convenient proxy for an insular group that is politically cohesive, historically stigmatized, economically depressed, and socially isolated.

2. Quoted in Manning Marable, *Black American Politics: From Washington Marches to Jesse Jackson* (London: Verso, 1985), 1.

Part I

The Electoral Arena:
From Exclusion to Access

Historical Overview: African Americans and the Evolution of Voting Rights

Sonia R. Jarvis

> We hold these truths to be self-evident that all men are created equal, that they are endowed by their Creator with certain inalienable rights, that among these are life, liberty, and the pursuit of happiness.
> —*The Declaration of Independence, 1776*

> We, the People of the United States, in order to form a more perfect union, establish justice, insure domestic tranquility, provide for the common defense, promote the general welfare, and secure the blessings of liberty to ourselves and our posterity, do ordain and establish this Constitution for the United States of America.
> —*Preamble to the U.S. Constitution, 1787*

INTRODUCTION

The principles upon which the government of the United States of America was founded—equality, liberty, and democracy—have served as a model that has stood the tests of time. In the late 1980s, the people of China, Hungary, Poland, East Germany, and the Philippines used the United States' vision of democracy as a basis for reforms in their countries. Unfortunately, when these principles were first enunciated in the American Declaration of Independence and Constitution, African Americans and other people of color who helped build the United States were excluded initially from the rights preserved in those documents. Yet if proof is needed of the continued vitality of both the Declaration and the Constitution over two hundred years, one simply has to review how well African Americans and other minorities have succeeded in transforming the politics of exclusion to that of significant political participation in American government.

During the colonial period, the exercise of the franchise was considered a privilege, certainly not a fundamental right preservative of all other rights of citizenship, as is now believed. How the right to vote evolved over time in response to demands made by the disfranchised and the impact of the African American voter on that evolution is the focus of this chapter. The influence of other minority groups (particularly Native Americans, Latinos, and Asians) and women on the process of evolution will also be discussed. Perhaps an examination of the difficulty African Americans, other minorities, and women have had in securing the right to vote will serve to remind all Americans of the importance of voting during a time when voter participation is seriously declining.

QUALIFICATIONS FOR VOTING: REVOLUTIONARY WAR PERIOD

Because the thirteen colonies that eventually became the United States were primarily settled by British subjects, it is not surprising that they continued the British system of restricting the franchise to those who owned property, namely freeholders.[1] As a general rule, qualifications for voting varied from colony to colony and were based on factors such as property ownership, status, gender, age, religion, and length of residence. The only qualification that was common to all of the colonies was the ownership of property, which was based on the English principle that the right to vote was derivative of possessing a material interest in the community.[2] Status referred to whether a person was a "freeman." In the northern colonies, a man had to be officially recognized by a governing body as a freeman, while in the southern colonies, the term referred to those who were not indentured servants or slaves. Women were not allowed to vote except in New Jersey (during the period 1776 to 1876) and Massachusetts (1691 to 1780).[3]

Voting was limited by age to adults over twenty-one in most of the colonies. Religious restrictions were also common. Roman Catholics were prohibited from voting in Rhode Island, New York, Maryland, and Virginia. Freeman electors in New Hampshire had to be Protestants; Jews could not vote in New York and South Carolina; Quakers could not vote in Massachusetts and Plymouth colonies (or other places where they had to take an oath to become freemen).[4] Others restricted from voting included convicts, debtors, servants, and those under guardianship. As a result of these restrictions, only 10 to 15 percent of the colonial population were even eligible to vote, and less than half of those actually participated, because voting was viewed as the privilege of the upper classes.

Of the original thirteen colonies, only Georgia and South Carolina adopted state constitutional provisions expressly limiting voting on the basis of race to white males.[5] However, voting restrictions based on race soon became the norm as the number of Africans increased dramatically following the institu-tion of slavery. It is important to note that the first Africans brought to this country, specifically to Jamestown, Virginia, in 1619, were not slaves but in-dentured servants. Initially, blacks were able to work off their period of servi-tude like white indentured servants. As a result, free blacks during the period prior to the Revolutionary War had the right to own property, attend church, pay taxes, and exercise the franchise like other colonials.[6]

But as their numbers greatly increased in response to the demand for labor, especially in the South, Africans soon found themselves in a state of perpetual servitude. Because of their color, blacks could not escape from service as easily as white servants; moreover, they were considered heathens who needed con-version to Christianity, and their supply seemed endless as compared to other nonwhite slaves. Thus, indentured servitude was slowly transformed into the profitable institution of slavery. With the increase in the number of African slaves and incidents of rebellion, white colonists became more apprehensive about insurrections and began instituting harsh slave codes in order to better control the slaves.[7] The imposition of these codes began to circumscribe the liberties of free blacks to prevent them from encouraging rebellion among those enslaved. Free blacks had to carry a certificate of freedom on their person at all times or risk being captured and sold as slaves. They could no longer vote (except in Tennessee until 1834 and North Carolina until 1835), hold public office, give testimony against whites, possess a firearm, buy liquor, assemble freely (except in a church supervised by whites), or immigrate to other states.[8]

As the colonies developed, so did slavery, but it developed differently de-pending on the region. New England was less dependent on the institution, and as a result slavery was less tolerated than in the Mid-Atlantic and southern re-gions, which depended heavily on slave labor. Free blacks in the northern colo-nies were subjected to less severe restrictions than those in the South because the size of the black population was much smaller, and the risk of free blacks in-fluencing blacks slaves to escape was not considered as important. However, northern blacks were regarded as inferior and undesirable and employment op-portunities were limited, while laws prevented their immigration to other re-gions on pain of imprisonment and enslavement. Massachusetts was the only place where blacks could serve on juries.[9]

During the Revolutionary War period, Africans, whether free or enslaved, served both the Colonial forces and the British as guides, messengers, spies, and soldiers; when the British left following the war, they took with them many of the blacks to whom freedom had been promised. Free blacks, some of whom gained their freedom by joining the local militia or Continental Army, were im-portant participants in the War for Independence from England. Initially, blacks were excluded from enlisting in the Continental Army (the military es-tablishment that represented all of the newly formed states) because their en-listment violated the property rights of masters and the use of slaves was viewed as inconsistent with the principles at issue with the British, namely freedom from tyranny.[10] One of the major benefits the Revolutionary War had for blacks is that many of the colonists who fought in the name of liberty began to realize that slavery was indeed inconsistent with the ideals of the new nation being formed, which in turn led to the formation of abolitionist societies and a growing anti-slavery movement.

It is against this background that the issue of slavery became part of the debates over the content of the Declaration of Independence. When Thomas Jefferson first drafted the Declaration, which was intended to justify the colonies independence from England, he included a specific charge against King George for his role in promoting slavery:

He has waged a cruel war against human nature itself, violating the most sacred rights of life and liberty in the persons of a distant people who never offended him, captivating and carrying them into slavery in another hemisphere or to incur miserable death in their transportation hither. . . . Determined to keep open a market where men should be bought and sold, he prostituted his negative (veto power) for suppressing every legislative attempt to prohibit or to restrain this execrable commerce.[11]

This section on slavery was unacceptable both to the southern delegates to the Continental Congress, because slavery was fundamental to their economy, and to the northern delegates who considered the slave trade a legitimate business, because they had profited handsomely as transporters of the slave cargo. The vote to strike this section was twelve to zero, with New York abstaining.[12] Thus, the founders of the United States failed in their first test of whether the ideals of equality embodied by the Declaration were intended to include those Americans who had been brought to this country from Africa.

During the drafting of the United States Constitution a decade later, the debate over slavery similarly influenced the final form this basic document took. When the framers of the Constitution met in 1787, it was clear that the institution of slavery would affect the issues of representation, apportionment among the states, direct taxation, and commerce.[13] A number of compromises were adopted that allowed the right of suffrage to continue to be a restricted one and that allowed blacks and Indians to be excluded from the protection of the Constitution.

The debate over qualification for suffrage occurred during a period when states were beginning formally to adopt their own constitutions. State constitutions varied widely in their suffrage requirements. The compromise reached was to leave voting qualifications to the states because it was too difficult to reduce the different qualifications in the states to one uniform rule.[14] The Constitution itself is silent on the franchise except in Article I, Section two, which provides that "the electors in each state shall have the qualifications requisite for electors of the most numerous branch of the state legislature." Thus, representatives to the House of Representatives (the lower house) would be elected directly by the people, and the Senate (the upper house) would be chosen by state legislatures (this was later changed by the Seventeenth Amendment in 1912).

While the Constitution was similarly silent on slavery, three compromise provisions protected the institution and set the stage for the conflict that culminated in the Civil War. Without an "eleventh hour" compromise on how to balance the South's reliance on the slave trade with the North's desire to regulate trade through the federal government, the Constitution as a whole might not have been adopted.[15] Article I, Section nine prohibited Congress from preventing any state from importing any such persons it wished for a period of twenty years. Article IV, Section two (the so-called fugitive slave provision) provided that any person held to service or labor in one state who escaped to another state shall not be discharged from such service or labor but shall be returned to the claimant. On the issues of representation and direct taxes, the framers compromised on the issue of apportionment in Article I, Section two, by including all free people (including servants), excluding Indians not taxed, and including three-fifths of all other people (those enslaved). The three-fifths compromise was reached when the delegates agreed that slaves should be treated both as property and as people. This twisted logic satisfied the issue of apportionment but failed miserably in settling the right of blacks, particularly those who were not enslaved, to vote.[16] The issue of black suffrage was left to the province of the states.

By allowing the states to determine voting qualifications, the architects of the Constitution set in motion a pattern of exclusion from the political process that extended to women, African Americans, Native Americans, and other minority groups. The argument made at the state level for excluding one group or another varied greatly, but the component common to all such exclusions was the element of fear. The white men who controlled their local and state governments were not about to allow their "inferiors" to challenge their authority through access to the ballot box. This policy of exclusion did not undergo any severe test until the Civil War and its aftermath.

MINORITY VOTER PARTICIPATION DURING THE PRE–CIVIL WAR PERIOD

By the end of the Revolutionary War, the population of the new nation was approximately 3.25 million, including 600,000 black slaves, 300,000 indentured servants, at least 50,000 convicts from English prisons, and numerous vagrants and debtors.[17] No attempt was made to count the native Indian population (estimates ranged from 1.5 to 2.0 million), since contact between the settlers and the native population had become increasingly hostile. Shortly after the adoption of the Constitution, the first census was taken in 1790. Slaves numbered 697,624, and free blacks numbered 59,557, or 7.9 percent of the total number of blacks. In 1800, the number of free blacks had increased to 108,435 while the slave population increased to 893,602. Indians who were taxed and other people of color were not separately counted.[18] By the time of the Civil War, the number of free blacks exceeded 488,000, or 11 percent of the black population in the United States.[19]

As the property qualification lost popular support with the growth of Jacksonian democracy, free blacks and other minority taxpayers became eligible to vote. During the period 1783 to 1838, various states in the southern and Mid-Atlantic regions (Connecticut, Delaware, Kentucky, Maryland, North Carolina, Tennessee, and Virginia) amended their constitutions specifically to prevent blacks and other "undesirables" from voting. Every state admitted to the Union between 1800 and 1860, except Maine, restricted the franchise to white males. Every southern state disenfranchised free black males from voting. By the start of the Civil War, blacks could only vote in the New England states of Massachusetts, New Hampshire, Vermont, Rhode Island, and Maine, states that had only 6 percent of the black northern population. Blacks in New York could vote only if they met a taxpaying requirement (limited to blacks) and if they registered their certificates of freedom five days before an election.[20] Of the northern states that permitted suffrage, only New York had a significant black population. This accounts for the additional restrictions in New York.[21]

Blacks, Native Americans, women, and children were generally treated the same with respect to the denial of the franchise.[22] The only two states that allowed women to vote if they owned property, Massachusetts and New Jersey, repealed women's suffrage in 1790 and 1817, respectively. The suffragette movement following the Civil War was needed before women could vote again. Native Americans were not considered citizens, or they were viewed as being under the guardianship of the State. Because "Indians not taxed" were not "free persons" under the Constitution, this term was used to exclude Native Americans from voting. Idaho, New Mexico, and Washington declared in their constitutions that Native Americans were not citizens, and Arizona denied Native American suffrage on the basis of guardianship.[23]

Although the first Naturalization Act passed in March 1790 granted citizenship as a matter of right to "free white" aliens who had lived in the United States for two years, immigrants from China and Japan were excluded from the franchise.[24] In short, while women, blacks, and other minorities were subjected to taxes and other obligations of citizenship, they were denied the right to political participation, which rendered them powerless to change their quality of life through laws and other processes.

Most especially, the political powerlessness of minorities and women prevented them from challenging the doctrine of white male supremacy that dictated all aspects of social and economic interaction within the United States. Blacks were subjected to segregation and restrictions on work and travel through the imposition of antebellum laws that were intended to maintain the inferior status of blacks.[25] The denial of political rights to blacks during this period can best be summarized by the infamous *Dred Scott* decision, in which the United States Supreme Court held that whether free or enslaved, people who were descendants of Africans initially imported into this country could not bring suit in federal court even if their state citizenship were unquestioned; the Constitution granted citizenship only to residents of states that formed the Union and the descendants of those initial residents.[26] Blacks did not recover their citizenship until the adoption of the Fourteenth Amendment following the Civil War.

Native Americans were treated even more harshly than blacks. Treaties to establish peaceful relations between tribes and the federal government were routinely violated or ignored. Indians were further isolated on reservations whose boundaries could be moved or changed upon the whim of the federal government. In 1831, the United States Supreme Court declared that Native American tribes were in a state of pupilage, with their relation to the United States resembling that of a "ward to his guardian." The denial of civil, political, and economic rights of Native Americans was blamed on their "wardship."[27] Because Native Americans were considered "domestic subjects" of the United States, they were not entitled to be treated as citizens.[28] The Supreme Court later refused to extend the right of citizenship conferred by the Fourteenth Amendment to Native Americans.[29] Native Americans had to wait until 1924 to be recognized as citizens of their native land through an act of Congress; the grant of citizenship was used to encourage them to abandon their tribal traditions.[30]

For women, their place of isolation was the home. Most professions were closed to them, and married women had virtually no legal rights. Women were regarded in the same category as children and idiots.[31] Higher education was considered unseemly, and women who rejected the sacred roles of wife and mother were ostracized and scorned.[32] While there is limited evidence of female voting prior to the Civil War, such instances were confined to local elections.[33] Following the Civil War, the Supreme Court recognized that the Fifteenth Amendment rendered inoperative a statute that limited voting to "free white male citizens." Yet, women were still not able to vote nationally until the adoption of the Nineteenth Amendment in 1920.

Despite the severe restrictions imposed on them, free blacks in states such as Pennsylvania, Ohio, and Connecticut continued to fight for the right to vote. If blacks had not tried to participate in elections, states would not have found it necessary to continue to disenfranchise them through amendments to their constitutions. There is evidence that blacks voted and participated in party conventions.[34] In fact, the first elected black officeholder was elected before the Civil War—John M. Langston, a Township Clerk in the state of Ohio.[35] Blacks became active in anti-slavery societies whose white members helped fan the sectional strife that erupted into the War Between the States.[36]

The decade before the Civil War manifested numerous political conflicts over the issue of slavery, represented best by the turmoil caused by the Kansas-Nebraska Act. Introduced by Illinois Senator Stephen A. Douglas, the act provided that Kansas and Nebraska should be organized as territories and that the question of slavery should be decided by the territories. A bitter and bloody fight ensued between North and South for the control of Kansas—making the territory a preliminary battleground of the Civil War. The Kansas-Nebraska Act persuaded many abolitionists that political action was necessary to stop the relentless drive of the pro-slavery forces to extend slavery. Those who were morally opposed to slavery in Nebraska (members of the Whigs, Know-Nothing, and Liberty parties, Free-Soilers, abolitionists, and others from the North) coalesced into a new party called Republican, whose basic principle was the nonextension of slavery.[37] The Democratic party became more regionally based in the South as the issue of slavery created a major political realignment.[38] When Abraham Lincoln, a Republican, was elected in 1860, the southern states chose to leave the Union rather than accept the outcome of the election.

POST–CIVIL WAR RECONSTRUCTION

It is beyond the scope of this chapter to detail the enormous changes that occurred in the country following the Civil War. The transformation of the status of African Americans from slavery to freedom culminated in the adoption of the Thirteenth, Fourteenth, and Fifteenth Amendments to the Constitution.

The Thirteenth Amendment, which formally abolished slavery on December 18, 1865, did not automatically grant freedmen citizenship or suffrage rights to vote, in light of prior Supreme Court decisions and constitutional recognition of states' right to determine voting qualifications. Because the Constitution had implicitly sanctioned slavery as an institution, amendments to the Constitution were viewed as necessary to establish black political rights conclusively. Yet, it is significant to note that support for the abolition of slavery did not automatically translate into support for black suffrage.[39]

Although they were basically opposed to the extension of slavery, the Republicans as a party did not stand for black suffrage. Only the "radical" faction of the Republican party supported the concept of full political equality for blacks, primarily as a means of solidifying control over the defeated southern states and punishing those who had lost the war.[40] Indeed, as freedmen left the South in large numbers following the War, whites in other parts of the country had to contend with large numbers of blacks for the first time. They responded by consistently voting against black suffrage in Connecticut, Michigan, Wisconsin, Ohio, Kansas, and Minnesota and by ignoring the issue in other northern states.[41]

During the period immediately following the war, southern states rejected all attempts to extend suffrage to their former slaves and instead enacted "Black Codes" that prohibited people of color from bearing arms or testifying against whites. Blacks were required to make annual written contracts for their labor and were subjected to terms of service if convicted of vagrancy, even though many whites refused to employ them.[42] But because the Democratic party was so adamantly opposed to black suffrage, the Republicans were able to consolidate their party by transforming votes on black suffrage into a test of party loyalty.[43]

This development was crucial to the passage of the Fourteenth and Fifteenth Amendments, as well as other postwar civil rights legislation. In response to the southern states refusal to extend suffrage to blacks, the Radical Republican-led Congress passed, over President Andrew Johnson's veto, the Civil Rights Act of 1866, which anticipated the Fourteenth Amendment by making United States citizens of all native-born people except untaxed Native Americans, and guaranteeing to all citizens regardless of race or previous servitude the right to enforce contracts, file lawsuits, testify in court, own property, and enjoy all benefits of law to which white citizens were entitled.[44] These protections, which were less emotional than political and social equality, became Section one of the proposed Fourteenth Amendment. Blacks, led by Frederick Douglass and George Downey, continued to lobby Congress for the elective franchise; however, framers of the Fourteenth Amendment feared northern rejection of the black franchise, so they left the decision on suffrage to the states in Section two of the amendment.[45] The former Confederate states were required by Congress to ratify the Fourteenth Amendment before readmission to the Union. Because most of those states refused, Congress placed the South under military rule in 1866 through various Reconstruction acts.[46]

Additional Reconstruction acts disenfranchised former Confederate leaders and soldiers and allowed blacks to participate in state conventions.[47] A situation unique in history emerged when the formerly suppressed class of slaves became, for a brief time, politically dominant over their former masters.[48] Reconstruction enabled the military authorities to register over 800,000 blacks to vote, which exceeded the number of southern whites then registered.[49] Southern whites resorted to violence and intimidation against blacks through the formation of secret societies best represented by the founding of the Ku Klux Klan. Congress responded with the Fifteenth Amendment, which explicitly provided that the right to vote shall not be denied on account of race, color, or previous condition of servitude. Ratification of both the Fourteenth Amendment (in 1868) and the Fifteenth Amendment (in 1870) was only accomplished through Congressional coercion of the southern states.

It is not surprising, then, that newly emancipated blacks were treated as pawns in the aftermath of the Civil War. The black vote was exploited by Republicans who wanted to radicalize and punish the South as well as take advantage of the South's cheap labor, and by Democrats who feared a further loss of power from an alliance between blacks and poor whites as represented by the emerging Populist party.[50] During the period 1870 to 1901, two blacks were elected to the United States Senate from the states of Mississippi (Hiram R. Revel and Blanche K. Bruce); one served as acting Governor of Louisiana for six weeks (P.B.S. Pinchback); twenty served as members of the House of Representatives from the states of Alabama, Florida, Georgia, Louisiana, Mississippi, North Carolina, South Carolina, and Virginia. Many blacks were also elected to state legislatures. It is important to note, however, that blacks never controlled any southern government; if they had, whites would not have been able to resume control of their legislatures with the departure of federal troops.[51]

When Reconstruction ended with the withdrawal of federal troops in 1877, blacks immediately found that their political participation was short-lived. While they were in power, blacks maintained a remarkable attitude of moderation rather than hatred toward their former masters, an attitude that was not reciprocated when white leaders resumed control of southern legislatures.[52] Southern white leaders sought to reestablish dominance over their former slaves through disenfranchisement (the Fifteenth Amendment notwithstanding) and imposition of mass compulsory segregation laws called "Jim Crow." Whites used segregation to maintain a system of control over blacks that prevented any significant social, economic, or political development.

The segregationists were assisted in their systematic subjugation of blacks by the indifference of the North to the plight of blacks and by the United States Supreme Court, which neglected to enforce the postwar Civil Rights acts.[53] More importantly, the Court legitimized the "separate but equal" doctrine in *Plessy v. Ferguson*.[54] Thus, the country proceeded to turn a deaf ear and blind eye to the southern political structure and its treatment of black citizens. Legal barriers to voting, such as the literacy qualification, the poll tax, the grandfather clause, and the white primary were administered to closely control the black vote. However, some blacks did vote after the Reconstruction period, but only when the white dominant faction needed them in order to win.

The poll tax actually originated prior to the Civil War. The tax, usually a head tax of one to three dollars levied against all males between the ages 21 to 65 years old, was popular in southern states because it aided them in their movement to disenfranchise blacks from politics.[55] The poll tax, which had to be paid months in advance of elections and which required each voter to bring a receipt of payment at the time of registration, reduced vote totals for both southern whites and blacks in each of the eleven southern states (for example, the 1903 vote was less than that of 1896.) The result was that the South had the lowest voter participation levels in the nation, a trend that continued for over one hundred years.[56] The real function of the tax-paying prerequisite was to restore control to the upper economic classes.

The literacy test, which required an applicant to interpret lengthy passages of a state's constitution, was also used to restrict voting. Illiterate whites were exempted from such tests through the use of the grandfather clause; that is, a person could vote if his grandfather had voted in the past. Most southern states amended their constitutions to require the literacy test in order to disenfranchise blacks, while northern states such as New York, Connecticut, and Massachusetts used literacy tests to protect them from "ignorant" foreigners.[57] The literacy test was one of the last of the various disenfranchising schemes to be ruled unconstitutional.[58]

The white primary was one of the fruits of the Civil War that made the Democratic party a "lily-white" party.[59] The unanimous support Republicans received from blacks during Reconstruction stemmed from the party's role in outlawing slavery. However, when southern whites assumed control after Reconstruction, the Republican party began a rapid decline until, in some of the deep-South states, it virtually ceased to exist. Thus, southerners and Democrats became synonymous with one another and transformed the South into a one-party region.

Party membership was added as a further voting restriction in the South (and in a majority of other states as well), based on the premise that only members of a party should take part in the selection of party nominees.[60] Thus, the Democratic party determined that blacks could not be Democrat, and they excluded them in most southern states. Mexican Americans were similarly barred from voting through this practice in Texas.[61] When blacks sought to have this procedure declared unconstitutional, blacks learned that the exclusionary practice was considered to be a voluntary action by a private organization and thus legal.[62]

During the time that blacks were being systematically disenfranchised, women began actively demonstrating for the ballot. Between 1874 and 1908, women suffrage was rejected by state legislatures in 17 states.[63] Feminist leaders responded by adopting more militant tactics (for example, picketing the White House, refusing to offer defenses to their arrests, and hunger strikes in jail) that became known as the Suffragette Movement. By targeting their political enemies and effectively campaigning against them in the congressional elections of 1914 and 1916, the Suffragettes became recognized as a potent political force. By 1920, women succeeded in securing enough votes to ratify the Nineteenth Amendment, which granted women the right to vote.

Meanwhile, actions were taken to curb the rights of even immigrant white males to vote. Widespread election fraud during the 1896 presidential elections ostensibly led many states to adopt methods (including registration procedures) to better control the electoral process; yet a more likely rationale for the adoption of registration systems was the mass influx of Eastern European immigrants at the turn of the century. Registration practices, including compulsory registration in person, lengthy residency requirements (from one to two years), and registration deadlines (eleven months before an election, for example), the adoption of registration lists, and so forth, appeared designed to prevent the newcomers from voting rather than to eliminating fraud.[64] The combination of these registration practices (by the 1920s, forty of the forty-six states required compulsory personal registration) with the literacy test, poll tax, grandfather clause, and citizenship requirement, operated to seriously restrict voter participation among blacks, poor whites, Native Americans, and foreign-speaking immigrants.[65]

THE IMPACT OF THE CIVIL RIGHTS MOVEMENT ON MINORITY VOTER PARTICIPATION

Minorities and women continued to press for the right to participate in the political system. Legal impediments to voting were thus subjected to constant legal challenges. The first to fall was the grandfather clause in 1915 when the Supreme Court ruled it violated the Fifteenth Amendment.[66] Similarly, the white primary was outlawed in 1944.[67]

Literacy tests and poll tax requirements were more resistant to constitutional challenges. In 1959, the Court unanimously sustained the validity of an English language literacy test in North Carolina, a holding that was not reversed until after enactment of the Voting Rights Act of 1965.[68] In *Breedlove v. Suttles*, the Court refused to rule the poll tax unconstitutional in Georgia in 1937 when a white male challenged its validity.[69] A constitutional amendment was required to prohibit poll taxes in federal elections; the Twenty-fourth Amendment was passed in 1964 directly in response to the Civil Rights Movement. The Supreme Court finally overruled *Breedlove* in 1966 when it ruled poll taxes in state elections violated the Fourteenth Amendment.[70]

The Civil Rights Acts of 1957, 1960, and 1964 began the long-overdue process of providing a mechanism to enforce the Fifteenth Amendment, a process that culminated with the Voting Rights Act of 1965. The Voting Rights Act provided direct federal intervention in state registration practices. Unlike the Reconstruction period, these Civil Rights acts were supported by Supreme Court decisions.[71] The Civil Rights Movement resulted in the enfranchisement of millions of blacks, particularly in the South. The significance of the Voting Rights Act to black and minority political development cannot be overstated.

Counties with federal examiners, mandated by the Voting Rights Act, immediately showed dramatic gains in black registration. Another critical provision of the act was Section five, which required states with a long history of discriminatory election practices to apply to the United States Department of Justice for preclearance before new electoral practices could be implemented. It was anticipated that the act would remedy the most egregious instances of voter discrimination, and as a result, the act was structured to expire after a five-year period.[72]

Symbolically, the act awakened black political electoral activism throughout the nation. Concomitantly, in 1965, Edward Brooke became the first black to be elected senator since Reconstruction, and in 1966, Carl Stokes and Richard Hatcher were the first blacks elected mayors of major cities. A year later, Robert C. Weaver became the first black to be appointed to a cabinet-level position (Secretary of Housing and Urban Development), and in 1967, Thurgood Marshall became the first black associate justice of the Supreme Court. Shirley Chisholm became the first black woman elected to Congress in 1968, and she was followed by nine other black men and women who were elected to Congress during the period 1966 to 1972. The Voting Rights Act was extended in 1970, suspending the use of literacy tests nationwide. Voters 18 to 21 years old were granted the right to vote nationally by passage of the Twenty-sixth Amendment in 1971.

Against this background, black leaders had a reasonable expectation that black voter participation would continue to increase as more African Americans became aware that the right to vote could be exercised without fear of physical violence or reprisals. Registration of southern blacks alone increased by two million during the decade following the passage of the Voting Rights Act.

Yet the results of the 1972 mid-term elections and the 1976 general elections revealed that black voter participation was declining nationally, and the gap between black and white voters was actually increasing.

In 1968, the first presidential election year following passage of the Voting Rights Act, blacks voted at the rate of 57.6 percent compared to 69.1 percent for white voters, a gap of 11.5 percent according to Census Bureau figures. By 1976, that gap had widened to 12.7 percent (48.7 percent of blacks voted compared to 60.9 percent of whites); the participation levels for all voters reached an all-time low. Registration rates for blacks also fell during this period from 66.2 percent in 1968 to 58.5 percent in 1976.[73]

One of the reasons for the continued wide disparity in black and white voting rates was the persistence of discriminatory electoral procedures. Not only were blacks subjected to rigid registration barriers (hostile registrars who closed their offices when blacks approached, "lost" registration applications, challenges at the polling place, and so forth), but also new discriminatory schemes were designed to dilute the black and Latino vote, such as gerrymandering of election districts to give more weight to white voters, creation of at-large rather than single-member election districts, annexation of black communities to large white populations lying outside the city limits, and similar discriminatory practices.[74] In short, although the Voting Rights Act did much to extend the right to vote to blacks nationally, new means of curbing the power (and, concomitantly, the enthusiasm) of that vote were devised and instituted.

CONCLUSION: THE POLITICS OF PARTICIPATION

The history of minority voting rights detailed above demonstrates a long and difficult struggle to realize the ideals of equality and democracy so eloquently expressed in the Declaration of Independence and the United States Constitution. African Americans were excluded from the protection of those documents, which made it easier to deny them participation in American society as equal partners. When the Constitution was finally amended to enfranchise blacks following the Civil War, they were prevented from exercising the franchise through violence, intimidation, and discriminatory registration practices. Blacks demanded the right to vote one hundred years later, but found that the rules were constantly changed through gerrymandering and vote-dilution tactics.

The treatment of the African American voter over time has adversely affected other minorities' ability to participate in the political process. State constitutional amendments restricting voting to white males intended to disenfranchise blacks but also prohibited other people of color and women from voting during the 1800s. Restrictive registration practices adopted to prohibit black voting in the early 1900s served to depress participation rates of poor whites and immigrants.

On the other hand, African Americans' struggle for the right to vote has positively benefited all Americans. So many of the rights now taken for granted— the right to vote, the right to privacy, the prohibition against discrimination— would have had no foundation without the Thirteenth, Fourteenth, and Fifteenth Amendments to the Constitution. Indeed, minority groups other than blacks have greatly benefited from the passage of the Voting Rights Act. The women's movement, which paved the way for greater participation of women in government and business, was greatly inspired by the Civil Rights Movement of the 1960s.

It is important that African Americans, other minorities, and women not lose sight of the historic struggle for voting rights or the continuing persistent influence of racism and sexism in the American political system. In the late 1980s, the Supreme Court decided a number of cases that seriously jeopardize gains made since the 1950s in the areas of affirmative action, employment discrimination, and privacy. It is important to remember that the majority of the Court in the 1980s and early 1990s sits as a result of decisions made by Americans at the ballot box. The challenge of the present and the future is to continue to remind people of color and women that they do have the power to improve the quality of life in the United States through active, consistent participation in the political process.

NOTES

1. For an in-depth discussion of colonial voting practices, see Albert McKinley, *The Suffrage Franchise in the Thirteen English Colonies* (New York: Burt Franklin, 1905) and C. F. Bishop, *History of Elections in the American Colonies* (New York: Burt Franklin, 1893). A Freeholder was the lifetime owner of property received by grant or purchase; the freehold had to have a specified value, which was determined by the British measure of land that could produce at least 40 shillings a year or by some other measure that was designed to confine the vote to the upper class. See Bill Severn, *The Right to Vote* (New York: Ives Washburn, Inc., 1972), 6.

2. *Report of the U.S. Commission on Civil Rights* (Washington, D.C.: United States Government Printing Office, 1959), 19–25; McKinley, *Suffrage Franchise*, 473–75.

3. The first woman who attempted to vote was Margaret Brent of the Maryland Colony, who had inherited property from Governor Calvert. In 1648, the Maryland Colonial General Assembly unanimously refused her demand for the right to vote based

on property ownership. See Marchette Chute, *The First Liberty* (New York: E. F. Dutton, 1969), 314.

4. Cortez Ewing, *American National Government* (New York: American Book Co., 1958), 130.

5. *U.S. Commission on Civil Rights*, 473-75.

6. John Hope Franklin, *From Slavery to Freedom* (New York: Alfred A. Knopf, Inc., 1974), chapter 5, and Charles H. Wesley, "Negro Suffrage in the Period of Constitution-Making, 1787-1865," *The Journal of Negro History* 32 (April 1947): 143.

7. Franklin, *From Slavery to Freedom*, 56-59. Franklin's work contains an excellent bibliography of major works that explain how white English settlers were able to exert and maintain control over Africans and other people of color by law. See also Winthrop Jordan, *White Over Black: American Attitudes Toward the Negro, 1550-1812* (Chapel Hill: University of North Carolina Press, 1968). In much the same way that the colonists inherited their concept of suffrage from the English system, they also brought to the New World the attitudes, prejudices, and opinions of the English toward Native Americans (who were already inhabiting the land and thus were an obstacle to conquest), Africans (who were brought here to supply cheap labor needed to build the colonies), and Spanish-speaking people (who lived in bordering lands and were competitors).

8. Benjamin Quarles, *The Negro in the Making of America* (New York: MacMillan, 1964), 88, and McKinley, *Suffrage Franchise*, 36, 146.

9. Quarles, *Negro in the Making*, 92-93.

10. Franklin, *From Slavery to Freedom*, 89-98, and Quarles, *Negro in the Making*, 52-59.

11. Franklin, *From Slavery to Freedom*, 88, and Chute, *First Liberty*, 215.

12. Ibid.

13. Wesley, "Negro Suffrage," 144-45.

14. Ewing, *American National Government*, 146, and Chute, *First Liberty*, 257. This difficulty is the reason we still have fifty disparate electoral systems.

15. Wesley, "Negro Suffrage," 146.

16. Ibid.

17. Ibid., 19.

18. Ibid., 146.

19. Carter G. Woodson, *The Negro in Our History* (New York: Associated Publishers, 1945), 244.

20. Chute, *First Liberty*, 313, and Wesley, "Negro Suffrage," 155. These certificates could be considered one of the earliest forms of a personal registration requirement.

21. See Emil Olbrich, "Development of Sentiment on Negro Suffrage," *Bulletin of the University of Wisconsin* (New York: Freeport, 1971), chapter 3.

22. Wesley, "Negro Suffrage," 148.

23. Theodore Taylor, *The States and Their Indian Citizens* (Washington, D.C.: United States Government Printing Office, 1972), 90.

24. Sidney Gulick, *American Democracy and Asiatic Citizenship* (New York: Charles Scribner's Sons, 1918), 77.

25. Franklin, *From Slavery to Freedom*, 169-71.

26. *Dred Scott v. Sanford*, 60 U.S. (19 How.), 393 (1857).

27. *Cherokee Nation v. State of Georgia*, 30 U.S. (5 Pat.), 1, 17 (1831).

28. 7 Op. Atty. Gen. 746 (1856).

29. *Elk v. Wilkins,* 112 U.S., 94 (1884).

30. 43 Stat. L 253 (June 2, 1924). See also the Dawes Act, 24 Stat. 388 (1887) and its Amendment, 31 Stat. 1447 (1901).

31. Chute, *First Liberty,* 314-15.

32. Ewing, *American National Government,* 139.

33. Ibid.

34. Wesley, "Negro Suffrage," 165-66.

35. Ibid.

36. Charles Wesley, "The Participation of Negroes in Anti-Slavery Parties," *The Journal of Negro History* 24, no. 1 (January 1944): 140-61.

37. See Paul Kleppner, "Partisanship and Ethno Religious Conflict: The Third Electoral System, 1853-1892," *The Evolution of American Electoral Systems* (Westport, Conn.: Greenwood Press, 1981), 59.

38. Ibid., 65-67.

39. William Russ, "The Negro and White Disfranchisement During Radical Reconstruction," *The Journal of Negro History* 19 (1934): 175.

40. Ibid.

41. Leslie Fishel, Jr., "Northern Prejudice and Negro Suffrage, 1865-1870," *The Journal of Negro History* 39 (1954), 12-15.

42. *Report of the U.S. Commission on Civil Rights,* 27.

43. Russ, "Negro and White Disfranchisement," 176.

44. Fishel, "Northern Prejudice," 15.

45. Ibid., 16-17. Section two provided for the reduction of congressional representation in the event of the abridgement of the right to vote in federal elections, a risk that was not significant in states with small black populations.

46. Ibid. The South was divided into five military districts, and each state was required to amend its constitution to provide for black suffrage, allow blacks to participate in constitutional conventions, and ratify the Fourteenth Amendment.

47. Ibid., 14 Stat. 428 (1867).

48. Russ, "Negro and White Disfranchisement," 181.

49. Forest Wood, "On Revising Reconstruction History: Negro Suffrage, White Disfranchisement, and Common Sense," *The Journal of Negro History* 51 (1966): 99.

50. Wesley, "Participation of Negroes," 167.

51. Wood, "On Revising Reconstruction History," 99.

52. Russ, "Negro and White Disfranchisement," 183.

53. In *United States v. Reese,* 192 U.S. 214 (1876), the Supreme Court ruled that the Enforcement Act of 1870 was unconstitutional in a case involving harassment of black voters; and in *United States v. Cruikshank,* 92 U.S. 542 (1875), the Court held that the Fifteenth Amendment did not guarantee citizens the right to vote but only provided the right not to be discriminated against on account of race, color, or previous condition of servitude.

54. *Plessy v. Ferguson,* 163 U.S. 537 (1896). The Supreme Court stated that "[t]he object of the [14th] Amendment was undoubtedly to enforce the absolute equality of the two races before the law, but in the nature of things it could not have been intended to abolish distinctions based upon color, or to enforce social, as distinguished from political equality, or a commingling of the two races upon terms unsatisfactory to either."

55. Ewing, *American National Government,* 134.

56. Ibid.

57. Derrick Bell, *Race, Racism and American Law* (Boston: Little Brown, 1980), 136.

58. Ewing, *American National Government*, 139.

59. *Report of the U.S. Commission on Civil Rights*, 35.

60. Ibid.

61. Ibid. See *Grovey v. Townsend*, 295 U.S. 45 (1935).

62. *Grovey v. Townsend*. In *Smith v. Allwright*, 321 U.S. 649 (1944), the Court later reversed itself on the white primary by holding that the party in holding the primary was acting in conformance with state laws and under the protection of the state, so that ultimately the white primary rested upon state action subject to the Fourteenth Amendment.

63. Ewing, *American National Government*, 139.

64. See John Harris, *Election Administration in the United States* (Washington, D.C.: Brookings Institution, 1934); John Harris, *Registration of Voters in the United States* (Washington, D.C.: Brookings Institution, 1929); and Frances Piven and Richard Cloward, *Why Americans Don't Vote* (New York: Pantheon, 1988).

65. See U.S. Commission on Civil Rights, 40, 67.

66. *Guinn v. United States*, 238 U.S. 347 (1915).

67. *Smith v. Allwright.*

68. *Lassiter v. Northampton Election Board*, 360 U.S. 45 (1959); Cardona v. Power, 384 U.S. 672 (1966). An English literacy test imposed on Puerto Rican plaintiffs was overturned; and *South Carolina v. Katzenbach*, 388 U.S. 301 (1966). Congress had the power to suspend literacy tests when those tests coincided with low voter participation.

69. *Breedlove v. Suttles*, 302 U.S. 277 (1937).

70. *Harper v. Virginia Board of Elections*, 383 U.S. 663 (1966).

71. See, for example, *Baker v. Carr*, 269 U.S. 186 (1962). The equal protection clause prohibited malapportionment. *Reynolds v. Sims*, 377 U.S. 533 (1964) prohibited malapportionment of either house of state legislature.

72. See *Voting Rights Act of 1965*, Pub. L. No. 89-110, 79 Stat. 437 (1965) codified at 42 U.S.C., sec. 1971, 1974; U.S. Commission on Civil Rights, *Voting* (Washington, D.C.: United States Government Printing Office, 1968).

73. See U.S. Department of Commerce, Bureau of the Census, *Current Population Reports, Voting and Registration in the Election of November 1988* (Washington, D.C.: United States Government Printing Office, 1989).

74. For a full description of dilution tactics, see Chandler Davidson, ed., *Minority Vote Dilution* (Washington, D.C.: Howard University Press, 1984). Registration barriers have been detailed in recent hearings before the House Administration Committee, Subcommittee on Elections, *Hearings on Voter Registration* (Washington, D.C.: United States Government Printing Office, April 19, 1988).

2

The Role of African American Political Organizations in the Mobilization of Voters

Dianne M. Pinderhughes

This chapter examines voter mobilization efforts and their effectiveness among African Americans in the United States. Specifically, strategies, tactics, and organizations that work best are considered; the role of voter education and the status of voter registration reform efforts and their potential impact are considered also. More broadly, the chapter addresses the nature and development of black political organizations (with a special emphasis on the role of black women's leadership), and places the evolution of voter mobilization groups and efforts within that context.

THE ORIGINS OF BLACK ORGANIZATIONS

Voter mobilization organizations evolved within the larger framework of black political organizations. In this context political organization means groups responsible for transmitting information about the concerns, beliefs, desires, and requirements of its members to elected or appointed representatives in the public sector. With even their most basic political rights moot for most of the nation's history, blacks' political organizations and interest groups were necessarily affected.

As Sonia Jarvis pointed out in chapter 1, there were few civil protections for blacks in the first decades of the nation's history. In addition to the lack of legal protection by state or federal governments, blacks faced threats of mob action with some frequency. Philip Foner reports that between 1812 and 1849, there were 207 major and minor riots in the North—many of them directed against blacks. "In each case, white mobs burned and looted Negro churches, meeting halls, and homes and clubbed, stoned, and sometimes murdered blacks."[1] It is within this eighteenth- and nineteenth-century context of the absence of legal rights for blacks and violent opposition to them from whites that blacks began to develop indigenous organizations.

The health and functioning of collective representation structures in U.S. society rests on the political status of the individual. Since blacks had little or no political status as individuals or as a group, understandably their efforts to create representative organizations encountered many difficulties.

Nevertheless, blacks formed religious, benevolent, fraternal, literary, social, and more explicitly political organizations early in their history in the United States. The oldest, first, and core organizations were religious bodies. While blacks worshipped with whites in the years before the Revolutionary War, they began to form their own churches and congregations in the face of great resistance by whites after the war. The African Methodist Episcopal Church, for example, evolved out of a Methodist Episcopal congregation in Philadelphia when, in 1787, Richard Allen, Absalom Jones, and William White "withdrew from the church in a body." By 1816, enough churches had been organized in cities on the eastern seaboard to form a congregation. The African Methodist Episcopal Zion Church was formed in New York City in 1800, and by the early nineteenth century, independent black churches existed in cities throughout the East. Churches also sprang up throughout the South, although there were more severe restrictions on them in that region, especially in rural areas.[2]

The churches became the center of a network of organizations for black communities, generating other groups linked to the church either because it was often difficult to secure meeting space elsewhere, or because their members were often also members of the church and interest groups arose out of the religious congregation.[3] The black church served as a community service center, an educational center, and an assembly hall for protest meetings. Shiloh in New York City could accommodate 1,600 people in its building at Prince and Marion Streets and was considered "eminently suited as a meeting hall" in a city where blacks could not ordinarily hire such halls.[4] Burial societies, school, fraternal organizations, anti-slavery, and literary societies had direct links to or through religious bodies.[5]

By all historical accounts, blacks founded a large number of many different types of organizations. They existed in spite of the environment within which they existed. While black organizations might have very specific public functions, whether religious, fraternal, literary, economic, social, or in some cases political, whites saw any and all such activities to bear explicit implications of rebellion at worst, or threats to the existing racial hierarchy at least. In other words, even when black organizations were not formally political or did not involve direct efforts to organize slave rebellions, any organization of and by blacks involved a challenge to the continued operation of the system of slavery and the hierarchical nature of relations between whites and blacks.

Taking into account the nature of the political, legal, and economic system in which blacks were nonpersons, their organization of large numbers of substantial religious denominations, and social and fraternal bodies posed a serious problem to this system. A meeting of such an organization might involve teaching a black person to read, a violation of the law in many states; or attendance by a runaway slave whose presence, even before passage of the fugitive slave law, could require local officials to assist southern parties in capturing the individual; the black codes of any number of northern states restricted association between free blacks and/or slaves.

After the slave rebellions in the first three decades of the nineteenth century, states significantly tightened laws restricting associations of blacks and forbade many such activities. State legislatures regulated both secular and religious activities, denied blacks the right to preach, and forbade meetings of slaves.[6] The civil authorities in Richmond, Virginia, were not content to jail a black man who had started a school for free blacks and had advertised it in the local paper, but lest anyone misunderstand their view of his actions, sent him to the "Williamsburg Lunatic Asylum."[7] Because of the regulation of religious meetings and organizations, as well as associations with other kinds of roles such as fraternal, benevolent, and literary, many black organizations conducted their business in secret for self-protection. Maryland (1842), Delaware (1842, 1855), and the District of Columbia forbade secret societies or otherwise restricted black activities.[8]

As a result of the harsh restrictions placed on black activities, black organizations tended to be complex in nature and holistic in concerns. More specifically, in addition to their formal or specific purposes, all black organizations, in the years before the Civil War, had to consider questions of standing regarding citizenship, property, racial hierarchy, violations of local and state laws regarding interaction of slave and free, and other more basic political aspects of their members' lives. All such organizations might find it necessary to address: the right of their members to own themselves, if they were or had been accused of being runaway slaves; the right to defend themselves against unfair charges of violation of the law or improper behavior relative to a white person with whom they had an interchange in the street; the right to their own property if whites sought to appropriate it unfairly; the right to seek employment and to practice a trade; the right to worship in the manner of their own choosing, and so forth.

Any of these issues might become a matter of conflict for one of their members, and even when there were formal political organizations, these were more likely to deal with broader, long-range questions such as the convention movement and abolitionist societies rather than simply day-to-day questions. Black religious bodies and fraternal, literary, and benevolent societies had to handle such long-range issues in relatively clandestine fashion, for to address them aggressively and too publicly invited violent attack by the white public or by law enforcement officials. The basic absence of formal legal status for blacks as full citizens imposed enormous constraints on black organizations. State and localities also enacted specific laws that outlawed the operation of black organizations of any kind, but especially of "political" organizations. These were not aberrations; in fact they were viewed in the South as necessary to maintain a legitimate status of white activities and an illegitimate status of black activities. In the North, whites and legal authorities were by no means more cooperative in recognizing the rights of blacks to meet, to petition, to organize, to represent their rights, or to vote. After all, they had no rights white men were bound to respect.

The character of black organizations in the nineteenth and early twentieth centuries were thus quite distinctive from other racial/ethnic groups for several reasons. First, the denial of citizenship to blacks seriously constrained the basis on which their political bodies and representation structures functioned. Second, the existence of separate black corporate structures was virtually required, given the racially hierarchical nature of the society in every respect. The maintenance of slavery required extraordinarily narrow limitations on the exercise of independent actions by blacks as individuals or in groups. Third, the formal and informal restrictions and attacks on black organizations by the state and by the population at large resulted in the formation of secret organizations for camouflage, which merged or superimposed several activities over a political role. Fourth, different black organizations often recruited the same people in slightly different arrangements. For example:

The leadership of the black conventions (in the nineteenth century) was drawn primarily from among Negro ministers. The ministry, the only profession easily accessible to blacks, was a natural training ground for black leaders not only for the churches but for all other spheres of black social life. From the church, a black activist might go into publishing and editing, the lecture circuit or business.[9]

Fifth, black organizations included diverse tasks and activities in several areas. Finally, black organizations addressed issues of great complexity, both ideologically and organizationally. While they were not always successful in surviving over long periods of time, the fact that they existed at all is probably more important.[10]

THE HETEROGENEOUS CHARACTER OF BLACK INTEREST GROUPS

As already indicated, black organizations have always been less likely to focus on a narrow sector of policy than to deal with a number of issues. Groups that appeared to be specialized, such as social or fraternal groups, were as likely to incorporate political issues as they were social. The very nature of discrimination in the American polity helped give rise to these types of groups. Without legal citizenship before the Civil War, and without continuing federal and state recognition of it after Reconstruction, without economic self-ownership before the Civil War, and with servitude after it, blacks were, as Mary Frances Berry and John W. Blassingame characterize them, "an unfree people." With so little in the way of property or wealth, with difficulties in education, health, social welfare, employment, and politics, the status of the black population in any one area was linked to that in every other area. Concomitantly, the activities of black organizations (for example, the Montgomery Improvement Association, the Southern Christian Leadership Conference, the National Association for the Advancement of Colored People, the Student Non-Violent Coordinating Committee, and the Congress of Racial Equality) often reflected this heterogeneous interconnectedness.

THE EFFORTS OF BLACK WOMEN

Another important factor in understanding the history of black political organizations is the role played by black women in their formation and maintenance. The Club Women's Movement, the activities of sororities and clubs of women in urban and moderate-size cities in the North and the South at the turn of the century, helped lay the organizational and strategic foundations for the Civil Rights Movement and political mobilization efforts over a half century later. Delta Sigma Theta, the National Association of Colored Women, the National Council of Negro Women, and various political groups such as the Alpha Suffrage Club were led and developed by black women with the education and economic resources to identify issues, set priorities, and attempt to reorder the extremely conservative and racist society in which they found themselves. They developed their own organizations that dealt variously with literacy, health concerns, economic status, and political interests, as well as created educational institutions and attacked segregation and discrimination. Their interests paralleled and were directly related to those expressed in more explicitly political organizations such as the National Association for the Advancement of Colored People (NAACP) and the National Urban League (NUL), which have survived to the present day. The same women who developed clubs to address a variety of issues on their own were also active in local chapters of the NAACP and NUL.[11]

For instance, Maggie Lena Walker, the first woman bank president in the United States, founded the Saint Luke Penny Savings Bank in Richmond, Virginia, in 1903. She was also grand secretary of the Order of Saint Luke, the mother organization, which with her leadership created a newspaper, the *St. Luke's Herald*, and a department store, the St. Luke Emporium. The Order of Saint Luke also affiliated with a women's economic association, the National Association of Wage Earners. She was a member of the Richmond chapter of the NAACP, the Richmond Urban League, and the International Council of Women of the Darker Races. With her assistance, the Order of Saint Luke led a boycott of streetcar segregation in 1904. Walker also ran for state superintendent of public instruction in 1921.[12]

Ida B. Wells Barnett, who is better known for her autobiography, *Crusade for Justice* (edited by her daughter and published posthumously in 1970), attacked lynching in 1892. She was also a clubwoman, as well as a newspaper reporter and publisher, member of the Afro-American Council, and founder of organizations such as the British Anti-Lynching Society, the NAACP, the Ida B. Wells Club, the Negro Fellowship League, and the National Association of Colored Women.[13]

Mabel K. Staupers was educated at Freedmen's Hospital's (now Howard University Hospital's) School of Nursing in Washington, D.C., in 1917. Staupers was executive secretary of the National Association of Colored Graduate Nurses from 1934 through 1949 and president from 1949 to 1951. She practiced a mixed effort of combining the organizations of blacks, the nursing profession, and geographically based groups to force integration of black nurses within the context of World War II, with the idea that if nursing was integrated within the military, black nurses would become integrated within the mainstream of American nursing. She was at least partially successful in 1945, for in that year nursing in the Armed Services was desegregated. Staupers died in November 1989.[14]

These are only a few examples of the integration and overlap of women's groups with somewhat more specialized organizations. Moreover, since the same people were often members of several different organizations, networks developed and expanded. In many instances, these networks were made possible and nourished by the church.

The work of historians and sociologists on the more recent Civil Rights Movement shows the link between the clubwomen's organizations, the specialized groups, the churches, and mass mobilization more clearly. People like Ella Baker, Septima Clark, Rosa Parks, and Joann Gibson Robinson served in various roles. Septima Clark, born in South Carolina, became a teacher in the Charleston schools. She taught on St. John's Island off the coast of Charleston, as well as in North Carolina and in the interior of South Carolina. During those years from 1917 to the early 1950s, she was involved in adult literacy education, the Parent Teachers Association, the Highlander Folk School, the YWCA, the Alpha Kappa Alpha Sorority, and eventually the NAACP, which led to her termination by the Charleston schools.[15]

Baker was president of the New York City NAACP, as well as director of membership for the national association. She later became second executive director for the Southern Christian Leadership Conference (SCLC), and she facilitated the independent organization of the Student Nonviolent Coordinating Committee (SNCC). Aldon Morris called her "one of the most significant and unheralded leaders of the Civil Rights Movement."[16] Baker and Clark found their roles in the movement "underappreciated," because as women they could not assume the traditional roles of sacred authority held almost exclusively by men in the black church.[17] More importantly, they challenged the organization of authority around charismatic religious male leaders in favor of more routinized networks.

Rosa Parks was a woman at the center of many interconnections in Alabama. She was a member and secretary of the Montgomery NAACP, as well as an officer in the Alabama NAACP. She worked with the NAACP Youth Council, and only a few months before she was arrested for refusing to give her seat on a bus to a white man, she had met Septima Clark at the Highlander Folk School.

Joann Gibson Robinson was president of the Montgomery Women's Political Council. This is one of the few specialized political groups formed to help women register to vote. It also unsuccessfully attempted to address the issue of segregation on buses by holding meetings with Montgomery's mayor and its bus company. The members developed a plan to notify the entire black population if and when a boycott was called.

CONCLUSIONS ON THE TYPES OF ORGANIZATIONS INVOLVED IN THE CIVIL RIGHTS MOVEMENT

These were the kinds of individuals and organizations that were active in the Civil Rights Movement in what Aldon Morris called organizations of organizations, coalitions of all the black organizations in a location or region. The Montgomery Improvement Association (MIA) and the SCLC were two notable examples of such coalitions of organizations. Morris identified three major black institutions in *The Origins of the Civil Rights Movement*. These institutions were the NAACP, the church, and black colleges. However, unlike many researchers, he also paid a great deal of attention to the work of women activists such as Baker, Clark, Robinson, and Parks, and showed the extent to which their involvement in the organizations mentioned above greatly facilitated the cooperative mobilization of blacks as a whole in the Montgomery crisis.[18] The MIA and the successive associations of the SCLC were mass-based and, according to Morris, in the latter case were the "decentralized arm of the mass-based black church."[19]

The SCLC was not an individual-membership organization. Only other organizations, such as churches or civic leagues, could become its affiliates. Here we see the impact of the MIA and the other local "organizations of organizations," which had demonstrated that community resources could be mobilized by uniting the various community organizations. Indeed, it was known that the Montgomery boycott had endured more than a year because the Women's Political Council, the Progressive Democrats, the NAACP, the Citizens Coordinating Committee, and dozens of churches coordinated by the MIA provided it with the necessary organizational networks and resources. The founders of the SCLC reasoned that it would organize a large Southwide mass movement if it were able to mobilize and coordinate community organizations across the South. The SCLC was to be a Southwide organization of organizations.[20]

In addition to the organization of organizations element, Morris said that an independent outside leader, local funding and resources, mass-based protest, and a local movement center are necessary to facilitate a successful challenge to the system of racial domination. All of these elements were present in locations where protest was successful.

MOBILIZING THE BLACK VOTER

The combination of local mass-based organizations of organizations can be seen in the Civil Rights Movement, and, as recently as the early 1980s, a similar event took place in Chicago, which made the election of a black mayor, Harold Washington, possible.[21] The Jesse Jackson campaigns for the Democratic presidential nomination and other mayoral campaigns in the early years of the Ronald Reagan administration are other examples of black organizations of organizations forming and inspiring rising black voter turnout. Since the earlier example of the Civil Rights Movement included protest but not voting and the second set of cases (the electoral campaigns) combined the two, it is important to explain the factors that facilitate voter mobilization.

Dianne Pinderhughes noted that the "bulk of the direct impediments to black political participation" had been removed by the 1965 Voting Rights Act.[22] The traditional socioeconomic status model of voting assumes "that people vote automatically if there are no obstacles to voting or if existing obstacles are removed."[23] As Lawrence J. Hanks noted:

The SES model of political participation states simply that the social status of an individual—his or her job, education, and income—determines to a large extent how much he or she participates. It does this through the intervening effects of a variety of "civic attitudes" conducive to participation: attitudes such as a sense of efficacy, psychological involvement in politics, and a feeling of obligation to participate.[24]

But,

The socioeconomic status model of political behavior assumes that individuals are living in a basically free and open society, that is, that one will not suffer reprisals for the exercise of the franchise. Under such circumstances, non-voting is usually attributed to apathy. Since the Voting Rights Act did not remove the threat of violence or economic intimidation, it is questionable just how open the new black belt South really is.[25]

And Pinderhughes concluded:

People vote not only when they have few or no obstacles but, more importantly, when positive incentives include three major factors: candidates who are attractive to black voters, which includes, but is not necessarily limited to black candidates; non-black candidates win black support, and black candidates win stronger (black) support if they espouse issues which appeal specifically to the black population.... Finally voter registration and mobilization campaigns carried out by, or linked to, indigenous community organizations advance a political campaign. The use of one or all of these factors significantly increases and transforms black electoral participation.[26]

In conclusions based on four case studies (the Chicago mayoral campaign of 1983, the Philadelphia mayoral campaign of 1983, politics in Birmingham, Alabama, in the early 1980s, and a congressional race in North Carolina's second district in 1982), Thomas Cavanagh summarized the factors that contribute to voter mobilization and turnout.[27] First, he noted that the "belief that a black could win" significantly enhances the effort of mobilizing black voters. Second, organizing around "existing networks of black political activists who had a long history of close collaboration in electoral and lobbying campaigns, . . . [that is,] building upon a social and political infrastructure already in place" offers a promising approach to mobilizing black voters.[28] Third, innovative voter registration techniques, including registration at public aid and employment offices, or registration sites where large groups concentrate or are located, such as shopping centers, church or tenant meetings, and rallies, significantly increases success rates and lowers costs of registration efforts.[29] Fourth, targeting age or economic sectors with relatively low rates of participation and developing specific strategies of reaching them, such as use of black music radio stations, is effective.

The next section provides a description of some of the organizations that are most active in voter mobilization and that have used one, some, or all of the approaches identified by Cavanagh.

VOTER REGISTRATION AND MOBILIZATION ORGANIZATIONS

The organizations discussed in this section were selected specifically because they represent different types of voter registration organizations. They span more than a half-century of voter registration activities, strategies, and constituency groups targeted. There is no one way to identify and attract voters and to mobilize them for political participation. Political activists and academics have continuously developed new strategies for voter registration and mobilization.

The League of Women Voters (LWV) was founded in 1920 by the leaders of the women's suffrage movement to help women register and vote, to encourage them to exercise the franchise, and to educate them to do so intelligently. The League is probably the prototypical voter registration organization, with an emphasis on the well-educated individual, and presumptions of a well-educated, well-informed, highly motivated voter. It was founded shortly after the height of the progressive movement with a belief that the ideal citizen is a highly educated one.

The members of the League have one most important interest in common, namely voting. As of the early 1980s, the League had 110,000 to 115,000 members in 1,400 local chapters; members joined only at the local level until 1982.[30] Members of the LWV are predominantly white, female, and college-educated. An important element of the League's activities is the development and evaluation of public policy positions—virtually every member of the organization is involved in a lengthy process of study and consideration. After this process, the membership is polled in a questionnaire, and the results are tallied. At the national level, it has also funded a voting rights project that has sponsored conferences, monitored the legislative campaign in the 1981-1982 Voting Rights Act reauthorization, and has supported the expansion of the electorate.

The earliest regional black voter registration education organization, the Voter Education Project (VEP) was very different from the League because its constituency had suffered from the consequences of racial and economic discrimination. While many of these constituents were highly motivated to vote, they might have been illiterate, have had no access to transportation to reach voter registration locations, found it difficult to register during regular working hours because of employment restrictions, and the like. The VEP thus faced an enormously complex task.

VEP was created in March 1962 as a bipartisan effort, the result of encouragement by John F. Kennedy's administration, the investment of significant resources by the Southern Regional Council (SRC), and the combined support of various civil rights organizations.[31] The Voter Education Project found both intentional efforts to block blacks from the ballot and distinctive patterns of alienation and resistance among blacks toward participation in electoral politics. Linked rather closely with SRC, the VEP's existence was based on infrastructural support from the SRC and on funding from foundation grants. It created a variety of regional projects and personnel to provide information and education for black elected officials as well as voters.

The VEP developed a variety of different types of projects, created its own state and local representatives, started its own offices in some areas, and maintained a research component. It contributed significantly to the increase in voter registration that occurred in the period, and assisted in the training of black elected officials in many locations. In 1971, it assisted in the registration of Mexican-American voters, in the distribution of bilingual education material, and eventually in the formation of the Southwest Voter Registration Education Project, which was "created to address political participation problems of Mexican Americans in the Southwestern states."[32] VEP is not a membership organization and has apparently not emphasized structural integration with existing civil rights and other black organizations in the South. In the late 1980s, its financial and organizational difficulties increased, and the Southern Regional Council and the foundations organized a working group to evaluate the VEP's goals and difficulties.

Operation Big Vote coalitions were created in local areas by the Joint Center for Political Studies (a Washington-based think tank) to work at increasing voter registration and turnout. In 1976, the National Coalition on Black Voter Participation was created by thirty-five national organizations "to reverse the decline in black voter participation."[33] In 1989, the nonprofit, nonpartisan National Coalition was composed of eighty-six diverse membership organizations. The National Coalition is an organization of organizations in the tradition of the MIA and the SCLC. The membership organizations include churches and other religious groups, labor unions, professional associations, political officials, policy groups, and social groups.[34]

In 1987, former executive director of the National Coalition, Gracia Hillman, observed:

The National Coalition had the foresight to develop a formalized coalition approach to nonpartisan voter participation ten years ago. Since then, we have proven that with the combined and cooperative leadership of national and local organizations with minimal resources, changes can be achieved through the political system. . . . Membership in the National Coalition is open to national organizations which subscribe to the Coalition's goals and objectives.[35]

Operation Big Vote, which became part of the National Coalition, operates local coalitions that "conduct intensive voter education, registration, and get-out-the-vote activities while bringing together a broad cross-section of the community."[36] In 1989, seventy-two or more chapters operated in twenty-nine states. The coalition also operates an Information Resource Center, provides assistance on voter education techniques to Operation Big Vote coordinators and conveners, provides public service announcements on voter participation to the media throughout the country, and sponsors the Black Women's Roundtable.[37]

Sonia Jarvis, executive director of the National Coalition, noted in 1989 that a more significant issue for the organization is that black voters are more often alienated than apathetic.[38] The task of voter mobilization is thus partly that of dealing with voter alienation from or even active hostility to the contemporary political system. To a certain extent, this is overcome by grounding the voter registration/mobilization functions within the existing network of organizations within the black population. This is a much less costly strategy for developing information flows and for ensuring that people are likely to receive the information. There are fairly powerful redundancies built into this system as earlier sections of this chapter suggested, because many activists in specific local communities are likely to be involved in two, three, or more of the organizations in question. Redundancy in this case is useful, for it means that the information conveyed through an interwoven political quilt of an organization of organizations is likely to be reinforced several times, and its impact on the individual recipient will be heightened.[39]

Of course, the question for the observer is to what extent these groups represent the full economic range of the black population.[40] If there is a class bias, if only the middle class is highly organized, if the poorer sectors of the population are organized but not linked to this network, then some groups might not be integrated into communitywide strategies. It is possible that the entire black community was more likely to be linked in the past than it is in the present because geographic separation by economic status might be growing among blacks. Thus, further study is required to calculate the impact of the socioeconomic spread of the black population on organizational links since the 1970s.

Human SERVE is quite different from those voter mobilization organizations previously described. It is a "national, nonpartisan, nonprofit voter registration and reform organization. It seeks to persuade public and private social service agencies to offer voter registration services as a way of broadening access to voter registration, particularly among low-income and minority citizens."[41] It was formed in 1983 with the understanding that "everyone has some dealings with public and nonprofit agencies of one kind or another, and poorer and minority people who are less likely to be registered, are more likely to have contact with health, housing, welfare, and unemployment agencies. If citizens could register in the course of using these services, access to voter registration would become nearly universal."[42]

Human SERVES's organizational strategy was developed to make use of the nation's federal governmental structure. "The fragmented character of the American state structure allows an agency-based registration strategy to be tailored to take advantage of the numerous openings provided by the different levels of government, the overlapping powers of different branches, and the vast network of nonprofit health and social service providers."[43] States such as Maine, Ohio, Michigan, Arizona, and Oregon operated motor vehicle voter registration systems as of 1983. Michigan's registration was quite high, 74 percent in 1984. Voter registration in other state or other governmental agencies could overcome the economic advantage given to those sectors of the population with the income to own a motor vehicle. Agency-based registration in federal, state, county, city, or town offices as a result of action ordered by state legislatures, or, failing their support, by executives in these jurisdictions, offers the possibility of multiple routes of access and opportunities for voter registration reform. Human SERVE has enlisted the support of the nonprofit health and welfare sector, both in efforts to encourage their clientele to register and to support agency-based voter registration procedures.[44] In general, voting rights activists supported congressional consideration in the late 1980s and early 1990s of reform legislation that for the first time would prohibit discriminatory registration practices and encourage automatic registration in federal elections.[45]

This has been a brief sample of some of the voter registration and voter mobilization organizations that have been active since passage of the Voting Rights Act of 1965. They cover a wide range of groups. The classic emphasis on the single highly educated voter was incorporated within the original conception of the League of Women Voters. Other organizations (such as the Voter Education Project, the Southwest Voter Registration Education Project, and the National Coalition on Black Voter Participation) target a specific racial or ethnic group in the population. The National Coalition and Human SERVE have adopted the interconnected network strategy of relying on existing groups of organizations to buttress them at the national level and to organize local groups by forming coalitions at the grassroots level as well. Human SERVE also has developed a particularly innovative effort at achieving universal voter registration by combining agency-based voter registration with use of federalism to increase the opportunities for expanding the electorate.

Finally, Jesse Jackson's contribution to voter mobilization in his 1984 and 1988 presidential campaigns cannot be overlooked. Like the National coalition and Human SERVE, Jackson built a national network out of existing organizational contacts; he also used his personal charisma to great effect in attracting supporters. While some commentators such as Adolph Reed have questioned Jackson's impact on voter registration, others such as Lucius Barker, Michael Preston, Fred Hutchinson, and Alvin Thornton have argued otherwise.[46]

DISCUSSION AND CONCLUSION

In comparison to the rest of the industrial world, the United States is quite pitiful in its level of voter registration and turnout. Frances Fox Piven and Richard A. Cloward show that in 1983, the United States (with a turnout of 53 percent of the voting age population) ranked twenty-third among democratic nations in voter participation in "most recent major national elections"[47] The United States ranked behind such countries as Portugal (84 percent), which ranked twelfth, Greece (79 percent), which ranked fifteenth, and Spain (68 percent), which ranked twentieth. When measuring turnout based on the population registered to vote, however, the United States jumps to eleventh. Eighty-seven percent of those registered to vote actually turn out to vote. However, most other nations in these rankings have almost universal voter registration, so the comparison base between the United States and other "democratic nations" relatively underestimates voter participation in the United States.

The levels of voter registration and mobilization are thus related to basic assumptions about political life. Is voting considered a duty or a privilege? In other parts of the world, governments seek to encourage and facilitate registration; in the United States, the assumption has been that it is a privilege.

The combined factors of regional and racial considerations raised an enormous barrier for the average black voter, but even with a significant amount of it removed by the Voting Rights Act of 1965 and its extensions, as well as by court decisions that have expanded voting rights protections to prevent discrimination based on vote dilution, significant differences remain in attitudes toward citizen participation that distinguish the United States from other countries.

Black, Latino, and white civil rights activists have developed a variety of strategies to remove the racial barriers and to encourage political participation in their respective constituencies. They have shifted from individualistic voter contact strategies to efforts that are group-based. They have merged their voter registration/voter mobilization organizations into existing networks of racially and ethnically based social/economic/professional/religious/political organizations. In other words, they have used racial and ethnic groups and the existing organizational patterns within each group to mobilize voters rather than to segregate voter registration/mobilization activity from specialized interest groups. In the black community, as this chapter has shown, interest groups have an organizational history distinct from whites, they function within multiple heterogeneous policy areas, they rely on overlapping elites, and they address ideologically and organizationally complex issues. Voter registration/mobilization strategies should therefore recognize and take advantage of this history. The Civil Rights Movement, the 1983 and 1987 campaigns of Harold Washington for mayor of Chicago, the 1984 and 1988 Jesse Jackson presidential campaigns, and the National Coalition incorporate elements that reflect this long-term political character of black organizational life.

Another important issue in voter mobilization involves how to identify and find the unregistered or inactive voter. The aforementioned campaigns have increased registration and turnout by expanding the reach of the registrars from official buildings to schools, libraries, shopping centers, and other locations where large numbers of people congregate. Human SERVE and other politically active groups set a long-term goal of universal voter registration and aimed at winning it through reform using every level of the federal government. This strategy implies that voting is not a privilege but a right, and that it is the responsibility of government to ensure that all citizens are registered and able to vote.

The alienation of some sectors of voters is also an important concern. The pattern of voter participation in the last decade and a half demonstrates that large sectors of the population have been mobilized toward voting with their behinds—that is, sitting out elections. Blacks, the poor in general, and the minority poor in particular, seem to be more and more discouraged from addressing their racial or economic interests in the electoral sphere. The chief indicator of this discouragement is the difficulty of expanding minority voter participation.

Political activists who seek to increase levels of voting among the previously disfranchised have at least partially identified reform strategies for raising voter registration and turnout rates. Voter turnout rates increase significantly among minorities when there are attractive candidates, issues that get the attention of voters, and aggressive voter mobilization organizations.[48] Important differences in turnout rates within minority communities continue to be based on socioeconomic status. Lower-income and less-educated blacks are especially likely to express alienation or apathy through nonparticipation. How political activists and black organizations address the factors that give rise to these attitudes of distance from the electoral system will shape the future of black participation patterns.

NOTES

I would like to acknowledge the work of Antonio Chico and Deirdré Cobb, who participated in the Committee on Institutional Cooperation and the University of Illinois's 1989 Summer Research Opportunity Program. Both participated in bibliographical research and also wrote research papers that provided supporting information for this paper.

1. Philip S. Foner, *History of Black Americans: From the Emergence of the Cotton Kingdom to the Eve of the Compromise of 1850* (Westport, Conn.: Greenwood Press, 1983), 203.

2. Carter G. Woodson, *The History of the Negro Church* (Washington, D.C.: The Associated Publishers, 1921), 73–77; Foner, *History of Black Americans,* vol. 2, 182–83.

3. Dorothy Porter, "The Organized Educational Activities of Negro Literary Societies, 1828–1846," in *The Making of Black America: Essays in Negro Life and History,* vol.1, edited by August Meier and Elliott Rudwick, *The Origins of Black Americans* (New York: Atheneum, 1969), 283; Ira Berlin, *Slaves Without Masters: The Free Negro in the Antebellum South* (New York: Pantheon Books, 1974), 73; and Mary Frances Berry and John W. Blassingame, *Long Memory: The Black Experience in America* (New York: Oxford University Press, 1982), 45.

4. Foner, *History of Black Americans,* 237.

5. Ibid., 184; Berlin, *Slaves Without Masters,* 73; and Berry and Blassingame, *Long Memory,* 45.

6. Henry W. Farnam, *Chapters in the History of Social Legislation in the United States to 1860* (Washington, D.C.: Carnegie Institute of Washington, 1938), 193–94, 221; Jeffrey R. Brackett, *The Negro in Maryland: A Study of the Institution of Slavery* (New York: Negro Universities Press, 1969), 199–200 (originally by John Hopkins Press, 1889).

7. Gabriel Prosser in 1800, Denmark Vesey in 1822, and Nat Turner in 1831. See Marion Kilson, "Toward Freedom: An Analysis of Slave Revolts in the United States," in *The Making of Black America,* vol. 1, edited by August Meier and Elliott Rudwick, 166–67; and Berlin, *Slaves Without Masters,* 78.

8. Brackett, *The Negro in Maryland,* 100–8; Farnam, *Chapters in the History of Social Legislation,* 206, 216; Worthington G. Snethen, *The Black Codes of the District of Columbia* (New York: A. & F. Anti-Slavery Society, 1848), 45 (republished by University Microfilms, 1988).

9. Robert Allen, *Reluctant Reformers* (Washington, D.C.: Howard University Press, 1983), 19–20.

10. This section of the paper was drawn entirely from a paper by the author, "The Political History of Black Interest Groups," presented at the American Political Science Association, Annual Conference, September 1–4, 1988.

11. Jeanne Noble, *Beautiful Also Are the Souls of My Black Sisters: A History of Black Women in America* (Edgewood Cliffs, N.J.: Prentice-Hall, 1978).

12. Elsa Barkley Brown, "Womanist Consciousness: Maggie Lena Walker and the Independent Order of Saint Luke," *Signs: Journal of Women in Culture and Society* 14 (1989): 921–29.

13. Thomas C. Holt, "The Lonely Warrior: Ida B. Wells-Barnett and the Struggle for Black Leadership," in *Black Leaders of the Twentieth Century,* edited by John Hope Franklin and August Meier (Urbana: University of Illinois Press, 1982), 39–62;

Darlene Clark Hine, ed., *Black Women in United States History: From Colonial Times to the Present*, vol. 15; Mildred Thompson, *Ida B. Wells-Barnett: An Exploratory Study of an American Black Woman, 1893–1934* (Brooklyn, N.Y.: Carlson Publishing, Inc., 1990).

14. Darlene Clark Hine, "Mabel K. Staupers and the Integration of Black Nurses into the Armed Forces," in *Black Leaders of the Twentieth Century*, 241–58; St. Clair Bourne, "Mabel K. Staupers, Spingarn Medalist Dies at 99," *The Crisis* 96, no. 10 (December 1989): 37, 39.

15. Cynthia Stokes Brown, *Ready from Within: Septima Clark and the Civil Rights Movement* (Navarro, Calif.: Wild Trees Press, 1986).

16. Aldon Morris, *The Origins of the Civil Rights Movement: Black Communities Organizing for Change* (New York: The Free Press, 1984), 83.

17. Ibid., 102–4, 109–15, 118.

18. Ibid.

19. Ibid., 51–53.

20. Ibid., 90.

21. Abdul Alkalimat and Doug Gills, "Chicago Black Power vs. Racism: Harold Washington Becomes Mayor," in *The New Black Vote*, edited by Rod Bush (San Francisco: Synthesis Publications, 1984); Thomas Cavanagh, ed., *Strategies for Mobilizing Black Voters: Four Case Studies* (Washington, D.C.: Joint Center for Political Studies, 1987).

22. Dianne M. Pinderhughes, "Legal Strategies for Voting Rights: Political Science and the Law," *Howard Law Journal* 28, no. 1 (1985): 525.

23. Ibid., 534.

24. Lawrence J. Hanks, *The Struggle for Black Political Empowerment in Three Georgia Counties* (Knoxville: University of Tennessee Press, 1987), 36.

25. Ibid., 38.

26. Pinderhughes, "Legal Strategies," 534, 535.

27. Cavanagh, *Strategies for Mobilizing Black Voters*.

28. Ibid., 140-41.

29. Ibid., 144.

30. Joyce Gelb and Marian Lief Palley, *Women and Public Policies* (Princeton, N.J.: Princeton University Press, 1982), 27.

31. "A History of VEP: The Voter Education Project—A Concise History, 1962–1979" and "Race and Class in Southern Politics," Voter Education Project Report, (Atlanta: Voter Education Project, 1979—estimated), 3.

32. Ibid., 13.

33. National Coalition on Black Voter Participation, pamphlet (Washington, D.C.: National Coalition of Black Voter Participation, 1989).

34. Types of organizations and specific examples include: religious (the African Methodist Episcopal, the Church of God in Christ, the National Baptist Convention—USA Inc., the National Black Clergy Caucus); labor unions (the American Federation of Teachers, the American Postal Workers Union, the Coalition of Black Trade Unionists); professional associations (National Association of Black Women Attorneys, National Bankers Association, National Bar Association, National Black MBA Association, the National Newspaper Publishers Association); political/policy groups (Congressional Black Caucus, Democratic National Committee, Joint Center for Political Stud-

ies, Leadership Conference on Civil Rights, Martin Luther King, Jr., Center for Nonviolent Social Change; NAACP, National Black Caucus of Local Elected Officials, National Conference of Black Mayors, National Urban Coalition, National Urban League, Operation PUSH, Republican National Committee, SCLC, VEP; social groups (the Alpha Kappa Alpha Sorority, Inc., Alpha Phi Alpha Fraternity, the Chums Inc., Delta Sigma Theta Sorority, Inc., Kappa Alpha Psi Fraternity, Inc., Las Amigas, Inc., the Links, Inc.). These examples are based on a National Coalition on Black Voter Participation pamphlet, 1989.

35. *Operation Big Vote Newsletter,* National Coalition of Black Voter Participation, no. 2 (February 1987): 1, 7.

36. Ibid.

37. Ibid.

38. Sonia Jarvis, "The Black Voter: Alienated or Apathetic?" Address at the University of Illinois, Champaign-Urbana, October 30, 1989.

39. Ibid.

40. A fuller listing of voter registration organizations include: ACORN, Center for National Policy Review, Churches' Committee for Voter Registration/Education, Committee for the Study of the American Electorate, Election Administration Reports, Frontlash Foundation, Inc., Funders' Committee for Voter Registration and Education, Human SERVE Fund, League of Women Voters Education Fund, Midwest Voter Registration and Education Project, NAACP Legal Defense and Education Fund, National Center for Policy Alternatives, National Student Campaign for Voter Registration, National Student Education Fund/US Student Association, Project Vote, Southwest Voter Registration Education Project, and U.S. Public Interest Research Group. This listing is based on Farley Peters, Sandra Martin, and Beth Kyle, *Voter Registration and the States: Effective Policy Approaches to Increasing Participation* (Washington, D.C.: The National Center for Policy Alternatives, 1986). Other organizations include: American Coalition for Traditional Values, Christian Voice, American Defense Foundation, Americans for Responsible Government, National Student Campaign for Voter Registration, Citizens' Leadership Foundation, National Coalition on Black Voter Participation (Operation Big Vote and eighty member organizations), Women's Vote Project, Institute for Social Justice, National Puerto Rican/Hispanic Voter Registration Project, Voter Education Project, and NAACP Voter Education Project. This second list is based on The Center for Responsive Politics, *Public Policy and Foundations: New Directions in Voter Participation* (Washington, D.C.: Center for Responsive Politics, 1986).

41. Peters, Martin, and Kyle, *Voter Registration and the States,* 116.

42. Ibid.

43. Frances Fox Piven and Richard A. Cloward, *Why Americans Don't Vote* (New York: Pantheon Book, 1988), 219.

44. Ibid., 222.

45. Legislation for registration reform (H.R. 2190 and S. 874) failed to pass in the 101st Congress; voting rights advocates such as Sonia Jarvis of the National Coalition report that they plan to continue supporting such legislation until passage.

46. Lucius J. Barker and Ronald W. Walters, eds., *Jesse Jackson's 1984 Presidential Campaign: Challenge and Change in American Politics* (Urbana: University of Illinois Press, 1988); Barker, *Our Time Has Come: A Delegate's Diary of Jesse Jackson's 1984 Presidential Campaign* (Urbana: University of Illinois Press, 1988); Lorenzo Morris,

Charles Jarmon, and Arnold Taylor, eds., *The Social and Political Implications of the Jesse Jackson Presidential Campaign* (New York: Praeger, 1990); and Adolph L. Reed, *The Jesse Jackson Phenomenon: The Crisis of Purpose in Afro-American Politics* (New Haven, Conn.: Yale University Press, 1986).

47. Piven and Cloward, *Why Americans Don't Vote*, 5, 19.

48. Pinderhughes, "Legal Strategies."

3

The Growth and Significance of African American Elected Officials

Theresa Chambliss

Two of the most important factors influencing African American political progress and power in the post-Reconstruction era are the "Great Migration" and the Voting Rights Act of 1965. The Great Migration of African Americans from the South to the North, beginning in the 1920s, transformed African Americans from a basically rural population into an overwhelmingly urban one. The urbanization and concentration of African Americans in northern central cities facilitated the emergence of political power in that region.

As pointed out in chapter 1, the Voting Rights Act of 1965 and its enforcement substantially ended disfranchisement throughout the nation. One of the first results of the politics of African American inclusion in the electorate was the growth in the number of African American elected officials (AAEOs). This chapter presents trends in the growth of AAEOs and explains some of the underlying causes of these trends. The chapter also comments on the significance of electing blacks to public office.

AFRICAN AMERICAN ELECTED OFFICIALS: AN OVERVIEW

In 1941, there were 33 black elected officials, mainly in the North. By 1965, the number was 280. Following the Voting Rights Act, the number increased to nearly 1,000 in 1968. Of this number, one was a United States senator, nine served in the United States House of Representatives, and more than 150 were members of legislatures in twenty-seven of the fifty states. The rest were officials elected to a wide variety of posts, ranging from county officials to city council members and mayors of large cities.[1]

In 1970, the Joint Center for Political Studies began its annual census of blacks holding elective office. This census resulted in the yearly publication, the *National Roster of Black Elected Officials*.[2] The roster shows a significant increase in the number of AAEOs since 1970.[3] As of January 31, 1989, there were 7,226 AAEOs, compared to only 1,469 in 1970, a nearly four-fold increase (see Table 3.1). Overall, African Americans have been elected to every major category of public office except the presidency and vice presidency. The most noticeable gains, however, have come at lower levels of government. African Americans elected to county office have experienced the highest rate of growth of all categories. Their numbers, since 1970, have increased 657 percent. This category is followed by mayors whose numbers have grown 523 percent, city council members (422 percent), and school board members (325 percent).

The change in the number of AAEOs by state (see Table 3.2) shows Alabama with the largest increase over twenty years. (Several other states—for example, Georgia, Texas, and Louisiana—had larger percentage increases, however). In general, more southern states showed numerical increases of 300 or more AAEOs since 1970.

Although the increase of AAEOs over two decades is impressive, it falls short of the ideal of equitable descriptive representation. While African Americans compose 12.2 percent of the nation's total population, they still hold fewer than 1.5 percent of its elective offices. In addition, the annual rate of growth for AAEOs has declined. For example, the number of AAEOs increased by 26.6 percent from 1970 to 1971, but the number rose only 5.8 percent from 1988 to 1989.

Geographic Distribution of AAEOs

The geographic distribution of the nation's AAEOs correlates with the distribution of the African American population.[4] Table 3.3 shows that the South had both the largest proportions of the African American population and AAEOs in 1970 and 1989. Similar correlations exist between the size of the African American population and the election of AAEOs in other regions. Thus, the Midwest has the second largest proportion of both African Americans and black officials, followed by the Northeast, and then the West.

The growth of AAEOs in the South is particularly noteworthy. Table 3.4 demonstrates that there are almost 8 times as many AAEOs in the South today as in 1970. Moreover, the rate of growth of AAEOs is substantially higher (at least 3.9 times) than in other regions.

African Americans in Congress

In 1970, 10 African Americans were members of the 91st Congress (see Table 3.5). This number represented 1.9 percent of the 535 United States

Table 3.1
Number of African American Elected Officials (AAEOs) in Selected Categories, 1970–1989

Year	Members of Congress	State Senators	State Representatives	County Officials	Mayors	City Council Members	School Board Members	Total AAEOs	Annual Percent Change in Total AAEOs
1970	10	31	137	92	48	552	362	1,469	
1971	14	36	162	120	61	653	465	1,860	26.6
1972	14	37	169	176	79	780	657	2,264	21.7
1973	16	42	196	211	82	840	744	2,621	15.8
1974	17	40	196	242	108	1,080	797	1,991	14.1
1975	18	53	223	305	135	1,237	894	3,503	17.1
1976	18	53	223	355	152	1,442	939	3,979	13.6
1977	17	56	238	381	162	1,560	994	4,311	8.3
1978	17	56	238	410	170	1,618	1,086	4,503	4.5
1979	17	70	237	398	175	1,696	1,085	4,607	2.3
1980	17	70	247	451	182	1,809	1,149	4,912	6.5
1981	18	76	257	449	204	1,818	1,211	5,038	2.6
1982	18	73	257	465	223	1,872	1,203	5,160	2.4
1983	21	85	290	496	247	2,030	1,305	5,606	8.6
1984	21	86	299	518	255	2,056	1,300	5,700	1.7
1985	20	90	302	611	286	2,189	1,368	6,056	6.2
1986	20	92	304	681	289	2,396	1,437	6,424	6.1
1987	23	99	311	724	303	2,483	1,475	6,681	4.0
1988	23	98	308	742	301	2,621	1,476	5,829	2.2
1989	24	101	315	696	299	2,882	1,537	7,226	5.8
PERCENT CHANGE 1970–1989	140.0	225.8	129.9	656.5	522.9	422.1	324.6	391.9	

Source: *Black Elected Officials: A National Roster* (Washington, D.C.: Joint Center for Political and Economic Studies, 1989).

Table 3.2
Numerical Changes in African American Elected Officials by State, 1970–1989

State	1970	1989	Change 1970–1989	State	1970	1989	Change 1970–1989
Alabama	86	694	608	Montana	0	0	--
Alaska	1	4	3	Nebraska	2	4	2
Arizona	7	12	5	Nevada	3	10	7
Arkansas	55	318	263	New Hampshire	0	3	3
California	105	276	171	New Jersey	73	119	46
Colorado	7	14	7	New Mexico	3	6	3
Connecticut	31	63	32	New York	74	252	178
Delaware	9	23	14	North Carolina	62	449	387
District of Columbia	8	242	234	North Dakota	0	0	--
Florida	36	179	143	Ohio	89	216	127
Georgia	40	483	443	Oklahoma	36	115	79
Hawaii	0	1	1	Oregon	0	9	9
Idaho	0	0	--	Pennsylvania	49	139	90
Illinois	74	444	370	Rhode Island	2	10	8
Indiana	30	68	38	South Carolina	38	373	335
Iowa	5	9	4	South Dakota	0	3	3
Kansas	6	23	17	Tennessee	38	146	108
Kentucky	41	68	27	Texas	29	312	283
Louisiana	64	521	457	Utah	0	1	1
Maine	0	3	3	Vermont	0	2	2
Maryland	43	118	75	Virginia	36	144	108
Massachusetts	8	38	30	Virgin Islands	NA	22	NA
Michigan	110	306	196	Washington	4	20	16
Minnesota	8	12	4	West Virginia	1	24	23
Mississippi	81	646	565	Wisconsin	7	24	17
Missouri	65	163	98	Wyoming	1	2	1

Source: *Black Elected Officials: A National Roster* (Washington, D.C.: Joint Center for Political and Economic Studies, 1989).

Table 3.3
African American Elected Officials and African American Population by
Region, 1970 and 1989

Region	1970		1989	
	Percent African American Population	Percent AAEOs	Percent African American Population	Percent AAEOs
North	19	23	15	10
South	53	39	60	68
Midwest	20	29	17	18
West	8	9	4	4

Source: *Black Elected Officials: A National Roster* (Washington, D.C.: Joint Center for Political and Economic Studies, 1989).

senators and representatives. One African American senator, Republican Edward Brooke of Massachusetts, held office at that time. None of the eight states that elected African American congressmen were in the South.

By 1989, there were 24 African Americans elected to the 101st Congress, the largest number of African Americans to sit at one time. In 1991, the number expanded to 26 African American members of the House. African Americans now comprise 5.8 percent of all voting members of the United States House. Since 1978, there has been no African American member of the United States

Table 3.4
Distribution of African American Elected Officials by Geographic Region,
1970 and 1989

Region	1970	1989	Percent Change
North	339	709	109.1
South	565	4,855	759.3
Midwest	432	1,272	194.4
West	131	355	171.0
TOTAL*	1,467	7,191	390.2

*Numbers for the Virgin Islands are not included.

Source: *Black Elected Officials: A National Roster* (Washington, D.C.: Joint Center for Political and Economic Studies, 1989).

Table 3.5
African American Members in the United States Congress by Region, 1970–1989

Region	'70	'71	'72	'73	Year '74	'75	'76	'77	'78	'79
Northeast	4	4	4	4	4	4	4	4	4	3
Midwest	5	6	6	5	6	6	6	5	6	5
South	0	2	2	4	4	5	5	4	4	4
West	1	2	2	3	3	3	3	3	3	3
TOTAL	10	14	14	16	17	18	18	16	17	15*

Region	'80	'81	'82	'83	Year '84	'85	'86	'87	'88	'89
Northeast	3	3	3	4	4	4	4	5	5	6
Midwest	6	7	7	9	9	8	8	8	8	8
South	4	4	4	4	4	4	4	6	6	6
West	3	4	4	4	4	4	4	4	4	4
TOTAL	16	18	18	21	21	20	20	23	23	24

*Numbers for Virgin Islands are not included.

Source: *Black Elected Officials: A National Roster* (Washington, D.C.: Joint Center for Political and Economic Studies, 1970–1989).

Senate. From 1970 to 1991, the number of states electing African Americans to Congress rose from eight to fifteen. Only 3 African American members of Congress, Alan Wheat of Missouri, Ronald Dellums of California, and Gary Franks of Connecticut, represent districts that are predominantly white. Currently, only 1 African American member of Congress (Franks) is a Republican; the other 25 are Democrats.

African American State Legislators

Between the years 1970 and 1989, African Americans have been represented in the legislatures of forty-three states and the Virgin Islands. In 1970, African Americans composed 2.2 percent of the 7,468 state legislators nationwide. In this same year, eleven states (Alabama, Arkansas, South Carolina, West Virginia, Alaska, Oregon, Wyoming, New Hampshire, Rhode Island, Vermont, and Nebraska) had no African American state legislators, but eight states (Missouri, Georgia, Illinois, Michigan, Ohio, New York, Maryland and Pennsylvania) had ten or more African American legislators (see Table 3.6).

In 1989, African Americans composed 5.6 percent of the nation's state legislators. There were black state legislators in every state except New Mexico.

Table 3.6
Numerical Changes in African American State Legislators by State, 1970–1989[1]

State	Total State Legislators 1970 & 1989	Black State Legislators 1970	Black State Legislators 1989	Numerical Change 1970–1989
Alabama	140	0	23	23
Alaska	60	0	1	1
Arizona	90	3	3	0
Arkansas	135	0	6	6
California	120	6	7	1
Colorado	100	3	4	1
Connecticut	187	5	8	3
Delaware	62	3	3	0
Florida	160	1	11	10
Georgia	236	14	30	16
Illinois	177	14	21	7
Indiana	150	3	8	5
Iowa	150	1	1	0
Kansas	165	3	4	1
Kentucky	138	3	2	-1
Louisiana	144	1	20	19
Maryland	188	11	27	16
Massachusetts	200	2	6	4
Michigan	148	13	16	3
Minnesota	201	1	1	0
Mississippi	174	1	22	21
Missouri	197	15	16	1
Nebraska	49	0	1	1
Nevada	63	1	3	2
New Hampshire	424	0	3	3
New Jersey	120	4	8	4
New Mexico	112	1	0	-1
New York	211	12	21	9
North Carolina	170	1	15	14
Ohio	132	13	13	0
Oklahoma	149	5	5	0
Oregon	90	0	3	3
Pennsylvania	253	11	18	7
Rhode Island	150	1	6	5
South Carolina	170	0	21	21
Tennessee	132	8	13	5
Texas	181	3	15	12
Vermont	180	0	2	2
Virginia	140	3	10	7
Virgin Islands	15	0	9	9
Washington	147	1	3	2
West Virginia	134	0	1	1
Wisconsin	132	1	5	4
Wyoming	94	0	1	1
TOTAL	7,468[2]	168	416	248

[1]States not listed had no African American state legislators during either year.
[2]Total includes state legislators of all 50 states.

Source: *Black Elected Officials: A National Roster* (Washington, D.C.: Joint Center for Political and Economic Studies, 1970–1989).

The number of African American state legislators declined in two states (Kentucky and New Mexico) from 1970 to 1989. The number of African American states legislators remained constant in six states (Delaware, Oklahoma, Arizona, Iowa, Missouri, and Ohio). The number of African American state legislators grew significantly in nine states during the period 1970-1989. Of these nine states, all in the South, four had no African Americans in their legislatures in 1970. Indeed, 68.5 percent of the overall gain in the number of African American state legislators in this period occurred in southern states.

African American Mayors

In 1970, the number of African American mayors was 48 (see Table 3.7). Of this number, 2 were mayors of cities with populations of 50,000 or more, according to the 1970 census. In 1989, the number of African American mayors was 299—more than five times as many as in 1970. Twenty-six African Americans represented cities with populations of 50,000 or more. The states with the biggest gains in the number of African American mayors in the period 1970-1989 were Alabama, Mississippi, Arkansas, and Illinois.

Regionally, the South led in the number of African American mayors in 1970 and 1989. However, the region showing the highest rate of growth between 1970 and 1989 was the Midwest. The Midwest had 8 African American mayors in 1970 and 58 (or 6.3 times more) African American mayors in 1989.

Female African American Elected Officials

Crossing the hurdles of gender discrimination as well as racial discrimination, African American females have run for and won elective offices. In 1975, extensive data on female African American elected officials were introduced in the *Roster*. During that year, females constituted 15 percent of the 3,505 AAEOs. In 1989, they constituted 25 percent of the AAEOs (see Table 3.8). The rate of growth for female AAEOs has exceeded the total AAEO growth rate in every year since 1975. Table 3.9 shows that from 1975 to 1989, the ratio of male to female AAEOs decreased from approximately six to one to approximately three to one.

By 1989, there were more female AAEOs in every category except federal offices. Instead, the number of African American females in Congress first declined from four in 1975 to only one in 1989, and then rose again to four in 1991. The regional distribution of female AAEOs reflects the pattern of all AAEOs.

In sum, the number of African American elected officials has grown steadily since 1970. The growth has been particularly impressive in the South, but all regions and levels of government have shown improvement. Although African

Table 3.7
African American Elected Mayors, 1970–1989

Year	Number of Mayors	Difference
1970*	48	--
1971*	61	13
1972*	79	18
1973	82	3
1974	108	26
1975	135	27
1976	152	17
1977	162	10
1978	170	8
1979	175	5
1980	182	7
1981	204	22
1982	223	19
1983	247	24
1984	255	8
1985	286	31
1986	289	3
1987	303	14
1988	301	2
1989	299	-2

*Number includes Vice-Mayors.

Source: *Black Elected Officials: A National Roster* (Washington, D.C.: Joint Center for Political and Economic Studies, 1970–1989).

American women continue to be underrepresented even when compared to African American men, their rate of growth has surpassed that of African American males. Despite these salutary developments, it is important to note that African Americans remain severely underrepresented among the nation's public officials.

FACTORS SUPPORTING THE ELECTION OF AFRICAN AMERICANS TO PUBLIC OFFICE

Approximately two out of every three AAEOs are elected in majority African American jurisdictions. Thus, the backbone of this progress is the African American vote. Since 1965, African American voter registration and turnout

when compared to white voter registration and turnout has increased significantly. For example, the overall gap in registration between whites and African
Americans closed substantially between the presidential election years of 1968
and 1988. The 1968, the proportion of African Americans registered to vote
was 9.2 percentage points lower than the proportion of whites registered to

Table 3.8
Growth in the Number of African American Female Elected Officials,
1975–1989

Year	Number	Percent Female AAEOs' Growth	Percent AAEOs' Growth
1975	530	----	----
1976	684	29.1	13.6
1977	782	14.3	8.3
1978	843	7.8	4.5
1979	882	4.6	2.3
1980	976	10.6	6.6
1981	1,021	4.6	2.6
1982	1,081	9.7	2.4
1983	1,223	13.1	8.6
1984	1,259	2.9	1.7
1985	1,359	10.8	6.2
1986	1,482	9.1	6.1
1987	1,564	5.5	4.0
1988	1,625	3.9	2.2
1989	1,814	11.6	5.8

Source: *Black Elected Officials: A National Roster* (Washington, D.C.: Joint Center for Political and
   Economic Studies, 1989).

Table 3.9
Total Numbers of Male and Female African American Elected Officials Since 1975

Year	Male AAEOs	Female AAEOs	Male AAEOs/ Female AAEOs Ratio
1975	2,973	530	5.61
1976	3,295	684	4.82
1977	3,529	782	4.51
1978	3,660	843	4.34
1979	3,725	882	4.22
1980	3,936	976	4.03
1981	4,017	1,021	3.93
1982	4,079	1,081	3.77
1983	4,383	1,223	3.58
1984	4,441	1,259	3.53
1985	4,697	1,359	3.46
1986	4,942	1,482	3.34
1987	5,117	1,564	3.27
1988	5,204	1,625	3.20
1989	5,412	1,814	2.98

Source: *Black Elected Officials: A National Roster* (Washington, D.C.: Joint Center for Political and Economic Studies, 1989).

vote. As Sonia Jarvis points out in chapter 1, at first the gap tended to widen in the mid-1970s; but by 1988, the African American-to-white voter registration gap had narrowed considerably. In 1988, the proportion of African Americans registered to vote was only 3.4 percentage points lower than the white proportion (see Table 3.10). Similarly, the gap between black and white voter turnout closed from 11.5 percentage points in 1968 to 7.6 percentage points in 1988. The gap in mid-term elections has narrowed even more. In the 1966 mid-term election, the proportion of African Americans who voted was 15.3 percentage points lower than the proportion of whites who reported voting; by 1986 the proportion of African Americans who reported voting was only 3.8 percentage points lower than the proportion of whites who reported voting. Between 1968 and 1988, almost 5.5 million additional African Americans registered to vote. During these same years, the number of African American voters who reported voting increased by almost 4 million.[5] In most places and in most instances, large majorities of African American voters supported African American candidates when and where they ran for office.

The root of these developments is first and foremost the Voting Rights Act of 1965, which removed many of the most serious obstacles to African American voter participation (see chapter 1). Organizations devoted to mobilizing African American voters have also played an exceptionally necessary and positive role (see discussion in chapter 2). Several other recent factors have heavily influenced African American voter participation. Three of these factors (Reaganomics, Jesse Jackson's campaigns for the Democratic presidential nomination, and the replacement of at-large election systems by single-member district systems) are discussed briefly below.

Reaganomics and African American Voters

Voter turnout often is stimulated by a candidate for whom voters feel either a great affinity or, conversely, a great hostility. President Ronald Reagan evoked the latter feeling among African Americans. During Reagan's eight years in office, rarely did more than 25 percent of African Americans approve of his job performance. The rating of Reagan's performance on economic issues was even more abysmal among blacks. Especially at the time of his 1984 reelection campaign, Reagan's job approval rating dropped among blacks. In July 1984, for example, a Joint Center for Political Studies (JCPS)/Gallup Organization survey found that only 8 percent of African Americans approved of the way the president was handling his job.[6] Seventy-two percent of African Americans surveyed in this poll reported that they believed Reagan was prejudiced. Other polls provided similar findings. For example, in a 1985 poll, 56 percent of African Americans reported that they believed Reagan was a racist.[7] Finally, the JCPS/Gallup survey demonstrated association between those who disapproved of Reagan's job performance and the reported likelihood of voting. Thus, hostility to President Reagan was one of the factors influencing the growth of African American voter participation after 1980.

Table 3.10
Reported Voter Registration and Participation as Percentage of Voting-Age Population, by Region and Race, 1964–1988

	1964	1968	1972	1976	1980	1984	1988	1966	1970	1974	1978	1982	1986
REGISTERED													
United States													
White	NA	75.4	73.4	68.3	68.4	69.6	67.9	71.6	69.1	63.5	63.8	65.6	65.3
African Amer.	NA	66.2	65.5	58.5	60.0	66.3	64.5	60.2	60.8	54.9	57.1	59.1	64.0
Difference	NA	9.2	7.9	9.8	8.4	3.3	3.4	11.4	8.3	8.6	6.7	6.5	+0.3
North and West													
White	NA	77.2	74.9	69.0	69.3	70.5	68.5	74.5	70.8	64.6	64.9	66.7	66.2
African Amer.	NA	71.8	67.0	60.9	60.6	67.2	65.9	68.8	64.5	54.2	58.0	61.7	63.1
Difference	NA	5.4	7.9	8.1	8.7	3.3	3.6	5.7	6.3	10.4	6.9	5.0	+3.1
South													
White	NA	70.8	69.8	66.7	66.2	67.8	66.6	64.3	65.1	61.0	61.2	63.2	63.2
African Amer.	NA	61.6	64.0	56.4	59.3	65.6	63.3	52.9	57.5	55.5	56.2	56.9	64.6
Difference	NA	9.2	5.8	10.3	6.9	2.2	3.3	11.4	7.6	5.5	5.0	6.3	-1.4
VOTED													
United States													
White	70.7	69.1	64.5	60.9	60.9	61.4	59.1	57.0	56.0	46.3	47.3	49.9	47.0
African Amer.	58.5	57.6	52.1	48.7	50.5	55.8	51.5	41.7	43.5	33.8	37.2	43.0	43.2
Difference	12.2	11.5	12.4	12.2	10.4	5.6	7.6	15.3	12.5	12.5	10.1	6.9	+3.8
North and West													
White	74.7	71.8	67.5	62.6	62.4	63.0	60.4	61.7	59.8	50.0	50.0	53.1	48.7
African Amer.	72.0	64.8	56.7	52.2	52.8	58.9	55.6	52.1	51.4	37.9	41.3	48.5	44.2
Difference	2.7	7.0	10.8	10.4	9.6	4.1	4.8	9.6	8.4	12.1	8.7	4.6	+4.5
South													
White	59.6	61.9	57.0	57.1	57.4	58.1	56.4	45.1	46.4	37.4	41.1	42.9	43.5
African Amer.	44.0	51.6	47.8	45.7	48.2	53.2	48.0	32.9	36.8	30.0	33.5	38.3	42.5
Difference	15.5	10.3	9.2	11.4	9.2	4.9	8.4	12.2	9.6	7.4	7.6	4.6	+1.0

Source: United States Bureau of the Census.

Jesse Jackson's Campaigns for the Democratic Presidential Nomination

Just as hostility toward Reagan encouraged higher African American voter registration and turnout, so, too, did affection for Jesse Jackson. One of the main goals of Jackson's campaigns was to encourage political empowerment through registering "the disenfranchised." The conclusion that Jackson was influential in increasing black voter registration and turnout is supported by evidence from the JCPS/Gallup surveys of 1984 and 1988. In both election years, more than two of every three first-time African American voter registrants reported that the Jackson campaign encouraged them to register to vote.[8]

Jackson's candidacies also prompted changes within the Democratic party— from rules and platform reforms to greater participation as delegates to the Democratic National Conventions of 1984 and 1988. The result of these reforms was an increase in black participation not only as voters but as delegates to the conventions. In 1984, 18 percent of all delegates to the Democratic convention were African Americans; in 1988, 23 percent were African Americans.

The Shift from At-Large to Single-Member District Elections

The election of African Americans is much more likely to occur under a system of district elections than under a system of at-large elections where candidates must compete citywide or countywide. Thus, although at-large electoral systems can be traced back to the nineteenth century and were devised as part of good-government reforms not specifically targeted to African Americans, they nevertheless stand as a bulwark inhibiting the election of African Americans where whites are the majority and are reluctant to vote for blacks. In single-member district systems, however, majority African American districts can be carved, thereby enhancing the probability of electing African American representatives. As a result of litigation, many areas switched in the 1970s and 1980s from at-large systems to single-member districts. Concomitantly, the number of African American elected officials grew.

In sum, access to the ballot made possible by the Voting Rights Act of 1965, the role of African American political organizations in registering African Americans to vote, the encouragement to vote generated by hostility felt toward President Reagan and his administration and affection felt for Jesse Jackson, and the switch from at-large to district election systems have all combined to support the election of more African American public officials.

It is important to add that in dozens of cities, congressional districts, and states, the growth in African American voting has often been the pivotal factor deciding the election of "more progressive" white candidates as well. In 1986, for example, the African American vote (which tends to be unified) was crucial to the election of five Democratic senatorial candidates in Alabama, Georgia, Louisiana, North Carolina, and California.

THE SIGNIFICANCE OF ELECTING AFRICAN AMERICANS TO PUBLIC OFFICE

African Americans, whether Democrats or Republicans, have a major stake in the political arena. According to Robert Dahl, ethnic/racial groups traditionally make their way into the American mainstream by moving from a position of powerlessness to empowerment in the political arena.[9] The advantages of full participation of African Americans in the political process are obvious: Being a part of the governmental process increases the likelihood of one's group securing its fair share of public goods and services. Attacks on affirmative action and other race-specific policies in the last decade present a clear danger to the hard-earned socioeconomic and political gains made since the 1960s. To overcome these dangers, African American political participation is imperative.

African American elected officials are in a unique position because they are usually only a small voting minority in the legislative bodies where decisions are made. Nonetheless, they have managed to make valuable contributions to the African American community, as well as to their jurisdictions as a whole. The key to overcoming their small numbers has been their willingness and ability to organize meaningful coalitions devoted to expanding civil rights and economic justice for all Americans.

For example, coming together as the Congressional Black Caucus (CBC), African American members of Congress have led in the initiation of social policies favorable to African Americans and other disproportionately poor groups, spearheaded legislation on South Africa, garnered support from other congressional caucuses (especially the Hispanic Caucus and the Women's Caucus) to moderate Reagan's draconian budget proposals; and led in the fight for maintaining or expanding civil rights protections for minorities and women during the George Bush administration. African American state legislators have initiated innovative legislation in a wide range of policy areas—for example, housing, minority business contracting, school desegregation, and so forth. They have also played a critical role in the redistricting process. Through their independent actions and participation in coalitions, they have helped determine where majority African American congressional, state, county, and local districts were drawn.

In cities (especially the nation's largest ones) where African American mayors hold office, African American-owned businesses expand, the rate of small business failure declines, and there are significant increases in both the numbers and proportions of African Americans employed in city government.[10] Hence, African American mayors have been instrumental in fostering the growth of the African American middle class through providing thousands of managerial and professional jobs in city government and contracts to minority businesses.

CONCLUSION

African American political participation and political effectiveness cannot be fully understood through quantitative data on AAEOs alone. These data do not show the total number of African American candidates seeking political office; they also do not reveal the influence of African American voters and officials on the electoral prospects of whites, Latinos, Asians, and others seeking office. Nor do these data show the contributions made by appointed African American officials at all levels of government or the influence of African Americans on public policies.

The data on AAEOs presented here do show, however, the progress made in winning elective office and the progress that remains to be made. For greater progress in electing African Americans to public office, there remains the necessity of building support for black candidates from other racial and ethnic groups and encouraging massive black participation at the ballot box.

NOTES

1. Joint Center for Political Studies, memorandum, April 9, 1981.

2. This publication contains listings for African American officeholders in the United States and the Virgin Islands. It provides statistical information on (1) the population of the states, and (2) the distribution of black elected officials by region, category of office, and gender. It also provides useful facts about the organization of the various state governments.

3. Cutoff dates for *Black Elected Officials: A National Roster* were as follows: February for the 1970 roster; March of each year for the 1971 and 1972 rosters; April of each year for the 1973 and 1974 rosters; May for the 1975 roster; June for the 1976 roster; July of each year for the 1976-1983 rosters, and January of each year for the 1984-1989 rosters. As of this writing, no roster has been published since 1989. However, the Joint Center for Political Studies reported in the May 1990 issue of its monthly newsletter, *Focus*, that there were 7,370 African American elected officials (AAEOs) in January 1990.

4. Geographic distribution is based on the following Census Bureau divisions: *SOUTH*—Alabama, Arkansas, Delaware, Florida, Georgia, Kentucky, Louisiana, Maryland, Mississippi, North Carolina, Oklahoma, South Carolina, Tennessee, Texas, Virginia, West Virginia; *WEST*—Alaska, Arizona, California, Colorado, Hawaii, Idaho, Montana, Nevada, New Mexico, Oregon, Utah, Washington, Wyoming; *NORTHEAST*—Connecticut, Maine, Massachusetts, New Hampshire, New Jersey, New York, Pennsylvania, Rhode Island, Vermont; and *MIDWEST*—Illinois, Indiana, Iowa, Kansas, Michigan, Minnesota, Missouri, Nebraska, North Dakota, Ohio, South Dakota, Wisconsin.

5. All statistics on voter registration and turnout cited in this chapter come from surveys conducted by the United States Bureau of the Census. These data reflect overreporting. Some analysts have concluded that African Americans overreport more than whites do.

6. Joint Center for Political Studies (JCPS)/Gallup Organization Survey, July 1984.

7. *The Washington Post* poll, January 1985.

8. JCPS/Gallup Surveys, July 1984 and August 1988.

9. See discussion of Dahl's ideas in Eddie N. Williams, "Perspective," *Focus* 11, no. 5 (May 1983): 2.

10. Peter Eisinger, *Black Employment in City Government, 1972-1980* (Washington, D.C.: Joint Center for Political Studies, 1981).

_____ Part II

The Present Legal, Economic, and Cultural Context of African American Politics

4

Eradicating the Continuing Barriers to Effective Minority Voter Participation

Frank R. Parker

In 1906, Greenville, Mississippi, held a referendum on how its city council members should be elected. The question was whether Greenville should retain its private charter under which all six city council members, then called aldermen, were elected citywide or whether Greenville should go under the state municipal code and elect its city council members by wards. Although most of Mississippi's African American voters had been disenfranchised by the state constitution of 1890, black citizens in Greenville had the potential to elect some city council members if voting was by ward, but none if elections were at-large.

One of the leaders of the opposition to the change to ward voting was State Senator J. L. Hebron, a prominent Delta politician, who told a crowd opposing the change: "I oppose the bringing of the Negro back into politics, which going under the Code and allowing the wards to select their Aldermen, will surely do."[1] The referendum was defeated and Greenville retained its at-large election system. Within nine years, all of Mississippi's major cities had switched from ward voting to at-large voting systems.[2]

When the Voting Rights Act was passed in 1965, enabling black voters in Mississippi to register and vote for the first time since Reconstruction, Mississippi had a majority black congressional district in the Delta area. This raised the possibility that the state's newly enfranchised black voters would be able to elect a black member of Congress in the 1966 congressional elections.

The Mississippi Legislature responded to what the *Jackson Clarion-Ledger* had called this "serious threat to 'white supremacy' " by adopting a new congressional redistricting plan.[3] This new plan split the Delta up among three districts, denying black voters a voting majority in any district. During the floor debate in the state legislature, State Representative Olie Trenor, an opponent of the plan, asked the legislators: "Did the Negro situation enter in this redistricting plan?" When he got no answer to his question, he said, "We all know the Negro situation was the main factor."[4] Nonetheless, a court challenge to the plan brought by the Mississippi Freedom Democratic party, a black political group, was rejected by the Federal District Court in Mississippi, and the United States Supreme Court affirmed its decision. This prevented black voters of Mississippi, who then comprised 42 percent of the state's population, from gaining black representation in Congress for twenty years.[5]

Two questions have arisen in the debate concerning barriers to effective minority voter participation. First, what role have structural barriers such as at-large elections and racial gerrymandering played as determinants of minority political success or failure in the period after the Voting Rights Act was passed? Second, have Congress and the federal courts gone too far in providing statutory and constitutional protection against minority vote dilution?

Structural barriers to effective minority voter participation, such as at-large elections and racial gerrymandering of district lines, have been a significant impediment to African American political success throughout the South and in other areas of the country for the past twenty-five years.[6] However, the extent to which southern states attempted to negate the black vote after passage of the Voting Rights Act is an issue that has been neglected by political analysts of the post-1965 period. Several important books have been written about southern politics and black voting after 1965, including Nunan Bartley and Hugh Graham's *Southern Politics and the Second Reconstruction*,[7] Jack Bass and Walter DeVries' *The Transformation of Southern Politics*,[8] Alexander Lamis's *The Two-Party South*,[9] Stephen Lawson's *In Pursuit of Power*,[10] and, most recently, Earl and Merle Blacks's *Politics and Society in the South*.[11] Although several of these books touch on the new barriers to the black vote maintained after 1965, none of them fully describe these barriers or analyze them as primary determinants of black political success or failure during this period.

In fact, it seems that the further the nation gets from 1965 and the more court cases that challenge these barriers, the less certain political scientists are that structural barriers ever were imposed to effectively disenfranchise blacks or ever had any impact on blacks' ability to vote. For example, Earl and Merle Black note that during the 1800s in the Reconstruction and immediate post-Reconstruction periods, at least sixteen discriminatory techniques were used to hamper black political power. They then write: "Similar techniques of minority vote dilution *appear to have been used* in the Second Reconstruction [emphasis added]."[12] The words used here are important. They do not write "were enacted to dilute black voting strength throughout the South," nor "were a primary deterrent to black electoral success after 1965," but "appear to have been used." They then dispense with this whole issue in a single paragraph.

In addition to the neglect of this issue in the literature concerning Southern politics, there is the question of the appropriateness of the legal standards that have been used by the courts in countering these structural barriers to minority political participation. In testimony opposing the extension of the Voting Rights Act in 1982 and in a book by Abigail Thernstrom, neoconservative scholars of the anti-affirmative action school began a concerted attack on most of the gains made in black voting rights since 1965. They focus particularly on the congressional legislation and legal standards used by the courts to eliminate at-large elections, racial gerrymandering, and other discriminatory voting devices.[13]

Thernstrom denounced the Supreme Court's decision in *Allen v. State Board of Elections,* a decision that is the *Brown v. Board of Education* for black voting rights, as a distortion of the original intent of Congress in enacting the Voting Rights Act. She criticized the *Allen* decision as the beginning of "the process by which the Voting Rights Act was reshaped into an instrument for affirmative action in the electoral sphere."[14] Thernstrom argued that eliminating at-large elections and creating majority black districts wrongly grants minority candidates "special protection from white competition."[15] The result, she argued, is to prevent biracial political coalitions and to distort the operation of democratic processes. Her solution is to cut back on legal protections for minority voting rights and to limit judicial intervention to rare and extreme cases.[16]

The raising of these questions—whether discriminatory structural barriers have in fact been used since 1965 to dilute black votes and whether the courts have gone too far in protecting minority voter participation—once again makes the issue of structural barriers to effective minority participation a central focus in the debate over minority voting rights and political participation in the United States.

This debate has the most profound implications for the future of black political participation in the country. It affects not only the continued viability of the Voting Rights Act of 1965, but also impacts on the 1990 census and the widespread redistricting at the congressional, state, and local levels that follows the census.

THE ROLE OF STRUCTURAL BARRIERS AS AN IMPEDIMENT TO BLACK POLITICAL PARTICIPATION

When the Voting Rights Act was passed in 1965, southern state political leaders knew that they could no longer deny blacks the right to register and vote. So they switched strategies from vote denial to vote dilution and introduced a second generation of disfranchising devices to negate the newly-gained black vote. Mississippi led the way by adopting a series of political "massive resistance" strategies.[17] Nine months after the Voting Rights Act was passed, the Mississippi Legislature enacted a series of laws that became models for post-1965 black disfranchisement throughout the South. These included:

- racially gerrymandering congressional district lines by dividing up the heavily-black Delta region

- increasing the number of multimember legislative districts that combined majority black counties with majority white counties to prevent the election of black state legislators

- making it easier to abolish majority black counties and combine them with majority white counties

- switching from district to at-large elections for county boards of supervisors and county school boards

- abolishing elections for county school superintendents and making the office appointive

- increasing the qualifying requirements for independent candidates to prevent black independents from getting elected.

The "open primary" was another device that first passed the legislature, then was vetoed by the governor in 1966, but later became law. The open primary law abolished party primary elections and instituted a majority vote and runoff requirement to win in the general election.

When the statute switching from district to at-large county elections was struck down by the Justice Department in a Section five objection under the Voting Rights Act, a majority of Mississippi counties switched tactics, and there was wholesale racial gerrymandering of county supervisors' district lines.

These techniques became models for black disfranchisement throughout the South. During the post-1965 period, all the southern state legislatures used multimember legislative districts and racial gerrymandering of legislative district lines to prevent blacks from getting elected.[18] Most southern states also retained at-large election systems at the county and local levels to dilute black voters.

Louisiana in particular followed Mississippi's lead and in 1968 passed laws switching from district to at-large elections for members of the parish governing boards and school boards. When that move was blocked by a Justice Department objection under the Voting Rights Act, at-large elections were replaced with widespread racial gerrymandering.[19] Louisiana also followed Mississippi's lead in adopting an open primary law that is still in effect.

These devices, combined with pre-1965 devices such as at-large municipal elections and the primary election runoff requirement, proved very effective in limiting the number of black candidates who could get elected. The primary technique most of them shared was to eliminate or minimize the number of majority black election districts from which black candidates could get elected.

The effectiveness of this vote-dilution strategy is demonstrated by the wide disparity between the high rate of black voter registration following implementation of the Voting Rights Act and the low level of black electoral success during the act's first years. Of all the southern states, Mississippi had the greatest percentage increase of black registered voters. Prior to 1965, only 6.7 percent of Mississippi's adults were registered to vote; by 1967 that number had increased to almost 60 percent, giving Mississippi the highest black voter registration rate of any state covered by the Voting Rights Act. However, in the first statewide elections held after the Voting Rights Act was passed, of the 127 black candidates who ran or attempted to run for state and local offices in 1967, only 22 were elected—a success rate of only 17 percent. Four years later, in the next statewide elections in 1971, of the 309 black candidates who ran, only 50 were elected—a success rate of only 16 percent.

Listing the structural barriers enacted by southern state legislatures to negate the black vote after 1965 does not imply that these structural barriers were the only impediments to black electoral success. Black political participation in the South also was hampered by depressed socioeconomic circumstances (low income, lack of education, unemployment, and economic dependency resulting in low black registration and turnout rates), harassment and intimidation from hostile whites, and vote fraud and election irregularities. But these structural barriers were and have been an important factor in determining black electoral success. Once they were eliminated, the number of black officeholders increased dramatically.

THE ROLE OF THE FEDERAL COURTS IN ERADICATING BARRIERS TO EFFECTIVE MINORITY VOTER PARTICIPATION

The black political movement in the South in the post-1965 period employed voting rights litigation in the federal courts as the principal means of overcoming the southern political massive resistance campaign. This litigation strategy encountered many obstacles, including the initial lack of direct constitutional or statutory precedent supporting a legal right to be free of racial vote dilution. Moreover, southern federal district judges were committed to maintaining the status quo of racial segregation in politics, and the Burger Court grew increasingly conservative beginning in the late 1970s. This new post-1965 voting rights movement was successful in influencing decision makers to make new laws protecting minority voting rights—both judicial and statutory—that were directly responsive to black voters' campaigns to overcome the southern political massive resistance strategy.

Initially, the Supreme Court and the lower federal courts, with some exceptions (such as District Judge Frank M. Johnson Jr. of Alabama) were resistant to claims of minority vote dilution.[20] But eventually, the Supreme Court responded to this southwide political massive resistance effort by expanding the federal statutory and constitutional protections for black voting rights. In 1969, the Supreme Court decided *Allen v. State Board of Elections*, involving Mississippi cases challenging three state political massive resistance statutes passed in 1966 (switching from district to at-large elections, abolishing elections for county school superintendents, and increasing the qualifying requirements for independent candidates). The Supreme Court construed Section five of the Voting Rights Act to require federal preclearance of all post-1965 voting law changes in states covered by the act, no matter how minor.[21] Since the *Allen* decision, Section five (under which certain "covered" jurisdictions are barred from instituting any new voting laws or procedures without first showing that the changes are nondiscriminatory) has become the most frequently used law to defeat new discriminatory voting laws.

Then in 1973, in a lawsuit challenging multimember legislative districts in Dallas and San Antonio, Texas, *White v. Regester,* the Court made a new law when it held that the Fourteenth Amendment prohibited any voting system that, under the totality of the circumstances, denied minority voters equal access to the political process and an equal opportunity to elect candidates of their choice.[22] This standard was applied in scores of lawsuits in the South throughout the 1970s to strike down discriminatory at-large election systems and racial gerrymandering.

As a result of personnel changes and increasing conservatism, the Supreme Court took a step backward in 1980 in *City of Mobile v. Bolden* when it ruled that plaintiffs asserting a dilution of minority voting rights under the Fourteenth and Fifteenth Amendments must prove discriminatory intent. This constituted a serious setback for the voting rights movement, since discriminatory intent is very difficult to prove in court and exceedingly easy for public officials to hide. In 1982, Congress in effect overruled the *Mobile* decision and strengthened the protections of the Voting Rights Act by amending Section two of the act to eliminate the requirement of proving discriminatory intent and to prohibit any voting procedure that "results" in racial discrimination.[23] Between 1982 and 1987, the Justice Department estimates that over 1,300 jurisdictions changed their methods of election to comply with Section two. In addition, there have been hundreds of lawsuits filed that have eliminated racial discrimination in congressional redistricting, state legislative reapportionment, and discriminatory election systems at the county and local levels. This litigation campaign to strike down discriminatory barriers to the effectiveness of minority votes has continued through the 1980s. Voting rights cases struck down racial gerrymandering in congressional redistricting in Georgia, Mississippi, and Louisiana; these decisions resulted in the creation for the first time of majority black congressional districts and produced three of the recently elected black members of Congress, John Lewis of Georgia, Mike Espy of Mississippi, and William Jefferson of Louisiana. Voting rights cases also resulted in the elimination of the remaining racially discriminatory multimember legislative districts in Arkansas, North Carolina, and Virginia, producing increases in black representation in the state legislatures of those states. Court decisions struck down at-large voting and racial gerrymandering in numerous counties and cities throughout the country.[24]

For example, the Alabama case of *Dillard v. Crenshaw County* indicates that there is a direct cause-and-effect relationship between successful litigation eliminating at-large voting (and other structural barriers) that submerge black voting strength, the creation of majority black districts as a remedy for that discrimination, and an increase in the number of black elected officials. The *Dillard* lawsuit challenged at-large county and city elections throughout Alabama. As a result of court decisions and settlements in that case, 180 counties and cities throughout the state were required to eliminate discriminatory at-large voting and to adopt single-member district plans. Switching from at-large elections to single-member districts produced 252 additional black county commissioners and city council members.[25]

THE NEOCONSERVATIVE CHALLENGE TO THESE DEVELOPMENTS

Despite the gains in black political participation that have been made as a result of voting rights litigation, neoconservative scholars in the political science community have mounted an increasingly visible campaign challenging these legal standards and court remedies. Immediately prior to the elections of David Dinkins to be mayor of New York and Douglas Wilder to be governor of Virginia, *U.S. News and World Report* ran an article reporting that "much of American politics is being ghettoized. Citizens are increasingly being cordoned off into electoral districts that are very black or very white."[26]

"There's a Jim Crow message in all of this," argues Abigail M. Thernstrom, author of the book *Whose Votes Count?* "We should structure electoral systems to create more interracial coalitions, not fewer." Carol Swain, a black political scientist at Duke University, agrees: "More blacks could be elected. It's just that there's a general perception among whites and blacks that blacks can't win in a majority white district." She argues that race is not insurmountable for black candidates; those who want to go it alone in separate districts should think again.[27]

These arguments were inadvertently given additional credibility following elections in November 1989 by some prominent political analysts who misinterpreted the results of those elections to imply that barriers that have prevented the elections of black candidates for the past twenty-five years no longer exist. Some political analysts were quoted as saying that the successful Dinkins and Wilder races show that strong black candidates working in the political mainstream now have a reasonable chance of getting elected in predominantly white jurisdictions throughout the country.[28]

The Dinkins and Wilder successes are indeed extraordinary, but the case can be made that they do not represent the typical experience of black politicians across the country. Two elections do not make a trend. What the neoconservatives and misinterpreters of the Dinkins and Wilder victories ignore is the widespread and stubborn persistence of racially polarized voting that historically has denied all but a few black candidates success in majority white constituencies. The Dinkins and Wilder successes should be compared with the results of the judicial elections in Mississippi in Spring 1989 that more nearly typify the experience of black candidates, particularly in the South. In Mississippi, the federal district court in 1987 found that at-large voting in eight judicial districts violated Section two of the Voting Rights Act and in 1988 adopted a judicial redistricting plan that subdivided those districts, creating seventeen new majority black judicial districts.[29] Although past experience in Mississippi showed that election districts usually had to be at least 65 percent black to give black voters an opportunity to elect candidates of their choice, the district judge in this case was more impressed with the recent elections of Mike Espy to Congress and Judge Reuben Anderson to the state Supreme Court in districts that were 58 percent black and less than 50 percent black, respectively. Accordingly, he ordered a 65 percent cap on majority black districts to avoid "packing" black concentrations. However, because of high black population concentrations in Jackson, Mississippi, three of the Jackson districts had to be slightly over 65 percent black.

In the Spring 1989 elections in these districts, seventeen black candidates ran for judicial seats. All of them were highly qualified candidates who were attorneys with five years of legal experience or more. Despite the qualifications of the black candidates, racially polarized voting patterns prevailed in these elections. Only five of these seventeen highly qualified black candidates were elected, three of them in the three Jackson districts that were over 65 percent black according to the 1980 census data and a fifth in a majority white multi-member district in Vicksburg. In this latter instance, black voters cast single-shot ballots (voting only for the black candidate, instead of for more than one candidate), enabling one black candidate to get elected. The limited number of black successes prompted one attorney, Carroll Rhodes, who was not a candidate but who represented black plaintiffs in the ensuing lawsuit, to remark: "In spite of some black leaders' allegations that there is not more discrimination in Mississippi, these election results are a clear indication that discrimination is alive and well in Mississippi and will probably be around for some time to come."[30]

The Mississippi experience demonstrates that, contrary to Thernstrom, the opportunities for black candidates in most of the country to get elected by forming interracial coalitions remain extremely limited. Swain, who has not produced any data to support her assertions, is wrong to assert that the inability of black candidates to get elected in white districts is merely "a general perception." For twenty-five years this has been the political reality recognized by both white and black political leaders alike, particularly in the South. Southern state legislators acted on this reality after 1965 with their political massive resistance strategy of eliminating and minimizing the number of majority black districts to prevent the election of black candidates. Minority

voting rights plaintiffs in hundreds of court cases have convincingly demonstrated to skeptical and conservative federal judges that black voters cannot
gain black representation in at-large voting in majority white districts or ger-
rymandered districts that eliminate black majorities, and that remedial majority black districts must be created to give black voters representation of their
choice.

This is not to say that biracial coalition politics is not a good thing or an ideal
to be pursued. However, the question of whether to pursue biracial coalition
politics is largely in the hands of white voters. Black voters for twenty-five
years have voted for, and frequently have formed part of the winning coalitions
for, successful white candidates in statewide and local races throughout the
South. But, particularly in the South, there are few instances in which a majority of white voters have supported a black candidate—other than hand-picked
blacks slated by whites to serve white interests.

For black voters, the notion of coalition politics is fraught with certain haz-
ards, including the price of admission to the coalition and the consequences to
black candidates of being electorally accountable to the white element of the
coalition. Dinkins and Wilder have been criticized by black political analysts
for being "sanitized" black candidates who did not make any special appeals to
black voters or include critical elements of the black political agenda in their
platforms. Although their white levels of support were less than 50 percent (reports indicate that only 30 percent of white voters voted for Dinkins and 38
percent for Wilder), their white support constituted a critical factor in their
successes. As a result, their continued political viability for future races requires them to retain that white support, and this might prevent them from
fully serving the interests of black voters on issues in which black and white
interests conflict.

CONCLUSION

The relatively few successes of black political candidates in general and
black political candidates in majority white jurisdictions in particular should
not divert attention from continuing and strengthening the nationwide movement to eliminate barriers to effective minority voter participation. Voter registration restrictions continue to produce disproportionately low minority
voter registration rates nationally. At-large elections in many states continue to
dilute black votes. For example, Virginia continues to have the lowest number
of black city council members of any state covered by the Voting Rights Act,
and this derives in part from the fact that, despite some litigation successes of
recent vintage, most Virginia cities continue to have at-large city council elections. Election runoff requirements in many states, where it takes a majority
vote to win party nomination or election, also disproportionately weaken black
candidates' prospects. These are all obstacles that continue to dilute the impact
of the black vote and hamper the electoral potential of black candidates.

Thus, as encouraging as some of the data on the growth, current number, and distribution of black elected officials presented in the preceding chapter is, the most startling statistic is the one that demonstrates that despite twenty-five years of progress, black elected officials still constitute only 1.4 percent of the total number of elected officials in the nation. This statistic indicates that there are continuing barriers to political equity for black people in the United States that must be overcome if the promise of American electoral democracy is to be fulfilled.

NOTES

1. *The Greenville Times,* November 24, 1906, 1, quoted in Frank R. Parker, *Black Votes Count: Political Empowerment in Mississippi After 1965* (Chapel Hill: University of North Carolina Press, 1990), chapter 5.

2. Bradley Rice, *Progressive Cities: The Commission Movement in America* (Austin: University of Texas Press, 1979).

3. Gene Wirth, "Study Negro in Politics," *Jackson Clarion-Ledger,* quoted in Parker, *Black Votes Count,* chapter 2.

4. *Jackson Clarion Ledger,* January 14, 1966, quoted in Parker, *Black Votes Count,* chapter 2.

5. Parker, *Black Votes Count,* chapter 2.

6. See, for example, United States Commission on Civil Rights, *Political Participation* (Washington, D.C.: Government Printing Office, 1968) and subsequent commission reports on voting rights.

7. Nunan V. Bartley and Hugh D. Graham, *Southern Politics and the Second Reconstruction* (Baltimore, Md.: John Hopkins University Press, 1975).

8. Jack Bass and Walter DeVries, *The Transformation of Southern Politics: Social Change and Political Consequence since 1945* (New York: Basic Books, 1976).

9. Alexander Lamis, *The Two-Party South* (New York: Oxford University Press, 1984).

10. Stephen R. Lawson, *In Pursuit of Power: Southern Blacks and Electoral Politics, 1965–1982* (New York: Columbia University Press, 1985).

11. Earl Black and Merle Black, *Politics and Society in the South* (Cambridge, Mass.: Harvard University Press, 1987).

12. Ibid., 145.

13. See Abigail Thernstrom, *Whose Votes Count? Affirmative Action and Minority Voting Rights* (Cambridge, Mass.: Harvard University Press, 1987), 21–27.

14. Ibid., 21–27.

15. Ibid., 5.

16. Ibid., 238–40.

17. This description of political "massive resistance" strategies and their impact on black political fortunes in Mississippi is taken from Parker, *Black Votes Count,* chapter 2.

18. Frank R. Parker, "Racial Gerrymandering and Legislative Reapportionment," chapter 5 in Chandler Davidson, ed., *Minority Vote Dilution,* (Washington, D.C.: Howard University Press, 1989).

19. United States Department of Justice, Civil Rights Division, "Complete Listing

of Objections Pursuant to Section 5 of the Voting Rights Act," Louisiana (April 30, 1988), photocopy.

20. Parker, *Black Votes Count*, chapter 3.

21. *Allen v. State Board of Elections*, 393 U.S., 544 (1969).

22. *White v. Regester*, 412 U.S. 755 (1973).

23. 42 U. S. C. Section 1973 (1982).

24. For a recent survey of voting rights litigation since 1965, see Laughlin McDonald, "The Quiet Revolution in Minority Voting Rights," *Vanderbilt Law Review* 42 (May 1989): 1249–97.

25. Joint Center for Political Studies Press release, "Number of Black Elected Officials Climbs to 7,226," October 31, 1989.

26. Matthew Cooper, "A National Dividing, The Return of Segregation," *U.S. News and World Report*, November 6, 1989, 24.

27. Ibid.

28. See, for example, Thomas B. Edsall, "Black Democrats' Victories Clouded by White Defections," *The Washington Post*, November 9, 1989, 1.

29. *Martin v. Allain*, 658 F. Supp. 1183 (S.D. Miss. 1987); *Martin v. Mabus*, 700 F. Supp. 327 (N.D. Miss., 1988).

30. AP, "Mississippi Elects Black Judges," *The New York Times*, June 22, 1989, 17.

5

African American Politics in the Era of Capitalist Economic Contraction

Walda Katz Fishman, Ralph C. Gomes,
Nelson Peery, and Jerome Scott

While there are far more African American elected officials than at any time in the history of the United States, African American workers find themselves disproportionately disenfranchised, dispossessed, unemployed, underemployed, poor, homeless, hungry, lacking access to health care and education, and faced with genocide.[1] In the South, where the majority of the African American people and elected officials reside, these conditions are most intense.

It is significant that today African Americans living in poverty are being joined by millions of U.S. workers and their children of all colors and nationalities, thus swelling the ranks of those in poverty. This concentration of poverty is dialectically related to the concentration of wealth at the other pole: the poor are getting poorer precisely because the rich are getting richer. Recent data from the Congressional Budget Office estimate that the poorest fifth of households in the nation lost 5 percent in average income between 1980 and 1990. Their $7,357 average income in 1980 was estimated to be $6,973 in 1990. Meanwhile, the richest fifth of United States households gained 33 percent in average income. Their $58,886 income in 1980 was estimated to have jumped to $78,032 in 1990. The very richest 1 percent gained 87 percent in average income, going from $213,675 to an estimated $399,697.[2]

CLASS POLITICS AND THE RACE QUESTION

Scholars and activists in the movement for social justice and equality must understand these phenomena—that is, the increasing numbers of African American elected officials, the increasing and disproportionate impoverishment of the African American masses, and the increasing polarity in wealth and poverty—in their historical and dynamic context of social development. The critical questions to answer are these: How did these circumstances develop? What is the significance of the Civil Rights Movement and the election of African American officials for the historical struggle for African American progress and equality? What does it mean that voter turnout in the United States is so low (roughly 50 percent of the voting age population in the 1988 presidential election and substantially less in state and local elections) and that few African Americans and other Americans in the lowest section of the working class bother to vote? What stage is it in the history of capitalist world development and its political expressions? How do the current conditions of economic contraction limit and constrain African American elected officials and affect the well-being of the African American masses? What social transformation is necessary if African American workers—and indeed, workers of all colors and nationalities—are to realize actual social, economic, and political equality? And, finally, what is the dynamic relationship between electoral politics and the revolutionary process of social transformation?

These are, of course, broad and complex questions that cannot be fully analyzed and answered in one chapter. However, we can examine the realities of history and current conditions within the theoretical formulation of dialectical and historical materialism. Politics is understood as the concentrated expression of economics. Thus, the Civil Rights Movement and the election of African Americans to office were possible during the stage of the expansion of the United States and the world capitalist economies after World War II. Similarly, the recent roll-back of civil and constitutional rights and the brutal attack on the African American people is the necessary expression of the current stage of contraction of that economy. In this period of economic contraction, African American elected officials and African American corporate and professional elites are especially constrained and limited (by the very dynamics of the capitalist economy) in their ability to deliver to the masses the goods and services they need. The capitalist political economy is rooted in the necessity to constantly maximize profits, to reduce the cost of production and labor, and to distribute goods and services through the market and wage system. The introduction of electronics and automation into the productive process in the 1970s and 1980s has already permanently displaced many workers from employment and decreased the wages of many more. This undermines workers' abilities to purchase the necessities of life and the ability of the capitalists to sell their commodities. The position of African American workers, conditioned by the legacy of slavery, places them at the heart of the United States working class as the most exploited or oppressed section, but also as the most revolutionary section for the very same reason.

At this stage of history, electoral politics is the form of political participation most often practiced by the American people. It is also the form of political participation that African Americans fought for and won in the struggles of the 1960s. Participation in electoral politics thus provides an invaluable learning experience about what is possible in the current electoral-representative system of the United States. At the same time, the mobilization of the masses through the electoral arena sets the stage for their political organization for other forms of activity, including those leading to the actual transformation of society.

THE "MASS" FRANCHISE—WHO HAS IT, WHO VOTES, AND WHY

Throughout the history of class society, the ruling class has held power and controlled the masses through a variety of political institutions, agencies, and organizations—the executive, legislative, and judicial branches of government, the military, domestic police forces, the administrative apparatus and procedures of society, and extra-legal forces such as the Ku Klux Klan. Dominant ideology and culture—the ideas, values, and beliefs of the ruling class—have justified and supported these power arrangements, as have the institutions of education, religion, media, philanthropy, and social welfare.

The revolutionary transformation of society from feudalism to capitalism set in motion important developments in the political relations between classes. The autocracy of the feudal monarchy was replaced by the "bourgeois democracy" of elected representatives of the capitalists, the new ruling class. Thus was born the notion of representative government based on the enfranchisement of "the people." Electoral politics was the only acceptable expression of mass sentiment and demands in the political arena conceded to the masses by the capitalists, who retained a tight grip on the entire process.

At certain historic moments—for example, periods of social warfare such as Reconstruction, the trade union struggles of the 1930s and 1940s, and the Civil Rights era—the interests of at least a section of the capitalist class and the masses in motion coincide. This results in the extension of the franchise and the passage of various legislative reforms. At other moments—for example, during the defeat of Reconstruction, and in the current period of the economic crisis and contraction—the capitalists move to protect their interests. They institute the process of disenfranchisement and roll back reforms for which many fought and died. The capitalist class has always had firm control over the major political parties, denying to U.S. workers in general and African American workers in particular any independent political expression.

In the United States (the so-called bastion of "freedom and democracy," to read the capitalists' press releases) very few of "the people" have actually had the franchise for any great period of time (see chapter 1). Over the years, especially in the last two decades, many who are now legally enfranchised have not found voting in bourgeois elections a useful means of expressing and obtaining their demands and needs. So they have not voted. Voting is, however, a gauge of the mood of the people. It is an indication of who, among the masses, has turned to the ballot box in search of resolution to their problems—equality, jobs, living wages, food, housing, education, health care, environmental protection, peace, and so forth. The results obtained in this manner are a further indication of the objective economic conditions within which political struggle is conducted, for the electoral stage of politics is an essential stage in the overall political and revolutionary process within society.

Moreover, when the "vote" is fought for and won by a section of the workers, the victory typically coincides with the strategy of a section of the capitalist class in its own internal class struggle. Thus, during Reconstruction, the northern industrialists, represented by the Republican party, supported the enfranchisement of the ex-slaves as part of their strategy to control the federal system and break the stranglehold of the slavocracy, represented by the Democratic party. Voter turnout by ex-slaves and southern white farmers and workers was extremely high. A significant number of African Americans won political office during this period. Some of the most progressive reforms, for example, free public education, were instituted by these Reconstruction administrations. Once the power of the former slavocracy was broken, however, the votes of the newly freed African Americans and the poor white farmers and workers were no longer needed. Further, cotton production, which had been carried out in large measure by the slaves, still required extensive manual labor. African Americans were virtually "re-enslaved," this time as sharecroppers. Thus began the process of disfranchisement of the masses and over a half-century of legalized terror in the South; the era of Jim Crow and "states rights" was on the rise.

THE POLITICS OF EXPANSION: THE POLITICS OF INCLUSION AND THE POLITICS OF REFORM, 1945-1973

In the first half of the twentieth century, the United States was preparing to assume its leadership in the world economy. The ruling class needed both class peace at home and support of the nation's workers for its imperialist domination of the Third World. The needs of capital coincided with the demands of labor at home. Through the Wagner Act, Social Security, unemployment insurance, and so forth, labor-capital relations were "reformed." Labor was brought into the Democratic party as part of the Franklin Roosevelt New Deal coalition.

The post–WW II period was the era of the greatest economic expansion of the world capitalist system. This is reflected in the "politics of inclusion" and the "politics of reform." For the first time, perhaps, women's votes were openly courted by the Democrats. They bribed sections of labor, predominantly white men in northern unionized industry with the best-paying jobs and benefits, with concessions under the leadership of the Democratic party. This section of labor was thus loyal to the interests of the capitalist class and was the key to capitalist control over the lower, unbribed section of labor—predominantly people of color and southern labor.

But with industry expanding in the South in the 1950s and 1960s, a new arrangement with southern workers, including black workers, had to be established. To fully exploit African American labor, as well as southern white labor, black workers had to be "integrated" into the workplace and into the larger society. African American people in the South thus won, at long last, their "civil rights." They won the legal, though often unrealized, right to equal and integrated education, the vote, and the freedom from discrimination on the basis of race and color. Other national minorities and women were included in the civil rights legislation of the period.

These civil rights reforms were the *last major reform of labor-capital relations* in the United States. African Americans were integrated into the existing class structure of American society. They were always found at the bottom of their respective classes. The vast majority of the African American people were black workers who integrated into the working class at the lowest level of unskilled and semiskilled labor. A smaller number of African Americans entered the ranks of the "middle class" as white-collar workers, as professional and technical workers, and as self-employed and small business owners. A still smaller number of African Americans entered the capitalist class as owners of enterprises.

The period of economic expansion and social inclusion was also a period of increasing voter participation. Voter turnout reached a twentieth-century peak of 62.8 percent of voting age population (VAP) in the presidential election year of 1960.[3] The turnout for congressional off-year elections reached a high of 48.1 percent of VAP in 1962 and again in 1970.[4] But as the economy turned downward, so did voter participation in electoral politics. The reforms of the era of expansion increasingly came under attack. At the same time, the quality of political participation of the masses in terms of the relationship between electoral politics and the revolutionary process was undergoing a transformation.

THE POLITICS OF CONTRACTION: THE POLITICS OF EXCLUSION AND REACTION

During the period of economic expansion and political inclusion, the Democratic party maintained firm control over the social, economic, and political aspirations and loyalty of the working class. Through its "liberal" reform agenda—the labor reforms of the Wagner Act, the expansion of the "welfare state," and the civil rights antidiscrimination legislation—the capitalist class, through the Democrats, was successful in containing the demands of the working class in all its diversity, but by the early 1970s, world capitalism was approaching the limits of its expansion. It was being forced to deal with the reality of the contraction of world markets and the increasing difficulty of circulating the glut of commodities being produced with less and less human labor. Massive extension of credit and mounting debt—for capitalist enterprises, for developing Third World countries, for consumers, and finally for First World countries—were the new realities of this period.

Markets were glutted. The revolution in technology was necessary to constantly increase workers' productivity and industrial competitiveness. Labor wages in the neocolonies and developing countries had been driven down to subsistence levels. Labor could not be further exploited. The capitalists of the United States had to turn inward to their own working class. They had no choice but to intensify the exploitation of the American worker to maintain their maximum profits. The revolution in technology leaped forward with the application of electronics to the productive process. By the 1980s, real wages were falling. Workers were being eliminated from the productive process. Mechanical production enhanced human labor in the past period. In the current period, however, human labor was being permanently replaced by electronics in the form of computerized and automated production. Human labor was becoming obsolete and workers were becoming superfluous. For instance, in the late 1940s, Ford's River Rouge auto plant employed 60,000 workers. In the late 1980s, it employed only 16,000.[5] Wealth and income were polarizing. Fewer and fewer capitalists were accumulating more and more wealth, while the workers received less and less in wages and benefits of the "welfare state."

In this process of economic contraction, white men lost the most because they had been the most privileged section of labor during the era of expansion. The African American workers, however, historically the most economically unstable part of the work force, felt the effects first and most profoundly. Young black men twenty years of age in major cities experienced a 42 percent decline in income since the mid-1960s. Black women twenty-five years old had a 35 percent decline in income.[6] Education, housing, health care, and all the necessities of life declined just as rapidly. Police brutality and imprisonment soared.

At the same time, the ruling class stirred up the historic divisions among labor. They pitted white against black, Americans against other nationalities, men against women, old against young, and the middle class against poor. Expressions of classism, of chauvinism, of racism, and of sexism surged in the media, in popular culture, and in the actual social relations among workers.

For the first time in United States history, there was not simply an unemployed group, but a growing group of permanently unemployable workers. The economic and social system of capitalism cannot and will not tolerate a section of society that does not contribute to the economy. In a previous era these unemployed and unemployable workers were "driven away." In the current setting, they face genocide. This is not a subjective question. It is built into the system.

In a capitalist society, everything must contribute to the functioning of the system or it must cease to exist. The decline of education is a direct reflection of the growth of this army of permanently unemployed. Education is to prepare the worker for employment. The same is true for health care. The society cannot keep in working order what it cannot employ. Similarly, all of the fundamental problems of African Americans are problems of class. They are confounded and masked by the historic evolution of a racism that tolerates the poor health, lack of education, and unemployment of the black worker.

It is quite clear that the black so-called "underclass" (the lowest section of the working class that is already outside of the productive process) is already caught in the objective process of genocide. African American women begin to outlive African American men at age 19, compared to age 45 for whites. Over half of the inner city black poor have no access to health care, education, or job training.

This new reality of a growing superfluous section of workers, including a disproportionate number of African American workers, demands a reexamination of strategy and tactics in the struggle for black liberation and equality. As dangerous as the material reality of this genocidal attack on the black worker is, even more dangerous is the growing isolation of the black section of the permanently unemployed from the larger grouping. These black workers are effectively isolated from white America and are increasingly isolated from blacks in the upper strata of the working class and, even more so, from blacks in the capitalist class.

This growing class polarization within the African American community raises questions about the call over the years for black unity. That call has always resulted in slogans of support for "black capitalism" or for "black political candidates." There has been very little talk of unity with that section of the African American people who are workers and of the whole U.S. working class more generally.

These realities have taken on an added urgency. The current economic contraction is expressed in the politics of reaction, the politics of exclusion, the politics of demobilization, and the politics of genocide. The Democratic party, led by its southern wing, made a clear "turn to the right" in the 1980s and 1990s. This rightward motion reflects the ongoing economic realignment rooted in the introduction of electronics into the production process. The Democratic party must realign politically to come into conformity with the restructuring of the economy—electronically based production using far fewer workers to produce more goods and services. It must abandon its "liberal reform agenda" introduced in the era of expansion. This means, of course, abandoning the constituencies brought together in the Roosevelt New Deal coalition—labor, ethnic and racial minorities, women, and the unemployed.

The southern wing of the Democratic Party organized its challenge to the party's liberal northern leadership (coalesced around the Democratic National Committee) through the formation of the Democratic Leadership Council (DLC) in the aftermath of the Mondale defeat in 1984. The DLC included both "Dixiecrats" of the "Solid South" and the "New South" politicians—both black and white. Originally labeled the "white boys club," the 30 founding members were all white and were from the South or Southwest. Today, the

DLC has over 175 members, including African American elected officials from North and South. The DLC understood they could and, indeed, must recruit into their ranks "moderate" African American leadership that was openly "pro-capitalist" (for example, Virginia Governor Douglas Wilder, and United States Representative William Gray) if they were to successfully realign the Democratic party to the right while keeping the black masses loyal to the Democrats.

The southern wing of the Democratic party historically has been the linchpin of capitalist rule. The election and reelection of right-wing southern Dixiecrats (also known as "boll weevils") to Congress year after year was guaranteed by disenfranchising the southern worker, especially the African American southern worker. These Dixiecrats controlled key committees and voted with whichever party was in power nationally to impose the political program of the capitalist class on both U.S. workers and workers throughout the world.

Thus, during the 1980s and in the first years of the 1990s, the bipartisan Congress, often under Democratic leadership, voted with the Reagan and Bush administrations time and again to pass regressive and reactionary budget and tax packages, to increase the budget for the military while cutting human and social services, to support U.S. militarism and interventionism in the Third World, to approve conservative Supreme Court justices, and to erode civil rights legislative protections. The motion to the right led by the DLC does *not* reflect a rightward drift in the attitudes and demands of the Democratic party's base constituencies—labor, ethnic and racial minorities, women, and the unemployed. It is, rather, an effort by the more reactionary forces within the Democratic party organized around the DLC to force the Democratic party to abandon its working-class constituencies. These include not only black workers, but workers of all colors and nationalities, and progressive women and men. This motion must necessarily intensify the contradictions developing between the capitalist interests in control of the party and the working-class base the Democrats have depended upon for their electoral victories since the New Deal.

Many of these working class and progressive forces at the forefront of the struggle for equality, jobs, housing, food, health care, education, a safe environment, and peace (including much of the New Deal constituency of the Democratic party) coalesced around Jesse Jackson's campaigns and the Rainbow Coalition in 1984 and 1988. To date, however, these efforts seem not to have resulted in the realization and formation of a truly independent political force with a strong grassroots base necessary to represent the interests of African American and other workers in the long-term struggle for survival.

Thus, the politics of contraction, unlike the politics of expansion, is the politics of *exclusion* and voter demobilization. The ruling class, including both those who are Democrats and those who are Republicans, is unable to grant any economic and social reforms because of the contracting economy. Consequently, they seek to narrow the base of those participating in the political and electoral process. They do not want to mobilize a large section of the workers to whom they can offer nothing. They do not want to be answerable and accountable to those in the working class, to those most oppressed in the African American community and among other nationalities, to women, or to children and youth. They make no promises for reforms and have no platforms addressing the issues of survival for the workers of all colors. The politicians representing the capitalist class run "issueless" campaigns, leaving unmoved and unmobilized the masses. They seek to be accountable only to the monied interests who finance their campaigns and whose interests they serve.

Elections, and those elected, are unable to respond to the survival needs of the workers. Thus, the form and content of the electoral process have deteriorated and degenerated. Elections are bought and sold by the capitalists for millions of dollars. Negative campaigns, mud-slinging, and personal scandals have replaced any semblance of discourse about the real economic and social problems facing the working class and the real solutions to these problems. Corruption, theft, and "unethical" ties to Savings and Loans institutions, bankers, realtors, corporations, and consultants are being uncovered and exposed as if these were the exceptions rather than the rule.

The capitalist class and its political representatives in Congress, in the White House, in the state and local executive and legislative offices—be they African American, white, or any other nationality; be they men or women—cannot expose the objective basis of the multitude of crises and problems confronting society and the working class. The reason is that the dynamics of capitalism itself are the "root cause" of the crises and problems. Sleaze, lies, deception, and confusion are the order of the day.

Is it any wonder, then, that participation by the masses in the electoral process is at a historic low? By the late 1980s, voter turnout rates plummeted to a dangerously low level—the lowest in the so-called "free world" and the lowest in the post–WW II period.[7] As the decade of the 1990s began, voter turnout in the mid-term election of November 7, 1990, was only 36.4 percent of the voting age population.[8] An estimated 67,660,000 Americans went to the ballot box out of the 186,383,000 the census estimated to be of voting age. Thus, more than 110,000,000 voting age people sat it out.[9] The dismal turnout in 1990 equaled the turnout in 1986, making it the lowest since 1942.

THE POLITICS OF SOCIAL TRANSFORMATION: FROM POVERTY TO POWER

In 1938, Curtis Gans, director of the Committee for the Study of the American Electorate, observed: "What we are witnessing is the decay of the impulse to civic duty on the part of the American citizen, not because of their dereliction, but because of the conduct of their political and institutional leaders. If allowed to continue, it will pose a threat to the health of the American nation."[10]

Gans further observed after the 1990 election: "American democracy will continue to erode at its base, and government of, for, and by the people will become more and more government of, for, and by the interested few."[11] Other political analysts suggest that when fewer than half of the eligible voters participate in the electoral process, the society in question is in a "pre-revolutionary" state. That is, a majority of the people no longer view the government as legitimate. The United States capitalists and their political parties (the Democrats and Republicans) are dealing with this situation by an active strategy of demobilization of the 50 percent of the people most in need. They are hoping that this mass will remain unorganized and thus unable to act in their own defense.

This is, however, not the history of human struggle. Many of those most affected by the economic contraction have already begun to move. As more and more workers are thrown out of the productive process, they are no longer able to engage in an economic struggle with their employer, but are forced to move into the arena of direct political struggle. Some have entered the electoral process searching for an answer to the survival needs at the ballot box. Others have taken to the streets, where they are confronting directly the capitalist state—the police, the national guard, the courts, and other agencies of the state. Real change has always come as a result of mass activity—in the community, on the job, in the churches, in the schools and universities, and in the streets.

Independent political activity, the heart of which is black political activity, is emerging as a reality in this period of economic crisis and contraction. The American people are registering their disgust with the bankruptcy of the two bourgeois political parties, the Democrats and Republicans. Not only did just over one-third of the eligible electorate bother to vote in 1990, but Gallup reported that in 1990 voter identification was roughly one-third Democrats, one-third Republicans, and one-third independents.[12]

The organization of this independent political motion representing the interests of African American workers and the entire working class is the task before progressive forces. This process must proceed from a strategy of working *both* inside and outside of the Democratic party at the moment. It must also proceed from the base of activity at the grassroots level. It must be built around local activity and electoral work, from the ground up, rather than being organized simply around presidential elections, top down. The specific form of this activity will and must vary according to local conditions. Thus, some may run as Democrats, some as independents, some as labor or under other banners (for example, as a socialist like Bernard Sanders, who was elected from Vermont to the House of Representatives in November 1990). In some instances the formations might be exclusively African Americans and in others multiracial. The historic experience of the South in independent progressive political formations—for example, the Mississippi Freedom Democratic party, the National Democratic Party of Alabama, the Alabama New South Coalition, and the recent struggle in Keyesville, Georgia, for political representation—must be summarized and must inform the efforts of progressive at this juncture in history. Other third-party experiences also must be examined for their relevance in the 1990s.

The new conditions of contraction of the United States and the world capitalist economy both demand and make possible the politics of social transformation. The African American workers cannot tolerate politics as usual, nor can the working class as a whole. The mobilization of the working-class base in the African American and other communities into independent political formations will provide an educational experience of the limits of electoral politics within the context of the contraction of the capitalist economy. But, more importantly, this activity provides the opportunity to develop organizational forms and links between groups that can and will lead to the social struggle for the necessities of life and for power itself.

Every society in human history is organized around its tools. Today, the revolution in the forces of production—that is, electronically based production replacing machine-based production—is the foundation of the social, economic, and political upheaval that is shaking up society in the United States and other nations. The capitalist organization of society around machine production, the private ownership of the productive forces, and the distribution of the necessities of life based on wages and the market system is no longer viable. The workers have lower and lower wages and the capitalists can circulate fewer and fewer of their goods and services.

Society has entered the epoch of an objective and historically necessary social revolution. The social relations of production and the organization of society must be brought into line with the new productive forces. In October 1990, Thomas Nkobi, treasurer and member of the national Executive Committee of the African National Congress, stated: "We are moving from the politics of protest to the politics of the challenge to power."[13] Similarly, black workers and their white counterparts in the United States and throughout the world are developing their forms of independent political organization inside and outside of the electoral arena. The African American masses, more and more of whom are superfluous workers within the contracting capitalist world economy, face genocide within capitalism. In order to avert genocide, they must prepare for the attainment of power in society. The working class, organized around the urgent lead of the black worker, must plan for and carry out the transformation of society necessary for human survival and human development.

NOTES

1. See chapter 3.

2. Robert Greenstein and S. Barancik, *Drifting Apart* (Washington, D.C.: Center on Budget and Policy Priorities, 1990), 17.

3. Curtis Gans, *Non-Voter Study, '88–89* (Washington, D.C.: Committee for the Study of the American Electorate, 1988), 130.

4. Curtis Gans, *Non-Voter Study, '85–86* (Washington, D.C.: Committee for the Study of the American Electorate, 1986), summary.

5. *Entering an Epoch of Social Revolution* (Chicago: Communist Labor Party, 1989), 4.

6. Gerald Jaynes and R. M. Williams, Jr., eds., *A Common Destiny: Blacks and American Society* (Washington, D.C.: National Academy Press, 1989).

7. Gans, *Non-Voter Study, '88–'89*, 13, and Curtis Gans, *Surges in Local Voting Don't Propel Turnout Upward in Messageless Election* (Washington, D.C.: Committee for the Study of the American Electorate, 1990), 1.

8. Paul Taylor, "Restive Voters Pick Change," *The Washington Post*, November 8, 1990, 1, 42; Gans, *Surges in Local Voting*, 1.

9. Gans, *Surges in Local Voting*, 1.

10. Gans, *Non-Voter Study, '88–'89*, 3.

11. Gans, *Surges in Local Voting*, 4.

12. S. Eizenstat, "No Cause for Democrats to Cheer," *The Washington Post*, November 12, 1990, 19.

13. "ANC Leader Charges: SA Wants Us to Grovel at Their Boots," *The Daily News*, October 1, 1900, Capetown, South Africa.

6

"Politics" Is Not Enough: The Institutionalization of the African American Freedom Movement

Robert C. Smith

This chapter has three major objectives: (1) to account theoretically and empirically for the transformation of the African American freedom movement from a direct-action style of politics seeking fundamental systemic change to a routine, bureaucratic interest-group style seeking payoffs within the system as currently structured;[1] (2) to describe quantitatively and qualitatively the institutionalization of black politics in the post–Civil Rights era—1965-1988; and (3) to demonstrate that institutionalized political participation is not enough to secure policies that alter or even substantially ameliorate the terrible conditions of the American "underclass."[2]

Although several social scientists have suggested that social movements decline as agents of change as they become institutionalized in the routines of interest group and bureaucratic politics, they have failed to give explicit, systematic attention to this phenomenon in regards to black politics in the post–Civil Rights era. This deficiency in the general literature on social movements is in part a function of the division of labor in social science between sociologists, who tend to focus on movements per se, and political scientists, who tend to focus on institutional politics (interest groups, parties, legislatures, electoral behavior, and so forth), leaving relatively unexplored the nexus between the two processes of politics. As sociologist Douglas McAdams concludes, "It is time the links between institutionalized and insurgent politics were established and the insights from both sociology and political science brought to bear on a complete analysis of the topic of power in America."[3] This chapter seeks to provide a comprehensive analysis of the relationship between black political activism in the sphere of protest *and* in the sphere of electoral-representative institutions.

The analysis is organized as follows:

1. The origins and evolution of the Civil Rights Movement are interpreted;
2. The transformation of the Movement in the late 1960s into its incipient state of institutionalization is traced;
3. The theoretical literature on the transformation of social movements in general is reviewed and related to the case of the Civil Rights Movement, using an analytical model;
4. The analytical model is applied to the process of black incorporation into the political system since the late 1960s, demonstrating that "politics," narrowly defined as participation in the electoral-representative system, can produce limited gains in *civil rights* but cannot produce fundamental social change or economic redistribution;
5. Theories and questions about institutional politics and its alternatives at the present historical conjuncture are reconsidered.

THE ORIGINS AND EVOLUTION OF THE MODERN CIVIL RIGHTS MOVEMENT

While the origin of the Civil Rights Movement (like any other social movement) cannot be identified in any exacting manner, the starting point of the following analysis is the early part of the twentieth century—that is, with the Niagara Conference in 1906 and the formation of the National Association for the Advancement of Colored People (NAACP) in 1909. This starting point is chosen because it is during this period that the basic goals, strategies, and organizational bases of the modern movement for civil rights were developed.

At the Niagara Conference, W. E. B. DuBois, William Monroe Trotter, and other African American intellectuals and political activists challenged the dominant conservative, accommodationist, anti-civil rights philosophy of Booker T. Washington and developed an alternative or complementary agenda of civil rights protest. The goals of the Movement were summed up in the Niagara Manifesto: "We will not be satisfied to take one jot or tittle less than our manhood rights. We claim for ourselves every single right that belongs to free born Americans, political, civil and social, and until we get these rights we will never cease to protest and assail the ears of America."[4]

The document raised specific demands for the right to vote, an end to discrimination in public accommodations, equal enforcement of the law, and quality education. As for strategy, the manifesto declared, "These are some of the things we want. How shall we get them? By voting where we may vote; by persistent, unceasing agitation; by hammering at the truth; by sacrifice and hard work."[5]

The formation of the interracial NAACP in 1909 provided a centralized organizational vehicle for the struggle, and by the time of Washington's death several years later, the Civil Rights leadership of DuBois and his NAACP colleagues was well on the way to displacing the accommodationist leadership of Washington's Tuskegee machine in the eyes of both African American and national white leaders. And despite sometimes vigorous challenges from both nationalists (most effectively, the Garvey Movement) and African American socialists, the liberal integrationist civil rights protest consensus endured and provided the intellectual and organizational groundwork for the coalition of white liberals, labor, religious groups, and blacks that ultimately won enactment of several of the items on the Niagara agenda in the mid-1960s Civil Rights laws.

The Civil Rights Movement (identified here as encompassing the years 1909–1965) may be divided according to the *dominant* form of activity.[6] From roughly 1910 to the mid-1930s, lobbying was the dominant form of black politics. During these years, the NAACP developed a campaign for education, propaganda, and lobbying in order to shape a favorable climate of public opinion on the civil rights of African Americans.[7] Some of the NAACP's lobbying campaigns were unsuccessful—for example, the 40-year effort to secure federal anti-lynching legislation (twice passed in the House of Representatives but defeated in the Senate).[8] Other of the NAACP's lobbying campaigns were successful—for example, the defeat of immigration legislation prohibiting the entry of people of African descent and the defeat of the nomination of an alleged anti-black, anti-labor judge to the United States Supreme Court.[9]

From the 1930s to the 1950s, litigation was the dominant form of black politics. In this phase, the NAACP sought to secure the rights of blacks in a series of important test cases. Successes included the invalidation of the white primary in 1944 and the "separate but equal" doctrine in the 1954 *Brown* school desegregation case.[10]

From the mid-1950s through the mid-1960s, blacks turned to protest-boycotts, sit-ins, mass demonstrations, and so forth. In this phase, the NAACP was displaced as the vanguard of the Civil Rights Movement by several new mass-based protest organizations (Southern Christian Leadership Conference, Student Nonviolent Coordinating Committee, and Congress of Racial Equality) and the charismatic leadership of Martin Luther King, Jr.[11] As a result of a series of mass protests and demonstrations beginning in Montgomery, Alabama, in 1955 and ending in Selma, Alabama, ten years later, the Movement was able to force the presidency and Congress to enact relatively comprehensive civil rights laws in the 1960s. Especially, the Civil Rights Act of 1964 and the Voting Rights Act of 1965 went a long way toward abolishing the legal basis of racism; concomitantly, in this new legal framework, protest politics began to dissipate. From then until today, institutionalized political behavior became the dominant form of black politics.

This study focuses on what happened next. Reform, repression, cooptation, integration, and incorporation developed hand-in-hand as the marching stopped. This chapter shows that these developments shape the present contours of African American politics. Before turning to a demonstration of these realities, however, the role of "black power" in the transformation of the Civil Rights Movement and the institutionalization of the struggle is explored.

BLACK POWER AND THE INSTITUTIONALIZATION OF THE AFRICAN AMERICAN FREEDOM STRUGGLE

The principal objective of this section is to examine the brief "black power" period (1966 and 1970) as an intervening phase between the Civil Rights era proper and the post–Civil Rights era. The chief question addressed is how the thrust for "black power" facilitated the Civil Right Movement's institutionalization.

With the passage of the Voting Rights Act in 1965, the Civil Rights Movement found itself at a crossroad, suffering from what A. Philip Randolph, its elder statesman, called a "crisis of victory." Simply put, the Movement had achieved its fundamental goals of equal rights under law, but blacks still were not the beneficiaries of equity and justice. Instead, the long-standing problems of racism and poverty in the big city ghettos (dramatically manifested in the 1965 riots in Watts, California) continued and in some instances worsened. Social and economic problems rather than legal ones now became the principal concerns of the Civil Rights leadership. As King put it in the title of his final book, *Where Do We Go From Here* was the question of the moment—a question that sparked much internal as well as public disunity.

One answer was provided by Dr. King. King sought to continue the movement style of politics, with a focus on economic rights, Vietnam, and the problems of poverty and ghettoization. He planned to conduct local marches and demonstrations in cities such as Chicago and envisioned a national poor peoples campaign culminating in a march on Washington for economic justice (specifically, a full employment program and a guaranteed income supplement).

This approach, a continuation of movement-style protest politics around the issues of war and economic justice, was opposed by Roy Wilkins and Whitney Young of the NAACP and NUL respectively, the young Jesse Jackson, and most vigorously by Bayard Rustin, the Movement's principal strategic planner.[12] Rustin called explicitly for the Movement's institutionalization. Specifically, he maintained that the 1964 Civil Rights Act destroyed the legal basis of racism; the Economic Opportunity Act of 1964 and the War on Poverty furnished the means for attacking the cumulative social and economic effects of racism; and the Voting Rights Act of 1965 provided the tools for the effective enfranchisement of millions of potential progressive voters. Thus, Rustin called for a shift from movement-style protest to systemic electoral activism in an effort to build "a coalition of progressive forces which become the effective political majority in the United States ... Negroes, trade unionists, liberals, and religious groups."[13] Although Rustin's position on the new directions of the Movement eventually prevailed, it did not do so without significant debate, violence, and turmoil sparked by the black power revolt, the ghetto rebellions, and a turn toward revolutionary activism by elements of the Movement's radical wing.

SNCC—the most self-consciously radical of the Movement organizations—sparked debate by introducing the rhetoric and symbol of black power during the 1966 Meredith March in Mississippi. For several years, the more nationalist (largely northern-reared) SNCC staffers had attempted to bring more separatist principles into the southern struggle, principles drawn from Frantz Fanon, Malcolm X, and the Nation of Islam.[14] Under the leadership of Bill Ware, a small group of SNCC's Atlanta staffers began to develop principles of nationalism for the organization. In 1966, the group prepared a position paper that set forth the fundamental themes and a rudimentary proposal that constituted the basic manifesto of black power. Although Stokely Carmichael initially joined the majority of the staff in rejecting the separatist themes of the position paper, he embraced the rhetoric of black power after he defeated SNCC's incumbent Chairman John Lewis in a bitter and divisive leadership election. Carmichael's victory was largely reported as a triumph of black radicalism and nationalism. He then persuaded SNCC to join the Meredith March in order to use the march as a forum to articulate and build support for the ideas of black power.[15] Following the march, black power immediately became the focus of widespread debate (elite and mass, black and white) and controversy regarding the future of the freedom struggle.

Black power was interpreted initially as composed of a variety of ideologies (cultural nationalism, interest group pluralism, and revolutionary nationalism). Later, Carmichael attempted to construct an intellectual rationale for the symbol of black power in a series of articles and a book written with Charles Hamilton.[16] Essentially, the black power period bridged the gap between the movement-style protest politics and institutionalized pluralist, interest-group style politics. Structurally, black power contributed to the development of race consciousness and solidarity, stimulated the formation of separatist black interest organizations, and sped up the process of black incorporation and cooptation into systemic institutions and processes.[17]

In effect, black power helped to create the ideological and institutional basis for the converging interests of the black and white establishments to incorporate blacks into the political system on the system's own terms. As a result, black insurgency declined. There might have been, as Frances Fox Piven and Richard Cloward suggest, a kind of inevitability to the demise of black insurgency as these developments unfolded, because the logic of the victories won by the Civil Rights Movement was integrationist.

If anything, the "black power" ideology aided in that transformation by providing justification of the leadership stratum (and a growing black middle class generally) to move aggressively to take advantage of these new opportunities. Despite the initial identification of the concept with nationalistic "extremism" and political "radicalism," it quickly came to have a much more moderate and conventional meaning. . . . As a result protest lost its legitimacy, undermined by the force of American electoral beliefs and traditions.[18]

Having discussed the role played by black power ideology in the transformation to institutionalization of the Movement, an explication of theoretical frameworks that seek to explain a movement's demise or transformation is discussed below, and a model is specified for studying post–Civil Rights era black politics.

SYSTEMIC RESPONSES TO SOCIAL MOVEMENTS: THEORETICAL PERSPECTIVES

As in the above passage quoted from Piven and Cloward, there tends to be unwarranted teleological reasoning in theories of social movement outcomes, suggesting that insurgencies inevitably exhaust themselves or are coopted or destroyed by what Max Weber called the "enduring institutional and material interests of modern society."[19] This logic is obviously unwarranted, in that some insurgencies are successful in transforming the "enduring institutions and material interests" of a society, either wholly (as in successful revolutions) or in part (as in successful reform movements, for example, the Civil Rights Movement's transformation of the de jure racist structure). In addition, some insurgencies have as their major goal cooptation—that is, integration into systemic institutions and processes in order to derive whatever symbolic and material benefits there are to get. Thus, it is important to consider theoretically the range of movement goals and available systemic responses in order to comprehend what happened (and why) to the African American freedom struggle after the marching stopped, as well as the probable future of this historic struggle, given its goals, resources, and available options.

Harry Scoble developed a "process model" to analyze systemic responses to insurgent movements.[20] The model essentially involved a modification of David Easton's systems analytic framework of the political process. On the input side, insurgencies (or even institutional interest groups) are specified in terms of (1) the substantive and rhetorical character of their demands (whether they involve changes in the social, economic or political systems); (2) the methods of the demands (whether routine, systemic regularized means of demand expression—for example, voting, lobbying, and litigation—or nonsystemic means in the form of strikes, riots, and organized force); and (3) the relative calculus of insurgent resources (money, weapons, status, size, and solidarity) regarding the government and oppositional groups. Depending on the relationship and the relative balance of these input variables, Scoble identified five logically possible systemic responses or outputs: neglect, symbols, substantive policy, cooptation, and repression. The systemic outputs Scoble emphasized are rarely (except possibly in the case of neglect) implemented exclusively; rather, there is, depending on the balance of forces, usually what he called a "judicious mix" of outputs, that is, some cooptation and symbols with a bit of repression and a dash of substantive policy in order to arrive at the appropriate recipe for system maintenance.[21]

Scoble's model may be fruitfully used in a study of the African American freedom struggle. If one dates the Civil Rights Movement from early in the twentieth century, then the basic systemic response until about the mid-1950s was neglect: In response to the black demand for civil rights (anti-lynching legislation, for example), the government did nothing; instead it acted as if there were no demands. This response was possible because blacks had not amassed the requisite resources (economic or political) to exert pressure on the system sufficient to counterbalance the enormous institutionalized resources of the southern-led opposition.

Once blacks gained political resources, the demands and pressures became so great that neglect was no longer a viable option in the context of the nation's economic prosperity in the immediate post-WW II era. As a result, the system responded with a range of available options, including major policy initiatives (judicial decrees, executive orders, and legislative acts), symbolic manipulation (as in the manipulation of images on television), cooptation, and repression.[22] As Scoble's model predicts, the systemic responses were not singular or sequential; instead there was the "judicious mix" of all four simultaneously. That is, at the same time the government was responding with a series of positive symbols and politics, it was engaged in widespread repression and cooptation. For purposes of understanding the Movement's transformation and its present status, the repression and cooptation responses warrant further examination.

As a result of extensive access to FBI files, it is now known that almost from the Movement's inception in the early decades of this century, the U.S. government (acting largely through the FBI and its forerunners) engaged in a systematic campaign of surveillance and repression of the freedom struggle. This campaign targeted not only radical groups and individuals such as the Garvey Movement and black socialists and communists such as DuBois, Richard Wright, and Paul Robeson, but also moderate conventional groups such as the NAACP and the black press. Indeed, the FBI targeted Dr. King almost from the moment he emerged on the national scene. The FBI appears to have had as its point of departure the notion that the entire Civil Rights Movement was subversive.

Thus, the Movement suffered from various forms of repression—denial of employment opportunities and access to the media, attempts to infiltrate, subvert, and disrupt political organizations, harassment of Movement leaders, and legal and extra-legal repression, including forced exile and murder. The employment of repression intensified in the late 1960s as a result of black power ideology, the ghetto rebellions, and the rise of revolutionary sentiments and organizations such as the Black Panther party, or in the evolving radicalism of Dr. King as he aggressively challenged United States imperialism in Vietnam and called for a system-challenging style of protest that addressed itself to "a radical restructuring of the whole of American society . . . raising questions about the economic system, about a broader distribution of wealth . . . about the capitalist economy itself."[23]

In this situation, repression by the government was predictable. There was a perceived threat to system maintenance in its present form. In the mind of the head of the system's police/domestic intelligence apparatus (J. Edgar Hoover), there was a danger that the African American struggle might be transformed into a genuine revolutionary force. Thus, a major goal of Hoover's campaign of repression against the Movement and its leaders was "to prevent the coalition of militant black nationalist groups . . . which might be a first step toward a real mau mau in America, the beginning of true black revolution."[24]

It is impossible to conclude whether Hoover's musings about revolution were well-founded. What is clear is that the government was by and large successful in its campaign to "expose, disrupt, and otherwise neutralize" the radical wing of the freedom movement, rendering it nearly impotent by the early 1970s. Thus, governmental repression of Movement activists explains in part the decline of insurgency. Cooptation, however, explains another part.

Phillips Selznick defines cooptation as "the process of absorbing new elements into the leadership-determining structure of an organization as *a means of avoiding threats to its stability*" (emphasis added).[25] Thus, structurally, cooptation and political repression are functionally equivalent, alternative mechanisms of restoring system stability. Yet, since every system wishes to govern by consent rather than force, cooptation is the preferred alternative because by publicly drawing leadership elements associated with the dissident group into highly visible systemic offices, confidence in the system is restored and respectability and legitimacy of governing elites are reestablished in the eyes of the dissident mass public. However, it is important to note that what is shared when dissident leaders are coopted is what Carl Stokes, the first black mayor of Cleveland, called "The Promise of Power" rather than its reality.[26]

Ample evidence of this formal cooptation process is available with respect to the black movement in the 1960s. There was an ongoing series of "first Negro who" appointments of black cabinet officers, judges, and ambassadors in Lyndon Johnson's administration. Especially important in this regard was the highly visible role the Congressional Black Caucus (CBC) began to play in national politics in the early 1970s (with highly flattering *Newsweek, Ebony,* and *Jet* cover stories) and the election of a string of big-city black mayors (again, widely celebrated in the black and white media. *Time,* for example, captioned its cover story on the election of Carl Stokes as "The Real Black Power."

Since the early 1970s, political repression abated, but the process of cooptation continued (for example, a conservative Republican president recently elevated a black, General Colin Powell, to the nation's highest military post, resulting in attendant media babble about a role model for young blacks). As a result, only marginalized remnants of movement-style black politics existed during the 1980s as the movement phenomenon had become nearly wholly encapsulated by elections, bureaucratic, and legislative routines, $100-a-plate dinners, and meetings and conventions in Las Vegas and Miami Beach.

Meanwhile, the daily headlines told of a black community characterized by poverty, emiseration, dispossession, and degradation.

Selznick argued that cooptation is often the "realistic core of avowedly democratic procedures."[27] In other words, it is part of the structural adjustment of democratic systems to the claims of new groups for inclusion, integration, or incorporation. Integration in this sense was certainly high on the list of priorities of the traditional civil rights agenda with its emphasis on the right to vote and participate in the decision-making process. While from the perspective of the Movement's radical wing, cooptation was pejorative, it was viewed, as Rustin argued, as the fulfillment of a long-held movement goal by the moderate wing.

This is also the view of virtually all students of protest and social movements in the United States. They tend to argue that protest is not enough, that if the causes represented by mass movements are to be sustained and advanced it must be through institutionalized structures and processes or not at all. For example, in their prize-winning study *Protest is Not Enough*, Rufus Browning, Dale Marshall, and David Tabb develop a framework for analysis of the process of minority group incorporation and systemic responsiveness. Although the theory was developed in a study of political incorporation at the local level, they argue that it is "universally applicable, . . . offering a way of studying group access and influence at any level."[28] Briefly stated, Browning, Marshall, and Tabb posit that effective minority incorporation requires three elements: (1) the mobilization of the minority electorate, (2) the development and maintenance of multiethnic coalitions of other minorities and progressive whites, and (3) the use of these unions to win elections and become the dominant governing coalition.[29] This should result in policy responsiveness to minority demands (at the local level in terms of increased minority appointments and government employment, increased minority access to city contracts, and the implementation of minority-oriented social and economic programs).

When applied to the national level, however, evidence suggests that, contrary to its authors conclusion, politics is *not* enough, because (1) the black electorate nationally is generally much smaller than at the local level in many areas; (2) it is more difficult to develop and maintain dominant multiethnic coalitions at the national level; and (3) when such coalitions come to power, as in the Jimmy Carter administration, they tend to be less responsive to the black agenda than similar governing coalitions at the local level.

The next section provides evidence from two cases demonstrating the above three conclusions.

BLACK INCORPORATION IN THE POST–CIVIL RIGHTS ERA: STATISTICAL AND SUBSTANTIVE OUTCOMES

This section, first, summarizes the statistical pattern of black incorporation into the structure of power in the United States. Second, it examines the substantive impact of black incorporation on policy outcomes, especially those relevant to the post–Civil Rights era black agenda. Third, it presents evidence from two case studies that demonstrate the possibilities and limits of black incorporation.

The first case deals with the post–Civil Rights era consensus on civil rights policy, narrowly confined. It shows that there is a governing coalition in Congress to sustain and in some modest ways even extend fundamental civil rights guarantees, even if a hostile president and Supreme Court object. The second case dealing with the post–Civil Rights era black agenda of fundamental economic and social change shows the exact opposite. Rather, on these issues (so fundamental to addressing the legacies of racism as they are reflected in discussion of the American "underclass"), black officials in federal positions find themselves increasingly isolated and nearly invisible.

Black Incorporation Revisited

Chapter 3 demonstrated that incorporation of blacks into electoral offices throughout the nation remains partial and incipient; given the slow rate of growth of black elected officials also demonstrated in chapter 3, it is unlikely that full incorporation (blacks holding about 12 percent of all elective offices, given their proportion of the population) will occur in the foreseeable future. While statistical equality in elective office does not necessarily result in equality of substantive outcomes, clearly the absence of such racial parity in public office is an important resource constraint.

For example, if blacks were democratically represented in the houses of Congress with a bloc of ten or twelve senators and forty-five congressmen, this could enhance enormously their impact on legislative outcomes. Blacks in Congress tend to act cohesively on most issues.[30] Thus, if they had higher numbers, they could act as a balance of power in the party caucuses, in committees, and on the floor on many issues. (See the discussion below of the caucus' role in exempting basic welfare programs from the Gramm-Rudman budget-cutting procedures as an example of an important legislative concession.) Yet, under present electoral conditions, this level of representation is not likely ever to be achieved. The Senate is likely to forever remain a largely white segregated body unless there are radical changes in white voting behavior or in the manner of allocating Senate seats. In the House, the level of black representation is not likely to go much beyond what it is in the foreseeable future, given again the general disinclination of whites to vote for blacks and certain structural features in the way House seats are apportioned and the single-member districting scheme.

Less is known about the number and distribution of black appointed officials, in part because there is no systematic standardized data source (akin to the Joint Center's annual rosters of black elected officials) and because there have been relatively few systematic studies. Especially at local and state levels, data are unavailable. However, since appointed officials get their jobs from mostly white elected officials, it is likely that their numbers in the aggregate are small. It is also likely that representation of blacks in appointive office varies by level of government, size of the black population in a state or locality, systemic racism, and black mobilization in a given jurisdiction, as well as which of the two major parties are in power.

Systematic data are available on the appointment of blacks to federal executive positions.[31] Prior to the John Kennedy administration, blacks were not appointed to high-level positions in the executive branch of government. Indeed, before 1960, only two blacks held subcabinet posts in the federal government—an assistant attorney general in the William Howard Taft administration and an assistant secretary of labor in the Dwight Eisenhower administration—although informal "racial advisers" were assigned to various agencies and departments under both Taft and Franklin Roosevelt. Under the latter, a "black cabinet" played an important symbolic function.[32] Given the paucity of black federal appointees before the Kennedy administration, statistical measurement of black incorporation at this level of power begins in 1960.

In Table 6.1, data are displayed on the percentage breakdown (by the principal functional policy divisions of the executive branch, including senior civil servants and federal court judges) on black presidential appointees from the Civil Rights era through the first Reagan administration. In the face of considerable delay and obstruction from southern racists in the Senate, President Kennedy appointed several blacks to high-level posts in the executive and judiciary. President Johnson made a number of historic "first Negro who" appointments to the cabinet, subcabinet, independent regulatory commissions, the judiciary, and the diplomatic service. These appointments, coming near the peak of the black power rebellion, were important symbolic manifestations of the formal cooptation of blacks. Yet at the end of the Johnson administration, blacks constituted less than 2 percent of executive branch appointees and only about 4 percent of the judicial ones.

In the post–Civil Rights era, a fairly steady increase in such appointments is observed: 4 percent in the Richard Nixon-Gerald Ford administrations (most by President Nixon), 12 percent under President Carter, and about 5 percent under President Reagan.[33] In fact, if one uses proportion of population as the measure of equitable incorporation, then by the end of the Carter administration, one may conclude that statistically, blacks had been fully incorporated. Yet, given that a traditional criterion for such appointments is the rewarding of loyal constituency groups, one might argue that blacks in Democratic administrations should have received 20 percent of party patronage, since they constituted roughly that percentage of the Democratic party national vote.[34] Similarly, employing this criteria, 4 to 5 percent black appointments in Republican administrations might be viewed as equitable, given the minuscule contribution of blacks to the party vote and the paucity of competent Republican loyalists (especially in the case of the Reagan administration, when a conservative ideological litmus test was also employed).

Table 6.1

Percentage Distribution of Black Presidential Appointees by Administration, 1960–1984*

	Kennedy-Johnson	Nixon-Ford	Carter	Reagan
Cabinet	9.0%	9.0%	7.0%	7.0%
Sub-Cabinet Agency	2.0	5.0	12.0	9.0
Non-Cabinet Agency Heads	14.0	0.0	14.0	0.0
Independent Regulatory Commissions	3.0	8.0	15.0	---
U. S. Attorneys	1.0	---	6.0	---
U. S. Marshals	---	---	17.0	---
U. S. Ambassadors	1.5	4.0	8.0	4.0
Assistants to the President	0.0	4.0	5.0	5.0
Senior Civil Servants	1.2	3.5	5.0	3.7
Federal District Judges	4.1	4.2	14.0	0.8
Federal Appeals Judges	5.0	0.0	16.0	3.2

*The percentages represent the black percent of the total number of appointments in each category. (The cabinet percentages in each administration represent one member. The fluctuations result from increases in the size of the statutory cabinet.)

Sources: Robert C. Smith, "Black Appointed Officials: A Neglected Category of Political Participation Research," *Journal of Black Studies* 14 (1984): 369-88; James Mock, "The Black Vote Output: Black Political Executives, 1961–1980," paper prepared for presentation at the 1982 Annual Meeting of the Midwest Political Science Association, Chicago; and United States Commission on Civil Rights, "Equal Opportunity in Presidential Appointments" (Washington, D.C.: Typescript, 1983).

In all administrations examined during this twenty-year period, black appointees tended to be concentrated in the civil rights and social welfare bureaucracies—Housing and Urban Development (HUD), Health, Education and Welfare (HEW), the Equal Employment Opportunity Commission (EEOC), Health and Human Services (HHS), and the Civil Rights Commission—rather than in the "inner" or "core" bureaucracies dealing with economic and internal and national security affairs (State, Treasury, Defense, and Justice).[35]

Statistical incorporation aside, what has been the substantive impact of black appointed officials on executive branch decision-making during this twenty-year period?

The difference it makes (or does not make) that blacks in the post–Civil Rights era are routine participants in executive branch policy-making is the critical issue to be assessed. Is politics of this sort enough to move the black agenda, or is it simply a matter of black faces in high places with little policy consequence for the black agenda?

An important assumption of proponents of black incorporation is that blacks will become advocates of black interests in the decision-making process. As Eddie Williams wrote on the eve of the Carter administration: "The inclusion of blacks would provide a much needed minority perspective in the early stages of policy development rather than after policies have been locked in concrete, when the only alternative is protest."[36]

The evidence, while mixed and at this stage somewhat tentative, suggests that Williams and other advocates of mere descriptive or statistical representation in government as a means to advance black interests are likely to be frequently disappointed. Space does not permit here a detailed consideration of the relevant data, but the pattern from the Eisenhower administration through the Reagan administration suggests that blacks in executive branch policy-making positions were frequent advocates of black interests as these are conventionally defined by the black establishment, but just as frequently, they were ignored, invisible to the president and his senior advisors.

For example, E. Fredric Murrow, the first black White House staff aide, tells in his memoirs the sad story of his tenure in the Eisenhower administration, where he could hardly get an office and secretary let alone advise the president on civil rights policy or other race concerns; he was the classic invisible man. Similarly, accounts of executive branch decision-making on civil rights legislation and Great Society antipoverty programs in the Kennedy and Johnson administrations show invisible black men and women, little consultation sought or given, and no discernible impact on outcomes.[37] In the Nixon administration, black appointees made an organized, concerted effort as a group to dissuade the president from pursuing its antibusing rhetoric and legislative proposals but to no avail; indeed the top black officials of the administration were only granted the opportunity to communicate with the president after press leaks about their displeasure and a hint of mass resignations.[38]

In the Carter administration, there was, from the point of view of black advocates of executive branch incorporation, the even more disturbing cases of black officials actively proposing and pursuing policies hostile to black interests as conventionally defined. For example, in preparation of the government's brief in the *Bakke* affirmative action case, Drew Days, the assistant attorney general for civil rights, and Wade McCree, the solicitor general, both black and the responsible agents of government on the matter, took the now familiar Reagan-Meese conservative view that it was impermissible for a university *ever* (their emphasis) to take race into consideration in its admissions decisions. Only the intervention of Vice President Mondale and other senior blacks in the administration (including United Nations Ambassador Young, HUD Secretary Patricia Harris, and EEOC Chairwoman Eleanor Holmes Norton) prevented this extreme position from being adopted by the United States.[39] (The position of the United States is traditionally given some deference by the Supreme Court.)

Another case of a Carter administration appointee—Emmett Rice on the

Federal Reserve Board—acting against perceived black interests involves the high interest rate policy pursued by Paul Volcker in order to lower inflation by generating a massive recession. This policy, which resulted in 1981-1983 in the worst recession since the 1930s Depression, was consistently supported by Rice, although blacks were predictably among its principal victims. Indeed, in Board deliberations only Nancy Teeters, its only female member, consistently opposed Volcker's policies as harsh. She was accused by her colleagues of being too soft, of bringing a "feminist perspective" to the decision-making process. One searches the record in vain for a trace of Rice's "black perspective."[40] (It is worth noting that governors of the Federal Reserve Board, unlike most other presidential appointees, do not serve at the president's pleasure but rather have fourteen-year fixed terms.)

The Reagan administration in a sense broke new ground in post–Civil Rights era black politics, in that for the first time a large number of blacks were recruited who not only did not actively pursue black interests in administrative decision-making but constantly opposed them as they are conventionally understood in the black community. In the Nixon-Ford administrations, black appointees were from backgrounds of civil rights activism and had close connections inside the black establishment.[41] In the Reagan administration, however, a new cadre of young ideological new right black conservatives were recruited with little if any connections to the Movement or the institutional black community.[42] And these people used their offices to join Reagan in attacks on the entire post–Civil Rights era black agenda. Thus, the experience of black appointees in the Reagan administration suggests that in the future a conservative administration might be able not only to recruit invisible blacks in the policy process but, more alarmingly, higher-visible ones working actively against the interests and agenda of black America.

The few studies of the behavior of black federal judges, though not conclusive, point in the same direction. Thomas Walker and Deborah Barrow, for example, found no significant differences between black and white judges in criminal cases or civil rights cases. Jon Gottschall's study of federal appellate judges appointed by Carter found significant differences in criminal cases (black judges were more likely than white judges to uphold the rights of criminal defendants and prisoners), yet there were no significant differences between the judges in race and sex discrimination cases.[43]

Overall, then, those who place hope in black appointees effectively pursuing black interests in bureaucratic decision-making are likely to be disappointed, because the results thus far show that this kind of politics is not enough.

The Black Agenda in the Post–Civil Rights Era: Consensus and Invisibility

Sometimes it seems that the principal activity of post–Civil Rights era black leadership has been identifying just what the "black agenda" really is. Since the late 1960s, a bewildering series of conventions, meetings, leadership summits, congresses, institutes, and so forth have replaced rallies, marches, demonstrations, and lawsuits as a principal routine activity. These meetings and other gatherings have yielded an equally bewildering set of documents variously described as the "black agenda."

The varied agendas produced in the last twenty years include the platform of the 1972 National Black Convention in Gary, Indiana, the CBC's sixty Recommendations to President Nixon and its watered-down version of the Gary platform called "The Black Declaration of Independence and Bill of Rights," a series of "True State of the Union" messages inserted in the *Congressional Record* in response to the annual addresses by Presidents Nixon and Ford, a series of recommendations developed by ad hoc meetings of black Democrats in 1976 and 1980 for presentation to the party conventions and nominees, a series of "mandates" issued by the National Institutes of Black Public Officials, meetings of several thousand people convened several times since 1973 by the Joint Center for Political Studies, and most recently the alternative CBC budgets developed in response to administration budget proposals since 1981 and the platforms developed by Jesse Jackson as part of his campaigns for president. Thus, if anything is clear in the post–Civil Rights era, it is "what black people want" (according to black leadership) in terms of an agenda of economic and social change.

As summarized in proposals of the Third National Institute of Black Public Officials (a 1976 assembly of about 1,000 black officials brought together by the Joint Center for Political Studies), the black agenda includes:

1. A full employment program that "guarantees the right to useful and meaningful jobs for those willing and able to work";
2. Welfare reform to include a "guaranteed annual income . . . not laden down with punitive counterproductive (forced) work requirements";
3. Comprehensive national health insurance;
4. Tax reform to remove loopholes that permit wealthy individuals and corporations to pay no taxes or less than fair rates;
5. Increased funding for higher education, elementary and secondary education, and vocational education, and support for busing as a "means to insure high quality education for children in integrated settings";
6. Minority business initiatives, including support for government set-asides and a "one year moratorium on federal loan repayments";
7. Support for international sanctions on South Africa, repeal of the Byrd amendment allowing the importation of Rhodesian chrome in violation of United Nations sanctions, and support for the new International Economic Order, specifically assuring "just and stable prices for primary commodities."[44]

With minor changes in emphasis and specifics (less concern with busing and successful repeal of the Byrd amendment for example), these items remain as key on the black agenda. The core item is the call for full employment.

Charles Hamilton forcefully articulated the analytic and strategic basis for the full employment priority in a paper prepared for the NUL's first national conference to consider the post–Civil Rights black agenda. He argued that full employment should become the "new major focus" of the Civil Rights Movement because of the obvious long-standing "crisis" of joblessness in black America and the correlation of joblessness with other socioeconomic problems. In addition, Hamilton concluded, a focus on full employment would facilitate moving beyond the limits of 1960s-style protest toward more efficacious forms of electoral activism. Hamilton also argued that this issue would create a consensus, and thus "rise above the devastating divisive ideological debates now wracking traditional Civil Rights circles." Perhaps more importantly: "It applies to the total society, not only to blacks and other traditionally stigmatized minorities, who are seen as wanting only hand-outs. It would, in other words, recognize the critical factor of race and racism, but it offers a *deracialized* solution" (emphasis added).[45]

The idea of "deracialized" issues and strategies of mobilization (which recalls Rustin's approach in his 1965 *Commentary* article) has been a hallmark of black politics in the post–Civil Rights era in terms of issues (employment, health insurance, tax reform, and so forth) and coalition formation, reaching a kind of peak (at least symbolically) in Jesse Jackson's efforts to build a "Rainbow Coalition" in his presidential campaigns.

The Black Agenda: Civil Rights Consensus

It is important to understand the difficulty of overriding presidential vetoes of civil rights legislation (for example, the failure to override President Bush's veto of the Civil Rights Act of 1990) and recent retrenchments in civil rights due to rulings of a Supreme Court now leaning rightward as a result of Reagan and Bush appointments. In *Croson v. City of Richmond, Wards Cove Packing v. Atonio, Martin v. Wilks, Patterson v. McClain Credit Union,* and *Jett v. Dallas Independent School District,* the high Court's rulings weakened civil rights protections.[46]

Yet, politics in the post–Civil Rights era does appear to be enough to maintain and preserve the basic structure of civil rights law. That is, a dominant coalition of blacks, liberals, and centrist forces in the Democratic and Republican parties has emerged in Congress on civil rights issues, narrowly defined. Or to put it another way, the coalition that emerged in the mid-1960s and facilitated passage of the three major Civil Rights acts of the decade remains largely intact and is usually able to control policy on these issues in the face of the opposition of even a popular president and Supreme Court majority. This suggests that there is a national consensus on civil rights. This consensus can be seen in congressional actions on such issues as rejection of antibusing legislation, renewals of the Voting Rights Act, passage of fair housing enforcement legislation, the Martin Luther King Holiday Act, the Civil Rights Restoration Act, and the refusals of the Senate to confirm the nominations of Robert Bork to the Supreme Court and William Lucas as assistant attorney general for civil rights.

On each of these issues, a major effort was undertaken by the black leadership establishment to activate the broad-based coalition that secured passage of the basic Civil Rights Acts of the 1960s, including labor, religious groups, other minorities, and the national business community. The result was a coalition in Congress that included substantial votes from centrist Republicans (following the leadership of Republican Senate leader Robert Dole) and virtually unanimous support from the Democratic party, including its large and influential bloc of southern conservatives.

For example, Bork's nomination was defeated in the Senate by the largest margin ever recorded for a Supreme Court nominee, and only one Democrat defected from the Civil Rights coalition, while several Republican senators opposed the nomination. Or take another example: On the vote to override Reagan's veto of the Civil Rights Restoration Act in the Senate, not a single Democrat supported the President while twenty-one Republicans supported the Civil Rights coalition. It should also be emphasized that on two issues—the Civil Rights Restoration Act and the 1982 reauthorization of the Voting Rights Act—the Congress explicitly overruled prior decisions of the Supreme Court, an unusual act given the Congress's traditional deference to the Court.[47]

Ronald Reagan's eight-year tenure in office represented the constellation at the summit of national power of the forces hostile to the civil rights reforms of the 1960s. These forces were intent on rolling back through executive, legislative, administrative, and judicial actions the important gains of the 1960s. This led many blacks in 1980 to talk openly of the end of a "Second Reconstruction," the effective repudiation of basic civil rights guarantees. That this did not occur in spite of the fact that there was a well-organized and well-financed anti–Civil Rights lobby and a highly popular president opposed to civil rights is evidence of the dominance of a broad Civil Rights coalition and suggests that in this important policy arena (an arena of *legal* rights), "politics is enough."[48]

The Black Agenda: Invisibility and Isolation Regarding Social and Economic Reform

Since 1981, the Congressional Black Caucus has embodied the fundamental elements of the black agenda of social and economic reform in a series of alternative budgets presented to the House for debate and vote.[49] This was done as a result of President Reagan's challenge to critics of his 1981 budget proposal to come up with a viable alternative of their own. In response, the Democratic party majority in the House proposed a diluted version of the Reagan budget that largely accepted prevailing conservative economic assumptions but with somewhat higher social welfare expenditures, somewhat fewer defense outlays, and somewhat fewer tax breaks for corporations and the wealthy.[50] Thus, it fell to the Congressional Black Caucus—the most progressive organized bloc in Congress—to fashion the only viable alternative to the conservative economic and social policies of the Reagan administration and the Democratic majority in Congress. In the words of *The Washington Post*, the Caucus was left to develop "the only truly liberal budget."[51]

With relatively few resources compared to the administration's Office of Management and Budget and the Democratic majority's Congressional Budget Office, and in 1981 with no black member assigned to the Budget Committee, the Caucus drew on staff from the offices of individual members, the expertise of their various committee roles, and the assistance of a few outside experts and groups to develop a budget proposal that was widely viewed as a comprehensive, economically sophisticated program, and the only real alternative to the social and economic policies embodied in Reagan's budget.

Prior to introducing their budget proposal in early April 1981, the Caucus sought to develop a broad coalition of support by talking to more than one hundred labor, environmental, social welfare, and peace groups. This process was employed, more or less, for each of the subsequent budgets proposed by the Caucus between fiscal years 1982 and 1986. The debate and roll call votes on these alternative budgets will be used as indicators or measures of the breadth and depth of the coalition in Congress sympathetic to the black agenda of progressive social and economic reform.

Within the planning framework established by the Humphrey-Hawkins Full Employment and Balanced Growth Act of 1978, each Caucus budget proposal has had as its centerpiece a major jobs program that would "address the problems of structural unemployment which affects such a large segment of the black population in America."[52] For example, in addition to a multibillion dollar direct job creation program, the Caucus budget in 1981 included a four billion dollar urban infrastructure program, a four billion dollar increase in mass transit and highway spending, substantial increases in Aid to Families with Dependent Children ($3.2 billion), and increases in a variety of health programs serving low-income citizens ($1.2 billion).[53] The Caucus proposals on tax reform were structured with an eye toward a balanced budget in the context of full employment and stable economic growth. To pay for these expenditures, the budget proposed fundamental changes in the tax code that shifted the burden more toward large corporations and individuals of substantial wealth (including withholding income tax on interest, repeal of dividend exclusion, limitations on some mortgage interest deductions, and repeal of tax subsidies for oil companies and other allowances for large corporations that resulted in their paying relatively little or, in a few cases, no taxes).[54]

Finally, and perhaps most controversially, the Caucus proposed substantial reductions in military outlays (in 1981 from $264 billion to $196 billion), including the elimination of Reagan's entire strategic weapons buildup (the MX missile, the Trident-2 submarine, the Trident-2 missile, the sea- and ground-launched Cruise missile, the Pershing 2 missile, and the B1 bomber) because, as Congressman Ronald Dellums (Democrat-California) said during the debate, such weapons are "destabilizing . . . irrational and insane."[55] In addition, substantial cuts were proposed in the Navy's 650 ship program, NATO, and the Rapid Deployment Force. As a result of these cuts in the military and tax proposals, the Caucus alternative budget, despite relatively large increases in social expenditures, projected a balanced budget by 1985, earlier than that of the administration or the Democratic majority.

Given this outline and overview of the basic elements of the Caucus budget, the outcome of floor debates and votes can now be considered. First, an analysis of the roll call votes is presented.

In 1981, the Caucus budget was defeated 356 to 69; in 1983, 322 to 86; in 1985, 333 to 76; in 1986, 361 to 54; and in 1987, 362 to 52.[56]

Using the 1983 vote (because it received the highest number of votes of the five) shows the limits of the progressive coalition in Congress. Table 6.2 shows the pattern of support for the black agenda in the House. This table reveals substantial support among the relatively small cadre of House liberals (in any given year, liberals constitute about a quarter of the House); 72 percent of the liberals (65 percent, excluding blacks) voted for the Caucus budget. In the House as a whole, not counting black members, support drops to 15 percent of the total and 27 percent of Democrats.

Analysis of the voting pattern is consistent with what is known about congressional roll call votes on issues of concern to blacks; that is, relatively little support from rural and southern districts with large black populations and some support from urban Democrats in other regions.[57] In 1983, for

Table 6.2
Distribution of Support on Roll Call Votes (in Percentages) for the Congressional Black Caucus's Alternative Budget, 1983

Group	Percent
All House Members	20%
House Members (excluding blacks)	15
All House Democrats	33
House Democrats (excluding blacks)	27
All House Liberals*	72
House Liberals (excluding blacks)	65

*Liberalism was determined on the basis of members score of 75 or more on the rating scale of the Americans for Democratic Action.

example, only five white southern Democrats supported the Caucus budget (Lindy Boggs of New Orleans, Claude Pepper of Miami, Wyche Fowler of Atlanta, Martin Frost of Dallas, and Steny Hoyer of Maryland) and each of them represented urban districts with majority or near-majority black or Latino populations.

In terms of region, approximately half of the votes in 1983 came from the Northeast, 24 percent from the Midwest, and 22 percent from the West. In terms of ethnicity, only three of ten Latinos and about a third of the Jewish members supported the Caucus budget.

Thus, the data here reveal that on the fundamental social and economic priorities of black America, there is support in Congress from only about one in seven members. Even this level of support is deceptive, since perhaps more than half of the whites voting for the budget in any given year did so while harboring strong reservations either about the tax proposals or the military cuts or both. Essentially, what many House liberals said during the debates was that they supported the Caucus proposals to increase social welfare spending but were opposed to the mechanisms to finance them through tax reform and cuts in military expenditures.[58] Relatively few members outside of the Caucus supported the alternative budgets without significant reservation, most notably Congresswoman Mary Rose Oakar of Ohio and David Bonior of Michigan. Indeed, if one strips away the votes of "commendation" and "faint praise" and those cast with "strong reservations," coalition support was probably no more than 10 percent of the House as a whole, 15 percent of House Democrats, and a third of House liberals.

What is more revealing about the status of the black agenda in the House than the outcome of the roll call votes on the budgets is the sense of isolation, frustration, anger, and bitterness felt by blacks in the House as they were routinely ignored by party colleagues and leaders. For example, during the 1982 debate, Congressman John Conyers of Michigan remarked:

Finally, Mr. Chairman, the most painful part of my remarks is reserved for those whom I love and respect and have worked for the most. The Democratic leadership, whom I have supported and voted for, worked with, cooperated with for every single year of which I have had the high privilege to serve in this Congress. The Democratic leadership has now for the second year in a row chosen to ignore this work product. It did not criticize it; leaders of the party will not praise it; they just do not see that it exists. It is the invisible document . . . but the time has come—as matter of fact long overdue—where we must address the critical underlying questions of why we cannot get more than 69 votes. . . . And it is about time we get a little bit of respect or criticism for the nature of our work product. We bring you millions of Democratic votes to the halls of the Congress and to the national ticket, more than anybody else on this side of the aisle, excluding nobody. And they are watching us and you. And I want to say that time is running out.[59]

Similarly, Congresswoman Shirley Chisholm of New York observed:

Why? Is it because of the terminology "black?" What would happen if we removed the term "black?" The fact is that months were spent putting this budget together. . . . Here we come again today, everybody wants to get rid of us, get us off the floor; we are taking up their time. Well, we are going to take up time because it is important to recognize that 18 members of the House of Representatives have been responsive in terms of accepting certain challenges. But because of inherent racism in the bloodstream of America, it becomes increasingly difficult to get beyond the color of one's skin.[60]

And finally on this point of isolation and invisibility, Congressman Ronald Dellums of California during the 1985 debate said: "Mr. Chairman, it is with some sense of sadness and pain that I rise this evening because as I look around this body including even to the press gallery, that at the time the Congressional Black Caucus offers its budget, it's break time, time to chat, time for the press to get a cup of coffee, read a newspaper, engage in conversation."[61]

What the budget debates document is not just the absence of a progressive coalition in Congress or the Democratic party that would support the black agenda of social reform, but more profoundly, the irrelevancy of that agenda and the Black Caucus itself in the congressional process.[62] As *Washington Post* chief political reporter David Broder wrote of the 1982 debate, "There is a perfectly good case to be made that it deserved to be defeated. A lot of people—myself included—would have gagged on the elimination of all new strategic weapons that it proposed. But this budget was not just defeated by the House of Representatives. It was ignored."[63]

Thus, as black power has nominally increased in the House in terms of seniority and important committee and subcommittee and party leadership posts (demonstrated most recently by the elevation of Congressman William Gray to Majority Whip, the third-ranking post in the Democratic leadership hierarchy), black substantive power is hardly greater now than it was twenty years ago when the Caucus was formed.

On the fundamental needs of the black community, "politics is not enough" in spite of two decades of agenda building and efforts at black voter mobilization and coalition formation.[64] This is not to say that the Caucus is not effective on incremental issues of importance to blacks; rather, it is to say that incremental changes are not enough.[65] Indeed, the so-called radical reforms embodied in the Caucus budget alternatives are only good first steps in the direction needed to reconstruct black America and end growing emiseration and dispossession.

One of the dangers of formal cooptation with the trappings of power rather than its substance is that over time it tends in a subordinate community to reinforce interpersonal and political alienation, cynicism, and despair at the mass level and tension and conflict among the group's elite.[66] This is well illustrated by the tenure of Congressman Gray as chairman of the Budget Committee. Despite his pledge to not "tolerate the vicious attacks we've seen over the past four years on those programs aimed at the least fortunate,"[67] as chairman, he consistently produced and defended on the House floor budgets that reflected the neo-Reagan consensus of majority House Democrats, sparking on more than one occasion a revolt by committee liberals.[68] The irony, of course, is compelling, since under circumstances other than his leadership role, Gray would have been among the committee rebels. Instead, he found himself defending the status quo—a status quo all his vaunted power as chairman found him helpless to alter.

Once he became chairman, Gray declined to support the Caucus budgets even with a symbolic "vote of commendation," as cast by Majority Leader Thomas Foley of Washington. Rather, he voted "present," raising the question of what good it is to have the "power" if one cannot "fight the power," in the memorable line from Spike Lee's film, *Do the Right Thing.*

Congressman Conyers "took exception" to Gray's failure to cast a symbolic vote of solidarity with the Caucus. "I draw the line where he actively campaigned against the Black Caucus resolution," Conyers stated.[69] Indeed, if politics were enough, Gray should have exercised his powers as chairman of the Budget Committee to advance the Caucus alternative. The extent to which Gray did not do this and, moreover, felt he could not do this, is a fitting piece of evidence to end an analysis that has demonstrated that "politics is not enough."

CONCLUSION

After two decades of the new black politics of institutionalized participation, the weight of evidence is quite persuasive that politics as routinely practiced in the United States by black Americans is not enough to alter the terrible conditions of the American underclass. Indeed, during this twenty-year period of the new black politics, the life-chances and conditions of the bottom third of black Americans grew worse by almost any measure of well-being.[70] In addition, the systemic response to the fundamental post–Civil Rights era demand (full employment) has been largely neglect and symbolism. This situation persists because blacks have been unable to obtain sufficient resources to pressure the system to yield a substantive policy output. That is, the kind of progressive coalition envisioned by Rustin in 1965 as a possible governing coalition has not materialized. Indeed, a progressive coalition is not likely to develop in the foreseeable future, given present conditions and politics as usual.

Hence, if politics is not enough and protest is not enough, the question becomes what is enough, or in the words of Browning, Marshall, and Tabb in a recent essay: "Is anything enough?"[71] More specifically, if black politics is not enough, will it be succeeded by a more radical movement, a higher stage in the historic struggle of blacks for their liberation in the Americas?

The prospects for a renewal of insurgency, for a revitalized mass movement style of politics as an integral part of the struggle, is a necessary but not inevitable or certain new direction in black politics. As Piven and Cloward forcefully argue, a mass protest movement is "not a matter of free choice; it is not freely available to all groups at all times, and much of the time it is not available to lower class groups at all. The occasions it must take and the impact it can have are delimited by the social structure."[72]

This is largely correct, but Piven and Cloward might underestimate the extent to which masses of people may exercise some degree of choice in these matters. The devastating conditions of the African American portion of the underclass in both rural and urban America are suggestive of conditions for the mobilization of insurgency. As Douglas McAdams concludes:

There is little question but that widespread black insurgency will develop again in the not too distant future. Jim Crow may be dead, but its legacy lives on in the form of grinding poverty, persistent institutional discrimination in jobs, housing, and education, and the continued social estrangement of blacks and whites in the country. Sooner or later organized black insurgency aimed at this litany of inequities will no doubt rise. And when it does we can expect it to be preceded by a fundamental shift in political alignments favorable to blacks, the mobilization of the indigenous organizational strength of the black community, and the transformation of existing feelings of cynicism and hopelessness in a shared vision of collective political power.[73]

One of the problems in the organization of black insurgency today, however, compared to the Civil Rights era, is that black leadership and would-be leaders are so thoroughly integrated into institutional structures and processes that they may be removed both physically and psychologically from the mass base of the community. Talented people who today might constitute the organizing cadre instead seek niches in relatively insignificant electoral office or in corporate and public bureaucracies (or increasingly work in the marketing and distribution of illegal drugs). Today, a young Stokely Carmichael might well end up with the equivalent of a GS-16 job in the Atlanta or the District of Columbia bureaucracies. Related to this, black institutional elites, acting in the classic tradition of middle-class liberal reform in the United States, pursue a top-down hierarchical model of social change. Elections, conventions, conferences, networking, media events, meetings with the president, and so forth are now the name of the game.

Most black leaders know that the conditions of the black underclass cannot be effectively addressed without changes in the structure of the national economy. Yet they act as if fundamental changes can come about as a result of playing the routine power games of Washington or city politics when clearly such changes, if possible, are *only* possible as a result of mass mobilization inside the black community.

This is not to say that routine institutional politics is not necessary; rather, it is to say once again that it is not enough. What is needed is what Ronald Walters calls a "balanced strategy." The limitations of the new institutional black politics might be overcome, Walters argues, if the leadership has the "honesty and integrity to admit openly that it cannot effect the necessary social change from within American institutions, and again support system-challenging strategies as a balanced plan of attack for the long run, involving electoral politics and protest."[74]

Yet viewed historically, one perhaps should not expect too much from increasingly comfortable, isolated middle-class institutional leadership. The masses might have to lead; inject themselves into the processes of history. Then the leaders might follow. There are some encouraging signs or at least hints that this might be occurring—for example, the developing patterns of rebellion in new music and other art forms popular among the young, such as the music of Tracy Chapman, Jackson Browne, and Public Enemy and the films of Spike Lee.[75]

It is also possible that the violence manifested in what has been called today's "quiet riots" might become not so quiet, exploding in another cycle of ghetto rebellions. It might be that by the year 2000, scholars of social movements will look back on the 1980s and 1990s as the seed-time for a new cycle of insurgency in the African American freedom struggle.

As Charles Hamilton pointed out, "serious periodic crises have attended every major achievement of black Americans—in housing, employment, education, public accommodations, voting. This has created an ethos in black political thought and action that strongly supports the contention that unless a crisis of major proportions is precipitated, there is little likelihood that any result will be forthcoming."[76]

Crises of kinds that have historically attended black progress in this country, such as the Civil War or the 1930s Depression are, of course, not situations that organizers can organize. Yet those involved in struggle must not simply wait for crisis. They must endeavor to do what they can.[77] The central lesson of this inquiry, however, is that by following the routines of politics as usual, the largely institutionalized leadership of black America in the closing years of the twentieth century is not doing what it can; it is not doing enough.

NOTES

1. Bayard Rustin called this a transformation "from protest to politics." See Bayard Rustin, "From Protest to Politics: The Future of the Civil Rights Movement," *Commentary* 39 (1965): 28–29. This conceptualization is misleading to the extent that it implies that protest is not politics but rather some irrational form of apolitical collective behavior.

2. This chapter is drawn from a larger project the author is completing.

3. Douglas McAdams, *Political Process and the Development of Black Insurgency, 1930–1970* (Chicago: University of Chicago Press, 1982), 1–3. See also Robert Salisbury, "Political Movements in American Politics: An Essay on Concept and Analysis," *National Political Science Review* 1 (1989): 15–30.

4. From the Niagara Manifesto as quoted in Lerone Bennett, *Confrontation: Black and White* (Baltimore: Penguin, 1965), 103.

5. Ibid.

6. There is, of course, overlap of the forms of political activism in each period.

7. See Charles Kellog, *NAACP—A History of the National Association for the Advancement of Colored People* (Baltimore: John Hopkins, 1957).

8. See Robert Zangrando, *The NAACP Crusade Against Lynching, 1909–50* (Philadelphia: Temple University Press, 1980).

9. On the legislation barring people of African origin, see Harold Cruse, *Plural but Equal: Blacks and Minorities in America's Plural Society* (New York: William Morrow, 1987), and on the lobbying effort leading to defeat of the Supreme Court nominee, see Gilbert Ware, "Lobbying as a Means of Protest: The NAACP as an Agent of Equality," *Journal of Negro Education* 33 (1964): 103–07.

10. The most comprehensive accounts of the litigation phase are Mark Tushnet, *The NAACP's Legal Strategy Against Segregated Education, 1925–50* (Chapel Hill: University of North Carolina Press, 1987), and Richard Kluger, *Simple Justice: History of Brown v. Board of Education and Black America's Struggle for Racial Equality* (New York: Random House, 1975).

11. There are numerous works, academic, popular, and participant memoirs, on the protest phase of the Movement, but the most theoretically sophisticated are Aldon Morris, *The Origins of the Civil Rights Movement* (New York: The Free Press, 1984) and Douglas McAdams, *Political Process and Development.*

12. David Garrow discusses King's dispute with Rustin about the poor peoples campaign throughout his *Bearing the Cross: Martin Luther King and the Southern Christian Leadership Conference* (New York: William Morrow, 1986).

13. Rustin, "From Protest to Politics," 28–29.

14. See Claybourne Carson, *In Struggle: SNCC and the Black Awakening of the 1960s* (Cambridge, Mass.: Harvard University Press, 1981), chapters 13–15.

15. Ibid.

16. Although there was initially a lot of disagreement among the black intelligentsia about the meaning of black power, early on the following elements elicited widespread consensus, bridging institutional and ideological gaps in the community: (1) black people should develop a greater sense of group solidarity and race pride; (2) the Civil Rights Movement had fallen short of benefiting the masses; (3) organizations and institutions in the black community should be controlled by black people; (4) white racism constitutes the core of the black man's problems; (5) the black movement must be led by blacks; (6) black people have the right and responsibility to defend themselves against violent attack; and (7) black power is sought as a means, not an end, to black liberation. See Solomon P. Gethers, "Black Power Three Years Later," *Black World* 23 (1969): 7–16; Dianne Pinderhughes, "A Retrospective Examination: The Failure of Black Power," *Journal of Afro-American Issues* 5 (1977): 253–56; and Harold Cruse, "Behind the Black Power Slogan" in *Rebellion or Revolution* (New York: William Morrow, 1988), 193–258.

17. See Robert Smith, "Black Power and the Transformation from Protest to Politics," *Political Science Quarterly* 96 (1981): 431–43.

18. Frances Fox Piven and Richard Cloward, *Poor Peoples Movements: Why They Succeed, Why They Fail* (New York: Random House, 1977), 243.

19. Max Weber, "The Sociology of Charismatic Authority" in *From Max Weber: Essays in Sociology,* edited by H. H. Gerth and C. Wright Mills (New York: Oxford, 1958), 54–55.

20. Harry Scoble, "A Process Model to Study Political Repression," unpublished manuscript, Department of Political Science, UCLA, 1971.

21. Some of Scoble's outputs are implicit in other work on social movement outcomes. See, for example, Piven and Cloward, *Poor Peoples Movements*, 27–32.

22. See McAdams, *Political Process and the Development of Black Insurgency.*

23. Martin Luther King, "Where Do We Go From Here," in *A Testament of Hope: The Essential Writings of Martin Luther King, Jr.*, edited by James Washington (New York: Harper and Row, 1986), 256.

24. Garrow, *Bearing the Cross*, 77.

25. Phillips Selznick, *TVA and the Grassroots* (Berkeley: University of California, 1949), 7.

26. Carl Stokes, *Promises of Power: A Political Biography* (New York: Simon and Schuster, 1973), 96.

27. Selznick, *TVA and the Grassroots.*

28. Rufus Browning, Dale Marshall, and David Tabb, *Protest Is Not Enough* (Berkeley: University of California Press, 1984), 242, 253.

29. A critical distinction overlooked in Browning, Marshall, and Tabb's analysis is between an electoral coalition constituted by groups necessary to win office and a governing coalition constituted by those groups necessary to govern.

30. See Arthur Levy and Susan Stoudinger, "The Black Caucus in the 92nd Congress: Gauging Its Success," *Phylon* 39 (1978): 39–46, and Charles Jones, "An Overview of the Congressional Black Caucus: 1970–85" in *Readings in American Political Issues,* edited by Franklin Jones, et al. (Dubuque, Iowa: Kendall/Hunt, 1987), 219–40.

31. James Mock, *The Black Political Executive and Black Interests, 1961–80,* doctoral dissertation, The University of Tennessee, 1981, and Robert C. Smith, "Black Appointed Officials: A Neglected Category of Political Participation Research," *Journal of Black Studies* 14 (1984): 369–88.

32. On Taft's black cabinet, see Louis Harlan, *Booker T. Washington: The Making of a Black Leader, 1865–1910* (New York: Oxford, 1972), 351–54; on the Roosevelt groups, see Nancy Weiss, *Farewell to the Party of Lincoln: Black Politics in the Age of FDR* (Princeton, N.J.: Princeton University Press, 1983), chapter 7.

33. Despite repeated requests to the White House Personnel Office, the Office of White House Assistant Melvin Bradley, the Republican National Committee, and the National Republican Council (an organization of blacks in the party), the Reagan administration refused to provide data on black appointments. Such data were readily available in the Nixon-Ford and Carter administrations. In the absence of up-to-date data from the administration, statistics supplied as of April 1983 to the United States Commission on Civil Rights for their report "Equal Opportunity in Presidential Appointments" (issued June 1983) are employed in this analysis. It is possible that it understates the number of blacks who served during Reagan's tenure, since at a comparable period in the Carter administration, blacks constituted 6 percent rather than the 1980 proportion of 12 percent of appointees in the Carter administration. Requests to the White House and to the Republican National Committee during the first three years of the Bush administration also failed to generate data. Although anecdotal evidence indicates that Bush appointed substantially more blacks than Reagan, statistics on the Bush administration are not included due to the lack of systematic data.

34. Robert Axelrod, "Where the Votes Come From: An Analysis of Electoral Coali-

tions," *American Political Science Review* 66 (1972): 11–20, and Axelrod, "Communications," *American Political Science Review* 76 (1982): 393–96.

35. Pointing to examples such as Colin Powell, chairman of the Joint Chiefs, Condoleeza Rice, former member of the National Security Council, and Constance Newman, head of the Office of Personnel Management, the Bush administration claims it has broken this mold of not appointing blacks to core bureaucracies.

36. Eddie Williams, "Commentary," *Focus* (November 1976): 2.

37. See the following studies of civil rights policy-making in the Civil Rights and post–Civil Rights eras: Richard Burk, *The Eisenhower Administration and Black Civil Rights* (Knoxville: University of Tennessee, 1985); James Harvey, *Black Civil Rights During the Kennedy Administration* (Jackson, Miss.: College and University Press of Mississippi, 1973); Harvey, *Black Civil Rights During the Johnson Administration* (Jackson, Miss.: College and University Press of Mississippi, 1973); and Alan Wolk, *The Presidency and Black Civil Rights: Eisenhower to Nixon* (East Brunswick, N.J.: Fairleigh Dickerson, 1971). On the formulation of Great Society antipoverty policies, see John Donovan, *The Politics of Poverty* (New York: Pegasus, 1967), and more recently, Nicholas Leman, "The Unfinished War," *The Atlantic Monthly*, December 1988, 37–46.

38. On the antibusing protests by black officials in the Nixon administration, see Robert C. Smith, "The Political Behavior of Black Presidential Appointees, 1960–80," *Western Journal of Black Studies* 8 (1984): 243–44. See also Paul Delaney, "Nixon is Seeking to Placate Black Aides Ready to Quit," *The New York Times*, January 4, 1971.

39. See Smith, "The Political Behavior of Black Presidential Appointees," 144; Eleanor Holmes Norton, "The Role of Black Presidential Appointees," *Urban League Review* 9 (1985): 108–09; and Bernard Schwarz, *Behind Bakke: Affirmative Action and the Supreme Court* (New York: New York University Press, 1988): 75–76.

40. See William Grieder, *Secrets of the Temple: How the Federal Reserve Runs the Country* (New York: Simon and Schuster, 1987), 75–76.

41. Social background data on black appointees are in Mock, "The Black Vote Output," and Smith "Black Appointed Officials."

42. Officials in the Reagan administration literally sought to create a sympathetic new black leadership through the appointment process and by bestowing publicity and prestige on alternative leadership through White House audiences and media events. For example, see Fred Barnes "Invent a Negro, Inc.," *The New Republic*, April 15, 1985, 9–10.

43. Thomas Walker and Deborah Barrow, "The Diversification of the Federal Bench: Policy and Process Ramifications," *Journal of Politics* 47 (1985): 596–616, and Jon Gottschall, "Carter's Judicial Appointments: The Influence of Affirmative Action and Merit Selection on Voting on the U.S. Court of Appeals," *Judicature* 67 (1983): 165–73.

44. "Seven Point Mandate," *Focus* (January–February 1976): 8.

45. Charles Hamilton, "Full Employment as a Viable Issue" in Hanes Walton, *When the Marching Stopped: An Analysis of Black Issues in the 70s* (New York: National Urban League, 1973), 90–91.

46. In *Croson v. City of Richmond* (#87-998), the Court invalidated the city's minority business set-aside program, thereby casting constitutional doubt on the validity of scores of such programs nationwide; in *Wards Cove Packing v. Atonio* (#87-1387), the

Court in effect overruled a 1971 opinion that placed the burden of proof on employers to justify policies that had the statistical effect of discriminating against minorities and women; in *Martin v. Wilks* (#87-1614), the Court allowed long-settled consent decrees involving racial discrimination to be opened to subsequent legal attack, threatening a costly, neverending round of lawsuits by victims of racial discrimination; in *Patterson v. McClain Credit Union* (#87-107), the Court held that the Civil Rights Act of 1866 provided no grounds to sue for racial discrimination or harassment once employed, and finally in *Jett v. Dallas Independent School District* (#87-2084), the Court further weakened the 1866 act by holding that it did not provide a legal basis for suits against local governments for acts of race discrimination. For a good overview of Supreme Court affirmative action jurisprudence (prior to the end of the 1988-89 term), see W. Avon Drake and Robert D. Holsworth, "Electoral Politics, Affirmative Action, and the Supreme Court: The Case of *Richmond v. Croson*," *National Political Science Review* 2 (1990): 65-91.

47. The Civil Rights Restoration Act overruled the Supreme Court's 1984 decision in *Grove City College v. Bell* (#84-7-811), which significantly narrowed the scope and coverage of Title VI of the 1964 Civil Rights Act. In renewing the Voting Rights Act in 1982, the Congress overruled the Supreme Court's decision in *City of Mobile v. Bolden* (#80-1-2089), which seemed to require direct evidence of discriminatory intent or purpose rather than simple effects in order to sustain a constitutional claim of vote dilution or discrimination.

48. The Reagan administration lost every legislative battle on civil rights that came to a vote in Congress, and Reagan declined, despite considerable right-wing pressure, to use his "stroke of the pen" authority to invalidate or even modify the executive order requiring affirmative action goals and timetables in government contracting. However, through administrative inaction, budget cuts, deregulation, and staffing patterns, the effective enforcement of civil rights law was blunted during this period. See Walton, *When the Marching Stopped* and *On the Federal EEO Administrative Process* (Washington, D.C.: Washington Council on Lawyers, 1978). Reagan's legacy is first and foremost, however, embedded in his judicial appointments. During his eight years in office, Reagan appointed almost half of the entire federal judiciary (district and appeal courts). And as noted earlier, he changed the political complexion of the Supreme Court. The 1988-1989 Supreme Court term suggests that considerable judicial rollbacks of civil rights laws should be expected. As Associate Justice Thurgood Marshall said, "It is difficult to characterize [the 1988–1989] term's decisions as anything other than a deliberate retrenching of the Civil Rights agenda." See Linda Greenhouse, "Marshall Says Court's Ruling Imperils Rights," *The New York Times*, September 9, 1989, 1. As indicated above, so far Bush has experienced more success in opposing the Civil Rights lobby. Still, it is important to note that his veto of the Omnibus Civil Rights Act of 1990 was upheld by only one vote. In all likelihood, the Civil Rights coalition ultimately will be able to secure this legislation.

49. For a discussion of these budgets, see Sula Richardson, "An Overview of the Congressional Black Caucus' Constructive Alternative Budget Proposals, FY 1982-FY 1986," (Washington, D.C.: Congressional Research Service, Typescript, 1985), and Alvin Thornton, "Alternative Budgets of the Congressional Black Caucus: Participation of an Ideological Minority in the Budgetary Process," presented at the 1983 Annual Meeting of the National Conference of Black Political Scientists, Houston, Texas.

50. Thornton, "Alternative Budgets," 13–14.

51. Ibid., 27.

52. Ibid.

53. *Congressional Record—House,* May 24, 1982, 11511–38.

54. Ibid.

55. Ibid., 11527. See also, Ronald Dellums, "Welfare State vs. Warfare State: The Legislative Struggle for Full Employment," *Urban League Review* 10 (1966): 49–60.

56. The debates and roll call votes on these budgets are reported in the *Congressional Record—House* on the following dates: May 6, 1981, May 24, 1982, April 5, 1984, May 22, 1985, and April 9, 1987. The Caucus' budget in 1986 was referred to the Budget Committee but there was no floor debate or vote.

57. See Michael Combs, John Hibbings, and Susan Welch, "Black Constituents and Congressional Roll Call Votes," *Western Political Quarterly* 40 (1985): 424–34.

58. See the comments along these lines by then Majority Leader Wright and Representatives Obey, Hoyer, Ottinger, and Scheur, among others, during the 1982 debate. Similar comments are to be found in floor discussion of each of the budgets. See, for example, the *Congressional Record—House,* April 9, 1987, 1981.

59. *Congressional Record—House,* May 24, 1982, 111524.

60. Ibid., 11530–31.

61. *Congressional Record—House,* May 22, 1985, 13090.

62. For a provocative exploration of the notion of the irrelevancy of post–Civil Rights era black leadership, see Mack Jones, "The Increasing Irrelevancy of Black Leadership," paper presented at the 1981 Annual Meeting of the National Conference of Black Political Scientists, Baltimore, Maryland.

63. David Broder, "Invisible Budget," *The Washington Post,* May 30, 1982, 21. Also see Robert Smith, "The Black Congressional Delegation," *Western Political Quarterly* 34 (1981): 220.

64. See Charles E. Jones, "Testing a Legislative Strategy: The Congressional Black Caucus' Action-Alert Communications Network," *Legislative Studies Quarterly* 12 (1987): 532.

65. For example, the Caucus has been effective in getting minority set-asides included in federal public works appropriations; in exempting basic welfare programs from the Gramm-Rudman budget reduction process; in welfare reform that established spouse-eligibility for Aid for Families with Dependent Children (AFDC) in every state (but with what Congressman Augustus Hawkins, one of its principal authors and then chairman of the Committee on Labor and Education, called work provisions so restrictive that they constituted "slavefare," conjuring up images of Victorian workhouses); and race specific support for black colleges in the form of The Black College and University Act of 1986. On the key role played by the Caucus in the Gramm-Rudman exemptions, see Edward Walsh, "Democrats Get Taste of Unity," *The Washington Post,* November 16, 1985. Hawkins is quoted on the welfare reform bill in Martin Tolchin, "Congress Leaders and White House Agree on Welfare," *The New York Times,* September 27, 1988, and the black college act's passage is analyzed in William Blakey, "A Legislative Victory," *New Directions* 14 (1987): 1–19.

66. On the saliency of interpersonal alienation, cynicism, and low political trust in African American culture, see Matthew Holden, Jr., *The Politics of the Black "Nation"* (New York: Chandler, 1973), 17-26, and Robert C. Smith and Richard Seltzer, *Race,*

Class and Culture: A Study in Afro-American Mass Opinion (Albany: State University of New York Press, Forthcoming): chapters 5–6.

67. William Gray, "Leadership in the Legislative Process, *Urban League Review* 9 (1985): 105.

68. See Tom Kenworthy, "House Liberals Balk at Budget Compromise," *The Washington Post,* June 5, 1987.

69. Eric Pianin, "Black Caucus Members Face Dilemma of Hill Loyalties," *The Washington Post,* September 23, 1987, 14.

70. For a penetrating summary of these measures as they relate to blacks in the aggregate and the lower third in particular, see Joel Feagin, "A Slavery Unwilling to Die," *Journal of Black Studies* 18 (1988): 451–69.

71. Rufus Browning, Dale Marshall, and David Tabb, "Is Anything Enough?" *PS* 18 (1986): 635–39.

72. Piven and Cloward, *Poor Peoples Movements,* 3.

73. McAdams, *Political Process and the Development of Black Insurgency,* 234.

74. Ronald Walters, "The Challenge of Black Leadership: An Analysis of the Problem of Strategy Shift," *Urban League Review* 4 (1981): 85–86.

75. See Stephen Holden, "Pop's Angry Voices Sound the Alarm," *The New York Times,* May 21, 1989; Nelson George, *The Death of Rhythm and Blues* (New York: Pantheon, 1988); and Michael Schwartz, *Visions of a Liberated Future: Black Arts Movement Writings* (New York: Thunder's Mouth Press, 1989).

76. Charles Hamilton, *The Black Political Experience in America* (New York: Capricorn Books, 1973), 155.

77. One thing that black leadership can do is challenge the dominance of the two-party system monopoly on electoral debate and choice. This could be done by forming a third party with sympathetic others in order to withhold the black vote from the Democratic party in presidential and congressional elections as punishment for its failure to support a progressive agenda of social reform.

Part III

Challenges and Prospects for the Future

7

Coalition Politics: Past, Present, and Future

Ralph C. Gomes and Linda Faye Williams

The objective of this chapter is to discuss the historical and current record of African Americans in coalition politics and the implications of this record for the future. The chapter is divided into five sections. First, the reasons behind the current high level of interest in electoral coalitions involving African Americans are discussed. Second, to provide a perspective for the following analysis, theoretical and methodological issues of coalition formation and maintenance are presented. Third, two historical examples of coalition politics involving African Americans are examined. Fourth, two current examples of coalition politics involving African Americans are examined. Fifth, based on the study of these four examples of African American involvement in coalition politics, an analysis of what worked, what did not work, and why is presented. Lessons are derived for building "winning coalitions" involving African Americans in the future.

INTRODUCTION: THE CURRENT INTEREST IN COALITION POLITICS

At least since Jesse Jackson campaigned for the Democratic presidential nomination with the goal of garnering the support of a "Rainbow Coalition" in 1984, there has been renewed interest in the possibilities and probabilities of garnering winning electoral coalitions for African American candidates.[1] Although Jackson was far more successful in 1984 and especially in 1988 than any other African American who had run for president of the United States, his failure to capture more than 5 percent of the white vote in 1984 or more than 17 percent of the white vote in 1988 was viewed most often by scholars, journalists, political pundits, and others as a direct indication of dismal prospects for African Americans' attempts at building multiracial/multiethnic electoral coalitions for candidates of their race.

What a difference a year makes: By November 8, 1989 (only a year after the last presidential contest and a day after the off-year local and state elections in 1989), most news analysts, political pundits, and scholars touted the dawning of an era of "new coalition politics" involving African American political candidates. The empirical evidence most often cited for this conclusion was the election of a number of blacks to prominent offices, most notably, L. Douglas Wilder to be governor of Virginia (the first black ever to be elected governor of a state in the continental United States), David N. Dinkins to be mayor of New York City, Norman Rice to be mayor of Seattle, Washington, and John Daniels to be mayor of New Haven, Connecticut (the first blacks to win these mayoralties). Not only observers of these elections, but the victorious candidates also, were likely to point to some element of coalition politics as the chief reason for these successes. For example, Dinkins concluded his was "a great victory against division and suspicion," made possible by capturing not only a nearly unanimous black vote but also a significant majority of the Latino vote melded with broad union and liberal white and Jewish support.[2] Journalists especially (for example, Mary Alice Williams on NBC's special election night broadcast and Ted Koppel on ABC's news show, "Nightline") focused on the new coalition politics.

The formula for building this new and successful brand of coalition for African American candidates, as some pundits saw it, consisted most importantly of the nature of the candidates' themes and messages and the candidates' targeting strategy.

Thus, the press repeatedly stated that the new code word for black political candidates was "moderation" or "new mainstreaming." For instance on November 9, 1989, *The Washington Times*' front-page carried a headline attributing this conclusion to one of the winners. In Jay Taylor's story, "Moderation Won the Day, Wilder Says," the new governor-elect was quoted as saying: "You don't need to make special appeals to special groups. The candidates who are mainstream, as we were mainstream here in Virginia ... the candidates who are not considered so far removed from what many middle-thinking people think, can be elected."[3] The "moderation" theme was undergirded by accounts of the candidates' route to power: It was reported that they worked their way up through the ranks of the Democratic party, as opposed to coming from the outside as a critic of the party. Similarly, the candidates' emphasis on independence from any particular constituency group and their backgrounds of electoral office experience were stressed.[4]

Another feature often emphasized in press accounts of November 1989 election results was the strategy of the successful African American candidates. The African Americans who became historic first black elected had emphasized unity and had campaigned throughout their jurisdictions—especially vigorously in places with low concentrations of African Americans. At the same time, these candidates, reporters concluded, were well served by demographic targeting. According to most conclusions reached, the liberal wing of young upwardly mobile white Americans (yuppies), not the working class or poor whites, had been targeted with moderate, pro-middle-class messages and had supported African American political candidates.

The 1990 mid-term elections further renewed interest in the possibility of new coalition politics. Although Andrew Young lost his bid in Georgia's Democratic gubernatorial primary and Harvey Gantt lost his bid for governor of North Carolina in 1990, Gantt's victory in the Democratic primary and substantial white vote in the general election (more than 30 percent of white voters) reinforced the view that coalition politics had positive prospects. The victory of Republican Gary Franks in Connecticut's fifth congressional district (a district where blacks composed less than 20 percent of the electorate) especially seemed to indicate promise for the black "mainstream" politician in building a winning coalition.

In short, the current interest in coalition politics is propelled by the results of the 1989 state and local and the 1990 mid-term elections. It has been advanced that what the nation is witnessing is a new coalition in support of African American political candidates in which not only African Americans and a majority of other minorities support these candidates, but also young upwardly mobile white professionals with high levels of education support such candidates if they profess to be moderates/mainstream.

The following analysis focuses on whether a new coalition for African American political candidates is emerging and what the implications would be of such a development for the African American mass public. The goals of the research are both theoretical and practical. Regarding theory, the goal is to seek conceptual clarity in analyzing coalitions in general and coalitions involving African Americans in particular. Regarding practice, the goal is to provide guidelines for African Americans to form more viable coalitions. The specific questions addressed in the analysis are:

1. Were the winning coalitions in 1989 actually new coalitions (in terms of their component parts and goals) in support of African American causes and interests?
2. What are the attributes and characteristics of electoral coalition partners of African Americans in historic and current relief?
3. What are the implications (entry price and consequences) for African Americans in joining electoral coalitions, per se? What are the payoffs when African Americans are members of winning coalitions?
4. What groups should African Americans target for coalition partners in the near future?

To begin to answer these questions, the next section explicates the nature of coalitions according to coalition theory.

THEORY: THE NATURE OF COALITION FORMATION

The search for guidance in social science literature for analyzing and under-standing political coalitions in general and African American involvement in coalitions in particular is not an especially satisfying one. Although theories of coalition formation were introduced in the social sciences over four decades ago,[5] the multiplicity of conceptualizations and usages emerging have resulted mostly in theoretical and methodological inadequacies.[6]

This section first introduces the main elements and types of coalition the-ory, then, briefly reviews the weaknesses and limitations of these formulations, and finally points to the elements of coalition theory that are salvageable for examining key examples of African American experiences in coalitions.

Eric Browne pointed out, "The most well-developed and insightful aspects of the coalition literature consist of several contributions."[7] Three distinct the-oretical models, each with its own vocabulary and mode of explanation, have been used to develop coalition theory. "They are: the mathematical-normative model, which derives 'rational' solutions to conflict situations; the economic cost-benefit model, which explains coalition formation in terms of cost-benefit calculations; and the social-psychological model, which explains coali-tion formation in terms of actors' calculations of their own personal advantage."[8] Two of these models (mathematical-normative model and cost-benefit) are applications of game theory, among other things, to political be-havior. Game theory is "a mathematical model of rational decision-making in situations in which the results depend on the decision of the actors involved."[9] The third model, social-psychological, seeks to explain coalition-forming be-havior as a result of specific modes of cognitive processing (psychological) or as a result of the interaction of group behaviors and individual cognitions (sociological).[10]

Although each model is responsible for some unique formulations, the over-lap in their fundamental content is considerable.[11] The basic idea of the theory is that a "coalition has to be formed and the outcomes have to be divided."[12]

Different and sometimes competing strands of theorizing based on the "input variables" were formulated to predict the basis upon which the deci-sion-making was based.[13]

Generally speaking, coalition theories "depend on three types of assump-tions: assumptions about the coalition situations, assumptions about the layers, and assumptions about formation outcomes."[14] Inherent in these assumptions are elements, conflicts, cooperation, and superordinate goals.[15] The approach utilized in these coalition theories is at the microlevel, and the unit of analysis is the individual or groups of individuals.

There are two basic questions involved in coalition theories: (1) how coali-tions are formed; and (2) once formed, how they are maintained. The vast ma-jority of the literature, however, has focused on the first question.

The tests of coalition theories can be grouped into three broad categories:

experimental, empirical, and historical-descriptive. Each test (as well as each model of coalition theory) has weaknesses and limitations.

The literature of the experimental approach shows only partial substantiation of its theoretical formulations. Many of the formulations have been criticized on methodological grounds in that they are nothing more than statistical artifacts, not guided by formal theory. In addition, it is difficult to assess the influence of the manipulated variables; the number of subjects studied are too small; and the formulations have been tested in only ideal situations. Thus, the mathematical-normative model has been deemed to be too much of an idealization to be realistic. That is, the assumptions of the theory itself are too far removed from reality to yield statements that can be used as predictions of actual behavior. Instead, the mathematical-normative model and game theory in general seem "to be concerned solely with ideal, closed systems in which real-life 'disturbances' are not allowed."[16] In sum, game theory in its present form does not provide models fitting most real-life social conflicts.

Reviews of the literature of empirical testing conclude that results are generally inconclusive and not guided by formal theory. Most of the research in this mode is plagued with methodological problems such as measurement problems, inability to logically relate variables into a holistic fashion, limited sorts of coalition situations, and so forth. No general conclusion can be drawn from the empirical findings, and results even seem to contradict each other now and then.[17]

The historical-descriptive literature has been plagued by its low level of systematic presentation and lack of methodological rigor. Henk Wilke concludes: "This approach almost distorts as much as it explains."[18]

In sum, the applicability and accuracy of most coalition theories is not impressive. One central problem is that it is difficult to know what constitutes winning in different coalition situations and what determines the weights of actors in different contexts. Another problem is the microlevel focus on individual behaviors when much that is interesting and important about coalitions is group behavior. These remain formidable problems in theory validation using empirical evidence.[19] Browne concludes: "This state of affairs prohibits us from making any confident statements about the validity of coalition theories either generally or within a specific context."[20] Additionally, according to Abram de Swaan, "Coalition theory walks a thin line between obviousness and implausibility. It may be for this reason that the field so enthusiastically developed in the years 1962-1975 has begun to be abandoned again."[21]

It has been suggested that a possible solution to these problems is one of cross-fertilization (interdisciplinary borrowing). As de Swaan concluded: "Formalizing theorists rarely display more than anecdotic knowledge of history and politics. . . . Traditional political scientists and historians, on the other hand, seem completely unaware of developments and findings in formalizing theory, including game theory and coalition theory."[22] In sum, the effective method of study and analysis is an interdisciplinary approach with intellectual borrowing from the established findings from not only coalition theory but history, as well as political and other social sciences.

This study is guided by such an interdisciplinary cross-fertilization approach. More specifically, the nature of coalitions involving African Americans, the reasons for and ways in which these coalitions are formed, the elements that determine whether they are maintained and become winning coalitions, the extent and kind of payoffs received by African Americans for their participation in coalitions, and other matters will be analyzed in the context both of coalition theory and of insights from historical, political, and sociological analyses.

Thus, the following analysis of coalitions involving African Americans is based on several points isolated from and specified in coalition theories:

First, the investigation builds on the fundamental feature common to all branches of coalition theories—that is, that they involve relations between individuals or groups of individuals, with different kinds of interests and different kinds of factors underlying cleavages—cultural (race), economic (class), political (issues), and so forth. The need for coalitions results from conflicts over the way resources are rewarded in society. From the perspective of African Americans, such resources include equality of opportunity, substantive/material equality (equality of results), legal equality, and so forth.

Second, coalition action is purposeful, although coalitions can be formed both intentionally and unintentionally.[23] When one (or a group) is sufficiently able to achieve a goal alone, he (or the group) is not likely to join or form a coalition. Thus, one (or a group) makes or joins a coalition because such behavior facilitates certain goals.[24] For African Americans, the problem is to find suitable coalition partners. At specific times and in specific places, African Americans might find no suitable nonblack coalition partners; in such instances, they have little choice but to rely on intra-African American coalitions seeking interracial third party reference publics (for example, the media, philanthropic foundations, public officials, and so forth). Thus, the following analysis features not only a concern for choosing the best coalition partner, but adds a concern for kinds of activities needed when one can find no coalition partner outside one's own group.

Third, having established the basic cause for formation of a coalition, it is important to define "coalition" as it is used in the following analysis. E. W. Kelley, in his critical essay surveying techniques of studying coalition behavior, writes: "By a coalition, we mean a group of individuals or groups of individuals who: (1) agree to pursue a common and articulated goal; (2) pool their relevant resources in pursuit of this goal; (3) engage in conscious communications concerning the goal and the means of obtaining it; (4) agree on the distribution of the payoff (benefits) received when obtaining the goal."[25]

Fourth, a winning coalition will be identified as a coalition that is large enough (or powerful enough, controlling enough resources) to determine the allocation of rewards among all members of a decision-making group. The goal of each member of a winning coalition is to maximize his or her (or the group's) payoffs.

In the context of these theoretical considerations, the next section examines and evaluates two key attempts of African Americans in the past to form winning coalitions. Of the variant coalition theories, the one borrowed from most is the sociopsychological; of the variant tests, the one most used is the historical descriptive.

THE PAST: THE NAACP AND THE MODERN CIVIL RIGHTS MOVEMENT

African Americans have always faced two possibilities in seeking to build a progressive movement to attain their goals. The first can be characterized as an intraracial coalition, a kind of "blacks alone for the sake of black development" strategy. The second is a progressive interracial coalition including whites and other ethnic groups. To be sure, African Americans have tried both strategies. Marcus Garvey's United Negro International Association (UNIA), Booker T. Washington's agricultural-economic nationalism, the Nation of Islam's religious nationalism, the formation of a black third party in the 1960s, and even electoral campaigns where black candidates targeted primarily or solely black voters are only a few of the instances in which African Americans have tried to "go it alone." Yet, African American attempts to develop and be a part of a progressive interracial coalition have as long (or longer) a history in the United States. Even before the end of slavery, legendary heroes in African American history such as Frederick Douglass participated in the abolitionist movement, which was a coalition of freedmen, ex-slaves, and whites—especially white women.

As posited in coalition theory, the decision on the part of African American groups as to whether to build a separatist/nationalist movement or to build an interracial coalition was conditioned by whether there was a chance of winning the group's goals without being in a coalition with other groups; whether there were available nonblack coalition partners; and whether there was more than one potential nonblack coalition partner (for example, another minority group or whites or working class whites versus affluent whites, and so forth) from which to make the choice.

Most often in African American history, there seemed (at least to many prominent African American leaders) to be no available nonblack coalition partner. Instead, as Frank Parker noted in chapter 4, whites were clearly in charge of the decision as to whether to form a coalition with African Americans. In these instances, some black leaders (for example, Garvey, Elijah Muhammad, and nationalist groups in the 1960s such as the Republic of New Africa) decided either that the potential payoffs for coalescing with whites were negligible and thus not worth pursuing or that blacks must rely only or mostly on their own numbers because no white coalition partners were available.

This section examines two instances in which African Americans sought to form coalitions. The historical instances chosen are the formation of the NAACP and the modern (1950s-1960s) Civil Rights Movement. In the formation of the NAACP, the goal from the start was to be an interracial coalition—a choice undoubtedly influenced by its formation in the northern section of the United States. In the formation of groups key to the modern Civil Rights Movement, particularly the Southern Christian Leadership Conference (SCLC), no interracial partners presented themselves, so the SCLC became "a coalition of coalitions" among African Americans.[26] The NAACP and the modern Civil Rights Movement by no means exhaust the historic instances of African American involvement in coalition politics. Instead, these two instances of interest-group coalition formation are chosen on the basis of their prominence; almost no intelligent observer would leave them out of any list of key coalition movements involving African Americans.

The NAACP

As indicated by Robert Smith in the preceding chapter, before the start of the modern Civil Rights Movement, the NAACP was clearly the dominant black protest organization.[27] It was founded in 1909 by a group of black and white intellectuals vehemently opposed to the racism that confronted African Americans, and was organized specifically to fight for equal rights of African Americans. With only one important exception (W. E. B. DuBois, who became the director of publicity and research), the top administrative positions of the NAACP were originally filled by whites.[28] Thus, from the beginning the NAACP was interracial. The white founders were highly educated, distinguished within their professions or business, and influential in the larger society. A number of them were wealthy white philanthropists.[29]

Not only were the poor and struggling white masses at the turn of the century not involved in the formation of the NAACP, neither were the black masses involved in shaping the organization at its outset. Instead, the black and white intellectuals who founded the NAACP sought through a top-down strategy to organize the poor black masses to struggle for their rights. Hence, from the start of the NAACP's struggle for equality for blacks, affluent whites (people who today might be called liberal yuppies or their betters) were part of a coalition with relatively well-off blacks (people who today might be called middle-class blacks) for justice for all.

The coalition partners in the NAACP brought unequal resources to the struggle at the coalition's formation. While both black and white founders were highly educated and brought with them substantial expertise, by and large only whites brought substantial economic resources and the ability to attract the attention of key reference publics such as political leaders, government officials, and the media. These differences, however, were precisely the reason behind the coalition. African American leaders of the NAACP had neither the status nor the economic resources to fight the battle alone. Whites could supply both status and financial resources for the group's agreed-upon goals, strategies, and tactics.

Both groups (white and African American intellectuals of the day) believed that much of American racism stemmed from white America's ignorance of African Americans. Behind this belief, NAACP officials of both races reasoned, was pernicious behavior on the part of the news and cultural media that promoted a demeaning picture of African Americans. Hence, an educational campaign consisting of a media strategy and lobbying became principal tactics. Legal action (for example, efforts to invalidate the grandfather clause, and integration of white universities) was also an agreed-upon strategy. As for the distribution of payoffs, this, too, was agreed upon. African Americans would receive legal benefits and improved social status as a result of both the educational and legal campaigns; whites would receive moral benefits (satisfaction) from aiding in the construction of a new, socially just America. Whether such a limited payoff for whites in the coalition would be enough to sustain the coalition was always a question—especially in the face of competing moral quests such as women's rights, World Wars I and II, and so forth. Similarly, there was always tension over who should lead the NAACP—African Americans or whites.

As long as the coalition was northern-based, these tensions were manageable, but as the coalition moved South, problems became more formidable. By the late 1910s and early 1920s when the NAACP organized branches in the South, some African American leaders openly decried not only the bureaucratic style and pace of movement of the NAACP, but also its white leadership.[30] First and foremost, the failure to find white coalition partners in the South underlay this development. Southern whites (educated and uneducated alike) not only failed to join the coalition, but instead labeled the NAACP as an "outside agitator" seeking to "stir up trouble" between the races. The differential roles of African American labor in the South compared to African American labor in the North had much to do with these different reactions on the part of white Northerners and white Southerners. The agricultural South had always relied on free or cheap labor from African Americans to a far greater extent than the industrial North with its large and growing stock of European immigrant workers. The South, prior to economic modernization, simply could not abide upgrading African American status or labor. Southern elite and mass opinion converged on the role, status, and opportunities of blacks.

Second, and concomitantly, the NAACP in the South was, out of necessity, closely tied to the black church. "The church, being independent of the white power structure, was often the only place the NAACP would meet."[31] As the NAACP in the South was forced to rely on sources internal to the African American community, the utility of a coalition with whites became more questionable. Third, unlike the reliance on white economic resources in the North, the NAACP in the South was largely financed through the black church and led by African American ministers.[32] This further intensified questioning of the worth of white leadership in the coalition. Taken together, these three differences between the northern-based NAACP and its southern wing began the transformation to an African American-led NAACP as well as reducing white involvement in the coalition. The more the NAACP's membership grew in the South, the more the NAACP's leadership positions were taken over by African Americans. Southern blacks soon became the majority of total membership in the organization. The more the NAACP became southern dominated, the more the NAACP provided organizing skills and developed networks through which resources within the African American community could be pooled. And the more African Americans relied on resources internal to their community, the less the NAACP existed as a multiracial coalition.

While the NAACP remains to some extent a multiracial coalition, the role of whites has been altered significantly. Today, whites occupy none of the NAACP's top leadership positions, and its board is predominantly African American.

Still, any fair observation of the formation of the NAACP and its sustenance as a coalition through the first half of the twentieth century would have to conclude that:

(1) The NAACP, a coalition between educated and professional whites and blacks at its formation, was the dominant protest organization of favor of equal rights;

(2) It was a coalition of blacks and whites in which affluent whites long held the important leadership roles and black leadership came in second;

(3) The NAACP's coalition members had agreed-upon goals, the most important of which was the achievement of legal equality for African Americans;

(4) The NAACP achieved significant payoffs in legal equality for its African American members (for example, invalidation of the grandfather clause in 1915, the first step in invalidating the white primary in 1927, invalidation of legal segregation in higher education in 1938 and 1944, desegregation in public education in 1954, and so forth)

(5) Its failure to find white coalition partners in the South ultimately weakened the organization as an interracial coalition while at the same time providing opportunities for the emergence of stronger African American leadership;

(6) It set the steps from which most of the leadership of the modern Civil Rights Movement would emerge.

The Modern Civil Rights Movement

The bureaucratic organization of the NAACP, the tensions over the role of whites in the NAACP, the legal attacks and white supremacist attempts at physical intimidation of the NAACP, the urbanization of African Americans and their transformation from sharecroppers to modern wage labor, and legal advances through cases won by the NAACP, among other factors, laid the basis for what is often called the modern Civil Rights Movement.

The modern Civil Rights Movement of the 1950s and 1960s began with a strong emphasis on an intraracial coalition of African Americans with limited support from whites (junior partnership in the coalition at best) and ended with an emphasis on a form of black nationalism almost exclusionary of whites.

The dominant organization of the period was the SCLC. As Aldon Morris points out, the SCLC from its inception was led by indigenous African American leaders—most particularly ministers of African American churches.[33] Indeed, SCLC was an arm of the African American church, an intraracial coalition of numerous African American churches (a southern organization of organizations) throughout the South. Although whites supported the SCLC, they never occupied leadership positions in the organization. The basic goal of SCLC was to build an organized force linking clergy activists and organized African American masses in churches. The role of the SCLC was to coordinate the activities and leadership of numerous local African American community organizations and provide a route for shared resources and experiences.

Financial resources for SCLC during its early years (1957-1960) came mostly from the northern black religious community, according to Rev. Ralph Abernathy, secretary-treasurer of the SCLC in those years.[34] Affiliate fees of twenty-five dollars, coming largely from southern African American churches, constituted the second largest source of money. Smaller contributions came from nonreligious African American organizations and from white individuals. These individual contributions from northern whites constituted only about 7 percent of the total finances, according to Abernathy.[35]

Dr. Martin Luther King was clearly the charismatic leader of the SCLC and the source of inspiration for money raised at the rallies, but, as Lerone Bennett wrote: "What is important is that King, like Franklin Delano Roosevelt, demonstrated in Montgomery and later a rare talent for attracting and using the skills and ideas of brilliant aides and administrators."[36]

Just as SCLC's mass strength stemmed from amassing support from numerous local churches and organizations, one of its central weaknesses stemmed from its inability to coordinate effectively and determine strategy for the various groups in SCLC's coalition. Preexisting organizations often went off on their own in actions, and approached SCLC recommendations (especially regarding direct action) with apprehension. In short, SCLC had a formal, centralized decision-making group headed by King, but this group had only weak powers in implementing or enforcing its policies.

Another problem for the SCLC as a coalition of organizations was that some preexisting organizations, especially the NAACP, perceived the SCLC as a threat. Problems between the two groups were based on issues of strategy (both whether there was a need for two or more organizations to lead the struggle for African American equality and whether working within the law as advocated by the NAACP or the direct confrontations with the law as advocated by the SCLC was more appropriate); issues of a leadership drain (from the NAACP to the SCLC); as well as division of the small financial base to support civil rights activities.

Ultimately, the NAACP, SCLC, and other groups such as the Congress of Racial Equality (CORE) engaged in coalition rather than competitive actions. Meetings were held that produced at least informal agreements to divide the labor of the groups in the loose coalition. SCLC would lead the nonviolent direct action; the NAACP would lead in the legal role; SCLC would not solicit for individual members and erode the NAACP's financial base; both groups would raise money jointly and divide it in many instances. CORE, whose membership and money came overwhelmingly from white intellectuals, would be a threat to neither the NAACP or the SCLC.

With the entry of black students as key players in the Civil Rights Movement, however, new tensions arose. The student sit-ins began in the late 1950s. The SCLC, assisted by CORE and the NAACP Youth Councils, spearheaded the organization that enabled the sit-ins to take hold.[37] The dramatic confrontations produced by the sit-ins not only garnered the Civil Rights Movement more attention, but also attracted more funds. Especially CORE and SCLC raised far more money following the sit-ins.

Rather than being a boon for all the organizations in the coalition, these new funds generated more tension. Many in the student movement came to believe that SCLC, in particular, used the funds to further its own organizational interests rather than for the good of the entire movement. Student activists argued that more money could be funneled by SCLC to the student movement— especially since SCLC had raised money specifically around the sit-ins. SCLC (as well as the NAACP) argued that they paid legal, transportation, and other expenses for the students and deserved the money.[38] Moreover, SCLC officials said 90 percent of their funds came as a result of King's speaking engagements.[39] These disagreements over who deserved how much money eventually led the way to a strengthened and relatively independent student coalition, the Student Nonviolent Coordinating Committee (SNCC).

SNCC began as a loosely structured coordinating committee with even less power and control over local groups that made up its coalition than SCLC had over organizations in its coalition. The central headquarters of SNCC provided important resources (education through its newspaper, organization of conferences) but not centralized leadership.

The emergence of SNCC had an almost immediate national impact, an impact that captured the imagination of white students. Kirkpatrick Sale captured the response of white students to SNCC's direct action strategy:

By the end of that Spring, students at perhaps a hundred northern colleges had been mobilized in support, and over the next year civil rights activity touched almost every campus in the country; support groups formed, fundraising committees were established, local sit-ins and pickets took place, campus civil rights clubs began, and students from around the country traveled to the South.[40]

Some of the rhetoric of SNCC from the beginning was more nationalist than the SCLC had ever propagated; yet, ironically, no previous actions of the southern Civil Rights Movement had brought so many whites into the moderate Civil Rights coalition.

It is important to note the kinds of whites that joined SNCC's coalition. Studies have shown that the typical white was an affluent student who excelled in scholarly pursuits, usually majored in the social sciences, and had liberal-to-radical political values.[41] Affluent young whites in larger numbers joined a coalition led by African Americans precisely at the time that there was a growing emphasis on black solidarity (intracoalition building among African Americans) and less emphasis on interracial-coalition building. White students appear to have joined SNCC because the organization's direct action techniques demonstrated to them how they could proceed actively and tactically to wrest power from older generations about a wide range of demands in a growing number of policy areas. Almost simultaneously, white students began their own organizations modeled after SNCC (most notably, Students for a Democratic Society—SDS).

Another source of growing white support was financial. SNCC had very little money when it began organizing in 1961. By the summer of 1962, it had received funds from the Taconic Foundation, the Field Foundation, and the Stern Family Fund.[42] These foundations worked in close conjunction with the John Kennedy administration and shared the administration's view that black activists should channel their energies into efforts aimed at acquiring the vote for southern blacks.[43] In the short run, however, the funds were used to expand and further invigorate SNCC's direct action projects across a wide variety of goals, not simply voting. Ultimately, the organization fell apart over the issue of whether to engage in direct action demonstrations or the voter registration activities favored by the Kennedy administration.[44]

As white students turned their attention overwhelmingly to opposition to the Vietnam War, SNCC declined as an organization and as a coalition. In the vacuum, African Americans (especially students) became more antiwhite and exclusionary. To some extent, there was a feeling of betrayal by the white students. Questions surfaced over to what extent sustained coalitions could be built between whites and blacks—at least at that historical conjuncture. There is no book more a scholarly marker of the times than the 1967 publication of Stokely Carmichael and Charles Hamilton's *Black Power*. Carmichael and Hamilton urged the development of group solidarity among blacks in order to bargain from a position of strength in what they basically accepted was a pluralist society. They emphasized that "before a group can enter into the open society, it must first close ranks."[45] They urged African Americans to first do so before trying to join interracial coalitions. The reason, as they put it euphemistically: "A midget cannot make a coalition with a giant."[46]

The modern Civil Rights Movement left in its waning several lessons about coalitions: An intraracial coalition among black organizations could produce significant payoffs. Important legislation flowed from the Movement's efforts in the context of economic modernization of the South and relative prosperity throughout the nation—for example, the Civil Rights Act of 1964, the Voting Rights Act of 1965, fair housing and education legislation, the War on Poverty and other Great Society programs, an executive order for affirmative action, and so forth; The Movement also taught that an intraracial coalition through acts of mass defiance and civil disobedience could attract important third reference publics—for example, the mass media, affluent white students, government leaders, and foundations. The more these reference publics were aroused, the more some of them, at least, sought to reshape the goals of the coalition in order to derive payoffs for their own interests—for example, Kennedy and Lyndon Johnson sought to reshape general demands for racial equality to demands for voting rights that would help shore up defections of white southerners from the Democratic party. Similarly, white students tried to enlist African Americans in order to gain support for opposition to the Vietnam War rather than because of concerns with domestic (including civil rights) policy. The weaker that internal organization and clear articulation of goals were, the more easily efforts on the part of reference publics (especially governmental authorities) toward cooptation and repression worked to divide and ultimately decimate the intra-African American coalition. Finally, the Civil Rights Movement showed that as reference public support declines, intraracial coalitions are likely to pursue more race-specific or black nationalist goals.

Preliminary Conclusions

The resurgence of black nationalism led away from the emphasis on interracial coalition politics in African American history. Only the increasing focus of African Americans on the electoral arena (after winning the right to vote nationwide) caused coalition politics to again become a widely popular prescription.

From the brief exegesis into the historical background of coalition politics involving African Americans, a number of conclusions can be drawn:

First, the emphasis on coalition politics is nothing new in the African American experience; the presence of indigenous resources (formal and informal organizations, leaders, money, people, and communication networks), as well as the availability of coalition partners from nonindigenous groups, determine whether an interracial coalition forms. In the case of the NAACP, resources were available to make an interracial coalition possible. The organization of the coalition, that is, the fact that the coalition was made up of individual (versus organizational) members, also contributed to its interracial nature. However, the SCLC located in the South found few interracial partners; it became an intraracial coalition. The fact that the SCLC was made up of organizational affiliates also contributed to its difficulty in finding interracial partners and dictated its nature as an intraracial coalition.

Second, coalition politics always involve a tension about which group should lead as well as a tension about just how and what each group should receive in particularized gains or payoffs. The resources each group brought to the coalition lay behind these tensions. Thus, in the case of the NAACP, as southern African American membership became key, southern black leaders demanded more of a leadership role. In the case of the SCLC, as student leaders claimed they generated most of the economic resources and as SCLC leaders claimed that they still generated these resources, tensions mounted over the direction of leadership per se and payoffs. Clearly, coalition partners had not agreed in advance about the relative resources or payoffs each expected to generate or receive. This lack of agreement led to the demise of the coalition—especially in the face of strategies of cooptation/repression by government sources.

Third, the group of whites that has been more likely to participate in coalitions with African Americans either as actual members (for example in the NAACP) or as significant supporters (for example in the SCLC or SNCC) has not been African Americans' most "natural allies"—the exploited white working class—but rather, affluent, more highly educated whites. Although in many ways this is simply a direct outgrowth of the role of race in the American political economy as one of the greatest of all sources of differential levels of exploitation between white versus black members of the working class as well as mystification and ensuing false consciousness regarding class divisions, it is not surprising. Even Marx, Engels, Lenin, and other leaders of the socialist revolution were not at the time of their most important leadership contributions members of the working class. They, too, were the "petty bourgeois" intellectuals of their day.

Fourth, the interests of petty bourgeois whites in coalitions with African Americans might be fairly fickle when other issues arise or even when African Americans demand to be leaders of their own struggle. Thus, thrust out of leadership positions in the NAACP, membership of whites in the coalition declined, and as white students turned to interests more sacred to their own well-being (staying out of the Vietnam War), their interests in SCLC, SNCC, and civil rights in general waned.

THE CURRENT EMPHASIS ON ELECTORAL COALITIONS

As African Americans in the South gained access to the ballot, civil rights coalitions splintered and protest subsided. (Voting rights for southern blacks was the most enduring product of the Movement.) African Americans moved from what Bayard Rustin epitomized as "protest to politics."[47]

The move to electoral politics understandably reawakened the emphasis on interracial coalition formation and building. After all, how could 11 percent of the potential electorate nationally, the lack of a majority in any state, and only a majority in a few cities, intelligently ignore the importance of creating a winning coalition by allying with other races/ethnic groups?

At first, however, the emphasis post-1965 was intracoalition politics in the electoral arena. Thus, in the immediate aftermath of the Voting Rights Act, African Americans first targeted winning elections in those cities and districts where they were (or near) a majority. Hence, between 1970 and 1976, African Americans moved quickly to win key offices in heavily populated African American cities. As the jurisdictions where African Americans were a majority but not the holders of key elective positions became more and more scarce, the rate of growth of African American elected officials declined (see relevant data in chapter 4). Moreover, even in jurisdictions where African Americans were a majority of the potential electorate but African American voting rates remained low, African American political candidates tended to desert a "blacks alone for the sake of blacks" strategy. Instead, many of these candidates appealed increasingly to white voters, who might (and sometimes did) prove even in majority black cities to be the pivotal factor in deciding election results.[48]

There was nothing amazing about the necessity to focus on interracial and large coalitions in the electoral arena. The American two-party system has always been based on putting together such large coalitions of diverse interests. More important, for the analysis here, is to remember that whenever the focus has been on the electoral sphere, African Americans have participated in coalitions.

Throughout most of the history of African American voting, these interracial coalitions have been in support of white candidates at all levels of government. Thus, the great bulk of the African American experience in electoral politics is made up of African Americans voting for the "lesser of two evils" white candidate. And these coalitions were rarely concerned with rights for African Americans.

Prior to the New Deal, for example, those African Americans who could vote joined northern business interests and northern ethnics in an electoral coalition for Republican candidates because of the image of that party as being the "party of Lincoln" and the sparse patronage positions the Republicans once awarded to African Americans.[49]

In the crucible of economic despair, known as the Great Depression, a large majority of African Americans joined a motley crew of industrial and finance capitalists, Jews, Catholics, northern ethnics, and southern whites by shifting to the Democratic party. Although it did almost nothing for the direct civil rights and social justice agenda of African Americans, the party did (through its failure to totally exclude African Americans from its economic agenda) improve African American lives economically.[50] It was not, then, the politics of race that led African Americans into the Democratic party's winning coalition beginning in the 1930s, but the economic benefits African Americans derived from the New Deal, even though these gains were relatively small.

When the Democratic party finally turned its attention to the civil rights of African Americans (largely to preclude its international embarrassment in a world in which the decolonization of Africa was occurring and to shore up defections of southern whites from the party), a healthy African American majority became nearly unanimous support for the Democratic party.[51]

For a good while, as long as the political candidate was white, blacks and poor whites maintained a coalition at the ballot box whether they knew it or not—in Kelley's terms, an unintentional coalition.[52] Nowhere was this more evident than in southern states where blacks and poor whites could be counted on to vote for the same white candidates who were usually economic welfare liberals. While differences over the Vietnam War put a damper on this likelihood, this coalition continued to be a prevailing pattern as long as the candidate was white and not dramatically pro-civil-rights.[53] Indeed, through the current period, there are many white southern Democrats who would not be senators or congressmen were it not for the coalition at the ballot box between African Americans and less affluent whites.[54] In addition, the presidential elections of Harry Truman, John Kennedy, and Jimmy Carter demonstrate this pattern.

The latter instance, the election of Carter to be president of the United States in 1976, demonstrates the temporal viability of a "new coalition" under white leadership. What became known in some circles as "the new coalition" in the mid- and late-1970s was in part responsible for Carter's election. The new coalition was composed of such important groups as women's organizations, environmental groups, peace proponents, organized labor, and African Americans. Most notably, African Americans, albeit disproportionately backers of Carter (compared to the other groups in the new coalition) were considered to be junior partners. Their votes were needed, but they were expected to acquiesce to following white leadership and this leadership's pressing concerns, which less and less included civil rights or increasing social spending goals.

Importantly and concomitantly, the historical record shows that when the candidate was black, the new coalition not only frayed at the white end, but actually fell apart in most instances. This returns the focus to the present day. Is there a new coalition led by blacks including white members? Is it really the dawn of new coalition politics? Based on the answers to these questions, what can be learned about electoral coalitions in general? To begin to answer these questions, the remainder of this section first analyzes Jesse Jackson's thrust for a new coalition in his presidential campaigns and next analyzes several key races in the off-year elections of 1989.

Jesse Jackson's Attempt to Build a "Rainbow Coalition"

Dissatisfied with the growing inattention of the national government and both major parties to problems afflicting African Americans in the post–Civil

Rights Movement era, a select and secretive group, "the Black Leadership Family" met in early 1984 to discuss the potential impact of running an African American candidate for president of the United States.[55] This candidacy, some reasoned, could bring a new focus to the plight of African Americans in general and poor African Americans in particular. Although this group never reached the decision to field an African American presidential candidate, Jesse Jackson, then president of Operation PUSH (People United to Save Humanity)—an organization devoted to African American economic advancement—decided to run for the Democratic nomination for president of the United States in 1984.

With the decision to run for president, Jackson, like every other electoral candidate, had to decide on his key objectives, his programmatic concerns, and the chief potential constituencies to target. In determining the constituencies toward which his campaign would be primarily directed, Jackson faced two choices.

First, he could seek to build a primarily intraracial coalition—a kind of "blacks alone for black development strategy." If he selected this option, his candidacy would continue the tradition of protest activism discussed above. Running a protest campaign could have met several of Jackson's objectives (increasing black voter registration and turnout, allowing Jackson to speak out on issues of great concern to blacks, and perhaps curtailing the rightward drift of the Democratic party).

What a "blacks-alone" strategy could not do, however, was garner enough votes outside the African American community to make Jackson and his supporters a central bargaining bloc within the Democratic party through which the interests he represented might have a critical impact on convention proceedings including the fashioning of the platform and the selection of the eventual nominee. Nor, given the small size of the African American electorate, could Jackson be perceived as a serious contender for the nomination if he appealed only to African Americans. If Jackson had not presented himself as a serious candidate, he and his representatives would not have been allocated places in the major party convention committees. They would not have been included in national Democratic party mailings and fundraisers, nor would Jackson have been included in Democratic party presidential debates. If he were not a serious candidate, he would have been denied much needed media exposure. The perception of Jackson as a serious contender rested on his repeated insistence that he was in the campaign to win and to win by building a majority coalition in support of his candidacy.

Second, given a decision to seek a majority coalition, two other strategy alternatives remained. Jackson could attempt to develop a coalition of African Americans and middle-class whites with a vague emphasis on "progress." Such a strategy had been demonstrated successfully by African American congressional and mayoral candidates, including Andrew Young and Wilson Goode, among others.[56] Alternatively, he could seek to align African Americans with

low-status whites and other minority groups in an interracial coalition empha-
sizing economic justice.

To have chosen the middle-class coalition approach, even if successful,
might have negated Jackson's concerns for a fairer and more humane domestic
and foreign policy agenda. Moreover, he would have found it difficult to differ-
entiate himself from other Democratic contenders, especially Walter Mondale,
and he would have lost some, if not most, of his appeal to his nearly guaranteed
voter base, African Americans. Thus, Jackson was largely compelled to choose
the economic justice strategy. It had the potential of achieving all of the objectives of a protest candidacy, plus providing Jackson with enough relevancy to
other constituencies to be perceived as a serious candidate.

In an effort to coordinate African American protest objectives with a wider
constituency, Jackson in his announcement speech declared:

This candidacy is not for blacks only. This is a national campaign growing out of the
black experience and seen through the eyes of the black perspective—which is the experience and perspective of the rejected. Because of this experience, I can empathize
with the plight of Appalachia because I have known poverty. I know the pain of anti-
Semitism because I have felt the humiliation of discrimination. I know first hand the
shame of breadlines and the horror of hopelessness and despair because my life has been
dedicated to empowering the world's rejected to become respected. Thus, our perspective encompasses and includes more of the American people and their respective interests than do most other experiences.[57]

To attract people with diverse interests, Jackson sought to identify key issues that he could use to assemble a Rainbow Coalition. The roots of his issues
agenda were in the Great Society and the poor and minority groups it had
helped to politicize. Hence, his early proposals included a massive public employment program and renewed federal spending on social services. To appeal
to antiwar activists whose political orientations had been formed in the 1960s,
Jackson's foreign policy centered on the Third World and on his pledge to reduce defense spending and secure the nuclear freeze. To attract women voters,
from the start he argued that political tickets should be "balanced" by gender
and race, not simply regionally or on the liberal-conservative continuum. To
win the support of Native Americans, Jackson said he recognized the rights of
Native Americans to represent nations, not just reservations, and that he would
take the money that now goes to the Bureau of Indian Affairs and give it directly to the tribes. To appeal to farmers, he attacked the Reagan administration's farm policies, particularly the payment-in-kind program (PIK), which he
described as a "pickpocket program" benefiting large and wealthy farmers. To
win the Latino vote, Jackson discussed the common interests of African Americans and Latinos and pledged programs to end the additional discrimination
Latinos suffer due to the language barrier. In short, Jackson sought to build a
coalition by offering payoffs to each major group that became involved.

This strategy did have a good deal of appeal to several leaders of non-African American groups. For example, Jackson garnered support from Mario Obledo, then president of the League of United Latin American Citizens (LULAC), the nation's largest Latino organization, as well as farm leader Cesar Chavez and past LULAC president Tony Bonilla. The Rainbow Coalition staff included leaders from Native American, women, Arab-American, organized labor, peace, and environmental groups, among others.[58] Yet, Jackson met with only limited success in building an interracial, interethnic coalition at the ballot box in 1984. While Jackson won 3.4 million votes nationwide and almost 80 percent of the African American vote, he won only 5 percent of the white vote and small minorities of the Latino, Asian, and other ethnic groups' votes. Racism and internal weaknesses in Jackson's campaign, such as disorganization, limited financial resources, gaffes and blunders, and poor issue development, significantly limited his appeal.[59]

Jackson sought again in 1988 to bring the Rainbow Coalition to fruition. This time he ran a far more well-organized campaign, raised substantially more campaign funds, spent far more time campaigning in predominantly white areas (for example, among the farmers of Iowa) and portrayed his issues and himself to be closer to the "mainstream" of American politics. As a result, he substantially improved his showing in the primaries and came in second in number of votes received and delegates won in the Democratic nomination contest.

Still, it is important to point out that while more members of each ethnic and racial group voted for Jackson in 1988 compared to 1984, a broadly representative number of coalition voters failed to materialize. Jackson was left without sufficient strength to make the coalition a strong bargaining bloc at the Democratic convention (outside of a few procedural matters) and a significant force in the general election. For all the originality of both the 1984 and 1988 campaigns and all of Jackson's magnificent eloquence and dramatic flair, the Jackson campaigns were mostly significant for their lack of influence on the outcome of the presidential contests of 1984 and 1988 and the direction of national policy that followed those campaigns.

Another particularly disappointing result of both campaigns was their failure to produce a coalition between African Americans and poor whites. Although Jackson emphasized a class-based lower income coalition, less affluent, less educated, and blue-collar whites tended to support Jackson even less than did younger, more upwardly mobile whites. In both contests, Jackson did better among whites 30 to 49 years old, midwestern and western whites, college-educated whites, whites in white-collar occupations, and whites with household incomes of $25,000 or greater.[60] An interracial election coalition based on an economic justice appeal eluded Jackson in 1984 and 1988. In sum:

(1) Due to the two-party system in the United States, national electoral coalitions must necessarily involve many groups with numerous diverse interests;

(2) Maintaining a coalition of diverse interests is difficult in any case, but it poses an enormous burden on black candidates who not only suffer from racism but also are generally perceived to be concerned about only one interest (African American);

(3) An African American presidential coalition is likely to be supported by the kinds of groups that have supported African American issue-oriented coalitions—that is, professional, highly educated, upwardly mobile whites;

(4) this upwardly mobile group of whites is usually interested in payoffs other than directly economic ones—for example, policies toward environmental problems; peace and nuclear weapons; gay, women, and other civil rights. Thus, the candidate is likely to give a growing amount of attention to issues other than economic justice to prevent this group from deserting. This further mitigates the likelihood of winning the votes of less affluent groups;

(5) Concomitantly, in an effort to put together a diverse winning coalition in presidential politics, centrist, vague policy pronouncements tend to dominate; the more winning is the goal, the more African American candidates, too, tend to be drawn into this net;

(6) Currently, a black presidential candidate might prove more useful in producing alternative policy recommendations and influencing the policy directions of campaigns and regimes if winning is not his or her goal.

Interracial Electoral Coalitions in 1989

Conditions that hold true for national elections might not necessarily hold true for state and local ones. Hence, only a year after Jackson's most recent defeat, several African Americans were elected to prominent positions in state and local government in jurisdictions where African Americans were a minority. As pointed out above, the ability of these candidates to win public office stimulated emphasis in cross-racial, cross-constituency voting and a new willingness on the part of whites to joining winning coalitions for African American candidates. Such coalitions could develop, some posited, if African American candidates were experienced and mainstream/moderate in their campaign themes and strategies. Do the well-publicized elections of a handful of African Americans in 1989 represent the dawning of new coalition politics?

The evidence is mixed. First, other developments (rather than the development of new coalitions supporting moderate African American candidates) might explain more about why some African American candidates won in November 1989.

For example, for those who claim that moderation is the key to the birth of a new coalition in New York City, a brief comparison with the election results in the city's mayoral primary of 1977 call into question such a conclusion.

In 1977, Percy Sutton (the third black Manhattan Borough president) ran for mayor. Sutton, like David Dinkins, had not only served as a borough president, but like Dinkins, Sutton had established himself politically as a loyal Democrat, working his way up through the party system. Thus, like Dinkins, Sutton had carefully cultivated a relationship with the Democratic party and favor with white ethnic blocs. Further, like Dinkins, Sutton appealed to the "just" nature of the people in the city and requested that he be judged on his ability, character, and experience rather than his race. Like Dinkins's attempt to show that he could be strong against crime—pledging to put more cops in the neighborhoods and on subways—Sutton's television advertisements boasted of his role as an auxiliary police officer and claimed he would be the most effective of the candidates in combating crime. Like Dinkins, Sutton also touched on the theme of the plural nature of the city and the necessity to unite, while stabilizing, the neighborhoods. Like Dinkins, Sutton ran in an era of fiscal crisis for the city. Like Dinkins, Sutton ran in the midst of racial crisis in the city; and like Dinkins, Sutton ran on the heels of a presidential election primary in the city where the African American vote had been credited with playing a pivotal role in election results.[61]

But unlike Dinkins, Sutton lost and lost badly. According to Charles Green and Basil Wilson, Sutton received only 14 percent of the aggregate vote in the Democratic mayoral primary of 1977; Dinkins, however, won not only the primary but the general election outright.[62] Since both Dinkins and Sutton presented themselves to the electorate as moderates, it does not appear likely that ideology in and of itself was the key to the different results.

There are a number of other possibilities that explain Dinkins's victory versus Sutton's defeat. One is that the media played a different role in 1977 than in 1989. In 1977, the news media by and large ignored Sutton's candidacy. By and large, Sutton could not attract reporters to his press conferences and was usually left out of news discussions of major contenders. In short, from the vantage point of the media, Sutton was not part of the horserace and had no chance of winning.

Similarly, Sutton was hampered by his inability to secure endorsements from prominent New Yorkers. Dinkins, on the other hand, had the endorsements of practically every major union in the city, several of the most prominent leaders of the Latino community, the state's attorney general, and so forth. In sum, to the extent that formation of a winning coalition is presaged on winning support from important reference publics, Dinkins was clearly more successful than Sutton.

Behind the developments of better treatment by the press and important endorsements, however, was the impact of demographic change in New York City between the two mayoral contests. In 1977, African Americans composed only 21 percent of the city's population; in 1989, they composed 27 percent. Moreover, African American and Latino voter registration amounted to 45 percent of the total registration in 1989. Meanwhile Jewish registration, which was 45 percent of registered voters in 1977, had declined to 22 percent in 1989. This growth in the African American and Latino share of the electorate lay behind the seriousness shown in news analyses of Dinkins's campaign in 1989. In turn, the attention Dinkins received in the press helped to make him a viable candidate and aided him in securing endorsements. Most importantly, however, demographic change in the city reduced the proportion of the white vote Dinkins needed to win compared to the proportion of the white vote Sutton needed. Thus, building on near-unanimous support from African American New Yorkers and strong majority support from Latino New Yorkers, Dinkins narrowly won with 30 percent of the white vote. In short, Dinkins clearly succeeded in forming a winning electoral coalition; yet the more important observation might be that in a city where Democrats outnumber Republicans by a five-to-one ratio, Dinkins's small margin of victory (2.4 percent) demonstrated the continuing difficulties of producing winning coalitions of African Americans and other racial and ethnic groups.

The election of the first African American mayor in New Haven, Connecticut, is likely a result of similar developments. African Americans compose over 40 percent of New Haven's population. Thus, Mayor John Daniels, like Mayor Dinkins, needed to secure only a significant minority (20 to 30 percent) of the white vote to win.

Clearly, however, interracial coalitions were substantial in some places. How else could L. Douglas Wilder have won in a state where African Americans compose only 18 percent of the potential electorate and have a long history of lower voting rates than whites? Similarly, Norman Rice could not have been elected Seattle's first African American mayor without substantial white support. African Americans compose less than 10 percent of Seattle's electorate.

No undisputed ideological guidelines for building a winning coalition with substantial white support for African American candidates stem from Wilder's and Rice's elections, however. Wilder obviously slanted his campaign toward moderation and conservatism regarding many state policies, but it was his embrace of reproductive choice (usually considered to be a liberal position) that not only won him substantial white (women) support but helped defuse the "race" issue, according to most poll analyses.[63] In Rice's case, Jesse Jackson campaigned vigorously for the candidate, and Rice poised himself toward the liberal end of the ideological spectrum in building his winning coalition.[64] It is important to note that each of the African Americans who were elected in November 1989 ran to the left of their opponents. Finally, the elections of 1989 demonstrate more fruitful possibilities for building winning electoral coalitions in support of African American candidates at the state and especially local levels than in national presidential contests. The reasons appear to be mixed. On the one hand, elections such as Dinkins's in New York appear to be a result of growing minority proportions of the population more than anything else. Partially as a result of the size of the minority population, its proportion of the total population, and constant violent clashes between the races in New York City, whites who supported Dinkins were eager to get a payoff of racial and ethnic harmony as a benefit for their membership in the winning electoral coalition. Moreover, Dinkins's chief opponent in the Democratic primary, Edward Koch, not only had already served twelve years in office, but was considered to be a source of conflict and fraction. His chief opponent in the general election, Rudolph Giuliani, had never held office. On the other hand, elections such as Rice's in Seattle appear to fit the racial competition or tipping point hypotheses: That is, where African Americans make up so small a portion of the population that they are not even considered to be serious competitors for scarce resources, African American candidates have a better chance of building winning interracial electoral coalitions. Thereby, in considerations of whether to seek to form a winning electoral coalition for African American candidates, there is no shortcut to a "concrete analysis of the concrete situation." This analysis must include study of demographic factors (especially proportion of the African American population in the electorate); types of electoral systems; African American and other groups' voter registration and turnout trends; office being sought; the total number of candidates in an election (especially the total number of minority candidates); potential campaign strategies, tactics, messages, and financing; candidate strengths, experience, and background; incumbency advantages, prospects for media and leadership endorsements; political culture; and changing racial voting patterns (preferences) over time. The 1989 elections demonstrate no new components of the winning coalitions of African American candidates. At least in the case of Wilder and Dinkins, the whites most supportive were upwardly mobile ones. The payoffs expected by these coalition partners varied from place to place. For example, as stated above, racial harmony seemed to be the payoff expected in New York; support for abortion rights seemed to be the payoff expected by many of Wilder's supporters in Virginia. For African Americans, the most poignant goals remained what they have been in every instance of coalition building; that is, racial progress. It is too early to tell what payoffs (other than the symbolic ones of victory) African Americans will receive from their participation in the winning coalitions of 1989. Research on past successes in controlling local political regimes has produced inconclusive evidence, but most of the literature on African American governance has stressed the limitations of African American mayoral influence in the policy process and especially on improving conditions for the poor.[65]

CONCLUSION: LESSONS FOR THE FUTURE

The above analysis has examined African American involvement in coalition politics at different points in time. It has also examined two different types of coalitions: (1) issue-based coalitions as represented by the NAACP and the modern Civil Rights Movement and (2) electoral coalitions as represented by Jesse Jackson's campaigns and a few state and local campaigns in 1989.

Theoretical Conclusions

From the preceding examination of African American involvement in coalitions in the past and present, a number of conclusions can be drawn:

First, in the theoretical realm, coalition formulations must give more attention to instances in which the partners in a coalition are determined by which, if any, partner is available, rather than which partner is best, or which can maximize the payoffs to a particular group, as prescribed in coalition theory. Coalitions involving African Americans rarely have been determined by their own choice and decision-making but rather by the reality of a long history of racial domination. In most instances, African Americans have not made the decision to minimize the number of coalition partners; rather, where there have been no partners willing to join them, they necessarily have formed intraracial coalitions.

Coalition theorists should also conduct more studies of "unintentional coalitions" if they are to understand electoral coalitions. Poor whites and African Americans seldom have recognized their support for the same (white) candidates at the ballot box, even though such ballot box coalitions dominate the history of American electoral politics since the New Deal.

Another factor that needs to be given much more consideration is moral/symbolic payoffs to coalition activities. To understand why affluent whites sometimes joined African Americans in coalitions, one cannot focus entirely or primarily on cost-benefit style material inducements.

The dimensions of what it means to win and the relative importance of different resources required to win need to be specified more clearly. For example, internal organization, which is often treated in coalition theory as falling in a different category from resources, might instead be one of the most critical resources it takes to win. Coalitions involving African Americans have sometimes floundered in both the modern Civil Rights Movement and in electoral campaigns as a result of internal disorganization. To be sure, there is a ranking of importance among resources. Organization, for example, may depend upon other resources such as money and expertise and still be a resource in and of itself. These relationships between various kinds of resources need to be clarified.

Finally, coalition theory must be taken outside the realm of abstraction and applied to real life situations. The mathematical models of game theory might look beautiful, but they are meaningless if they fail to explain everyday occurrences of coalition formation.

Experiential Conclusions

Second, in the empirical realm of African American coalition formation and maintenance, a number of conclusions and lessons can also be drawn.

It can be noted, for example, that the winning electoral coalitions in places like Virginia, Seattle, New York, and so forth represent little that is new in terms of the component groups that made up the coalitions. From the formation of the NAACP to the elections of 1989, the whites who have consciously supported African American causes and candidates have been liberal, relatively affluent, well-educated white professionals.

Although emphasis on a class-based lower income coalition touches the heart of objective needs of the great bulk of African Americans, other minority Americans, and white working-class Americans, the history of interracial coalition building in the United States demonstrates the continuing difficulty of forming such a coalition. There is not only the problem of producing an alliance between African Americans and working-class whites. Even among ethnic and racial minorities, there is often a pattern of conflict and competition rather than cooperation; thus, African Americans often worry about ceasing to be the largest minority; Latinos often view African Americans as keeping them from getting their just due. In cities such as Philadelphia and Detroit, Arab Americans and African Americans often oppose each other; in other cities such as Washington, D.C., and New York, Koreans and other Asians sometimes find themselves in violent conflict with African Americans, and much attention has been given to the conflict between Jewish and African Americans.

Hence, just as in 1909 when the NAACP was founded, upwardly mobile whites are more likely than their more unfortunate brothers and sisters to support or join issue-oriented coalitions and electoral coalitions with African American partners today; nor has a minority-based coalition among Latinos, Asians, other minorities, and African Americans materialized in an effective way in many places. The means by which to build a class-based coalition in this nation remain to be discovered. In addition, as long as middle- and upper-status African Americans suffer from vestiges of racial discrimination, race-based coalitions remain the order of the day.

Meanwhile coalitions of African Americans with upwardly mobile whites have the potential for having high entry prices and consequences. Those who benefit from the economic status quo are hardly eager to support calls for the kind of fundamental restructuring of the economy that the vast majority of African Americans needs to move forward. The more economic issues dominate the political agenda, the more coalitions of African Americans and upwardly mobile whites have the potential for falling apart. This is especially true in an era (following legal civil rights gains) where the moral claims of African Americans for social justice are less clear and straightforward. In short, a coalition with either class of whites and some minorities remains fragile and difficult to maintain.

In attempts to build such coalitions, then, African American groups and candidates are often likely to downplay racial and economic issues. From the standpoint of poor African Americans, the question is whether what such coalitions win, when they win, is worth the effort.

To be sure, there have been significant payoffs flowing from African American involvement in past coalitions. The structure of legal segregation of the races has been mostly dismantled. Many public accommodations from schools to washrooms have been integrated or at least desegregated. In most places, blacks can now vote. The number of African American elected officials has grown from fewer than 500 in 1965 to more than 7,000 in 1989 (see chapter 4). Important changes in the social structure of African American communities have resulted from higher eduction and skills levels, rising incomes, and better occupations for a substantial minority of African Americans. Yet, it is important to thoroughly consider that as higher-status African Americans have moved upward in American society and sometimes out of African American communities, there has been increased class bifurcation among African Americans. While a substantial and influential minority of African Americans have benefited from the payoffs of past coalitions, a large majority of African Americans has fallen farther and farther behind. It is this bifurcation that accounts for much of the lack of progress revealed in important overall African American/white socioeconomic indicators, such as the median-income gap between whites and African Americans, residential segregation, and so forth.

It remains to be seen whether a winning coalition of African Americans, other minorities, and whites can be mobilized in the interests of the poor. Since African Americans remain disproportionately poor, this question has strong implications for the interests of African Americans as a whole.

Perhaps, only the emergence of a genuine coalition of the left with strong roots in working-class communities of all racial and ethnic groups could improve the chances for the bulk of African America.

This study of African American involvement in coalition politics suggests some basic lessons regarding the prospects for building a winning coalition in the interests of the poor, not just the middle class. First, coalition partners must agree to pursue common and clearly articulated goals. All strategy should flow from these well-understood goals. Thus, any specific decision to coalesce with any particular group(s) must be based on a thorough, realistic, and practical analysis of whether the alliance will in the long run advance the goals, rather than produce some temporary gain but ultimate stagnation or decline in long-range interests. For example, in decisions about which political party to form a coalition with during the redistricting process in the 1990s, it should be clearly established whether the premier goal is to elect more African American representatives, state legislators, and so forth, or whether the premier goal is to structure jurisdictions that will elect more progressive elected officials (devoted to advancing the policy interests of the poor) regardless of their race. The practical ramifications of such a decision may well affect which of the two major parties African Americans ally with, not only in the redistricting process but in the presidential election of 1992 and beyond. This type of decision-making should be at the root of all decisions about coalition partners.

African Americans must continue to seek winning coalitions for African Americans. Currently, minorities (especially their less affluent sectors) do tend to coalesce in a growing number of instances; poor whites, however, require substantial consciousness raising. Many poor whites vote diametrically opposite to their own economic interests (for example, they supported the Reagan administration, whose policies benefited the rich at the expense of the poor).[66] Progressive white coalition partners of any class must agree to take on the job of demonstrating the efficacy to poor whites of joining an economic coalition with African Americans, because poor whites are unlikely to listen to African Americans.

In general, future coalition politics should not be solely or even primarily organized around individual African American candidacies. Coalitions constructed around individual candidates, so that loyalties are to that candidacy and coalition members and groups are submerged after the election, tend to produce few payoffs. (For example, thus far, evidence indicates that issue-oriented coalitions represented by the NAACP and the modern Civil Rights Movement produced more long-lasting (even if predominantly "legal") changes than the candidate-oriented coalitions behind Jackson and local African American officials. Attention, then, should be given to issue-oriented coalitions that can be institutionalized. The coalition then chooses to support a particular candidate because of the candidates' agreement with the coalition's positions. Such a coalition would antedate the politician's campaign and would be expected to outlive the candidacy—win or lose.

Coalition partners must agree to pool their relevant resources in pursuit of the articulated goals. A high level of internal organization that uses all of the resources of the coalition must be established. Resources include money, number of participants, the climate of the larger environment, third-party reference groups such as the media, governmental authorities, philanthropic foundations, and the level of internal organization. Since he who pays the piper calls the tune, only an organization supported financially mostly by members of the coalition will be free to exercise its own choices and political will. These resources must be skillfully handled. It is the ability of the coalition to organize, mobilize, and manage valuable resources that determines whether it will secure payoffs.

Third, the coalition must engage in conscious communications concerning the goals and the means of obtaining them. From the start, agreements should be reached on the distribution of the payoff (benefits) received by coalition partners when obtaining the goals. Clearly, there must be give and take. Members of other racial and ethnic groups in the coalition who run for public office, for example, must be supported fully. Specific policy concerns of coalition partners, for example, bilingual education, and immigration policy, must be part of the coalition's thrust. It is the nature of coalitions that each component must find its own strength before the common cause is joined. To find its common basis for institutionalization, the coalition would have to include those leaders of various targeted groups who influence their own constituencies. This would mean including leaders of those groups suffering in the current status quo, for example, many Latinos and other minorities, poor whites, and so forth. Only if a clear vision of the payoffs involved for each coalition partner when the goal is achieved is agreed upon in the early phase of coalition formation, and only if this agreement holds when goals are achieved, will the coalition be sustained. After all, the goal of each member of a winning coalition is to maximize that person's (or that group's) payoffs.

Fourth, the coalition should not rely on simply one strategy. Rather than endless debates about whether more can be achieved through economic boycotts, black capitalism, protest, legal strategies, or electoral politics within and without the two-party system, it should be understood that all methods should be pursued in a well-organized, concerted effort. Just as the NAACP's legal strategy was complimented by the SCLC's and SNCC's direct action protests, so too can myriad tactics and strategies produce a winning coalition today. The choice is not between politics and economics or between community activism and electoral activism or any other particular brand of politics, but how each can be used to advance progress through bolstering each other. Cooperation between groups and strategies, not competition, must be the heart of the winning coalition. Cooperation and compromise, as well as long- and short-term planning, are unavoidable realities for winning coalitions.

The potential components of a new larger coalition capable of determining rewards in American society are still in the free political marketplace. They are not being coopted by the increasingly restrictive major parties. Given the strong prospect of continued political and economic retrenchment, the growing divisions between housed and homeless, employed and structurally unemployed, rich and poor, the coming fights over redistricting, presidential politics, taxation, the "peace dividend," budgetary priorities, Supreme Court nominations, and a host of other issues, the response to a coalition invitation might be stronger in the near future. Much depends on whether the friends of coalition politics have the courage, will, and skill to organize.

NOTES

1. For a discussion of Jackson's attempt to build a coalition of have-nots in American society, see Lorenzo Morris and Linda Faye Williams, "The Coalition at the End of the Rainbow," in *Jesse Jackson's 1984 Presidential Campaign: Challenge and Change in American Politics,* edited by Lucius Barker and Ronald Walters (Urbana: University of Illinois Press, 1989).

2. *The New York Times,* November 8, 1989, 1.

3. *The Washington Times,* November 9, 1989, 1.

4. *The Washington Post,* November 9, 1989, 1.

5. J. von Neumann and G. Morgenstern, *Theory of Games and Economic Behavior* (Princeton, N.J.: Princeton University Press, 1947).

6. See Abram de Swaan, "Coalition Theory and Multi-Party Systems" in *Coalition Formation* edited by H. A. M. Wilke (New York: Harcourt, 1985), 229–61. Also see Eric C. Browne, *Coalition Theories: A Logical and Empirical Critique* (Beverly Hills, Calif.: Sage, 1971).

7. Browne, *Coalition Theories,* 10.

8. Paul Hill, *A Theory of Political Coalitions in Simple and Policymaking Situations* (Beverly Hills, Calif.: Sage, 1973).

9. Abram de Swaan, "Coalition Theory and Multi-party Systems" in *Coalition Formation*, ed. by Henk A. M. Wilke (Amsterdam: Elsevier Science Publishing, 1985), 232.

10. Hill, *A Theory of Political Coalitions*, 13–14.

11. Ibid., 5.

12. de Swaan, "Coalition Theory," 232.

13. Ibid., 252.

14. Browne, *Coalition Theories*, 34.

15. See M. Sherif et al., *The Robbers Cave Experiment: Intergroup Conflict and Cooperation* (Middletown, Conn.: Wesleyan University Press, 1988).

16. W. J. van der Linden and A. Verbeek, "Coalition Formation: A Game Theoretic Approach," in Wilke, *Coalition Formation*, 91.

17. Ibid., 101.

18. Wilke, *Coalition Formation*, 170.

19. Browne, *Coalition Theories*, 10.

20. Ibid., 11.

21. de Swaan, "Coalition Theory," 252.

22. Ibid.

23. E. W. Kelley, "Techniques of Studying Coalition Formation," *Midwest Journal of Political Science* 12 (February 1968): 62–84.

24. Wilke, *Coalition Formation*, 5.

25. Kelley, "Techniques of Studying Coalition Formation," 62–63.

26. This term and concept comes from Aldon Morris, *The Origins of the Civil Rights Movement: Black Communities Organizing for Change* (New York: The Free Press, 1985).

27. See also Morris, *The Origins of the Civil Rights Movement*, 12.

28. Ibid., 17.

29. Ibid., 14.

30. Ibid., 15.

31. Ibid.

32. August Meier, "Negro Protest Movements and Organization," *The Journal of Negro Education* (Fall 1963): 445.

33. Morris, *The Origins of the Civil Rights Movement*, 114.

34. Ibid., 117.

35. Ibid.

36. Quoted in Morris, *The Origins of the Civil Rights Movement*, 234.

37. Richard Flacks, "Who Protests: The Social Bases of the Student Movement," in *Protest: Student Activism in America* edited by Julian Foster and Durward Long (New York: William Morrow, 1970), 137.

38. Morris, *The Origins of the Civil Rights Movement*, 214.

39. Ibid., 227.

40. Kirkpatrick Sale, *SDS* (New York: Vintage, 1973), 23.

41. Flacks, "Who Protests," 134–57.

42. Claybourne Carson, *In Struggle: SNCC and the Black Awakening of the 1960s* (Cambridge, Mass.: Harvard University Press, 1981).

43. Morris, *The Origins of the Civil Rights Movement*, 234.

44. Ibid., 239. See also Frances F. Piven and Richard A. Cloward, *Poor People's Movements: How They Succeed, Why Some Fail* (New York: Vintage Books, 1979).

45. Stokely Carmichael and Charles Hamilton, *Black Power: The Politics of Liberation in America* (New York: Vintage Books, 1967), 17.

46. Ibid., 21.

47. Bayard Rustin, "From Protest to Politics: The Future of the Civil Rights Movement," *Commentary* 39 (February 1965): 25–31.

48. Examples of this development are the election of Sidney Barthelemy to be mayor of New Orleans in 1984, the election of John Lewis to represent the fifth congressional district of Georgia in 1986, and the election of Mark White to be mayor of Cleveland in 1989. In each of these instances, the winning African American candidate received a majority of the white vote and a minority of the African American vote in jurisdictions that were more than 50 percent African American.

49. Nancy J. Weiss, *Farewell to the Party of Lincoln: Black Politics in the Age of FDR* (Princeton, N.J.: Princeton University Press, 1983).

50. Ibid.

51. Ibid. See also Piven and Cloward, *Poor People's Movements*.

52. Kelley, "Techniques of Studying Coalition Formation," 81.

53. For example, United States Senator Ralph Yarborough in Texas is a prime example. A rather consistent liberal on all fronts, Yarborough's constituency was composed of working class whites and blacks. Only after proponents of the Vietnam War skillfully opposed Yarborough's antiwar stance in this instance did poor whites desert Yarborough in large number leading to his defeat.

54. Consider, for example, the elections of four United States senators in Georgia, North Carolina, Alabama, and Florida in 1986. In each case, the victorious candidate for senator won with a minority of the white vote (disproportionately from less affluent whites) and a majority of the African American vote.

55. Gerald Jaynes and R. Williams, *A Common Destiny: Blacks and American Society* (Washington, D.C.: National Academy of Sciences, 1985), 187.

56. For example, see Robert Holmes, "The Andrew Young for Congress Campaign, 1972: Some Reflections on Coalition Politics and the Struggle," paper presented at the annual meeting of the National Conference of Black Political Scientists, New Orleans, Louisiana, April 1973.

57. Quoted in Morris and Williams, "The Coalition at the End of the Rainbow," 229.

58. Ibid., 234.

59. For discussion, Ibid., 227–48.

60. Linda F. Williams, "White Black Perceptions of the Electability of Black Political Candidates," *National Political Science Review* 2 (1990): 45–64.

61. African American voters were key to Jimmy Carter winning New York City's Democratic primary in 1976; similarly, African American voters were key to Jesse Jackson winning the New York City primary in 1988.

62. Charles Green and Basil Wilson, *The Struggle for Black Empowerment in New York City: Beyond the Politics of Pigmentation* (New York: Praeger, 1989), 41.

63. *The Washington Post*, November 9, 1989, 1; *The New York Times*, November 9, 1989, 1; and *USA Today*, November 9, 1989, 1.

64. Interviews with Washington state representative Jesse Wineberry, October–November 1989.

65. Ralph Gomes, Walda Fishman, Jerome Scott, and Robert Newby, "The Politics of Race and Class in City Hall: Race Politics and the Class Question," in *Research in Urban Sociology*, edited by Ray Hutchins and Ronald K. Baba (Greenwich, Conn.: JAI Press, Inc., 1989).

66. Kevin Phillips, *The Politics of the Rich and the Poor: Wealth and the American Electorate in the Reagan Aftermath* (New York: Random House, 1990).

8

Redistricting in the 1990s: Opportunities and Risks for African Americans

Walter Hill

In April 1990, the decennial United States census was taken. The results of that census have major ramifications for American politics in general and African American politics in particular.

The costs of taking a census every ten years are higher and higher, but it is clear that Americans are easily compensated for the costs, because the data are widely used. Constitutionally, a census is required to determine apportionment in the House of Representatives and to determine congressional district lines. In addition, the data are used to determine district lines in state, county, and city governments and to allocate governmental finances at all levels of government. There are many other uses of census data, including determining school district lines, some judicial district lines, potential sizes of markets, optimal cities for development, and so forth. Indeed, no other data are more widely used by government, business, and academia.

Given the many uses of census data in making important decisions that affect everyday life, disadvantaged minorities have an important stake in producing an accurate count. For example, the steady political empowerment of disadvantaged minorities that began with the Voting Rights Act of 1965 has rested partially on the ability of political leaders to transform local population majorities into political office. Knowledge of the location of minorities has been crucial in this regard. This knowledge is especially necessary for successful litigation against discriminatory voting plans. The official basis of knowledge of the size and location of minority communities is the decennial census.

This chapter presents some potential developments for black Americans in the context of the 1990 census and the ensuing redistricting process. First, the difficulty of simply counting the population is highlighted, and recent developments in computer technology for making and disseminating the count are also discussed. Second, the academic literature dealing with public choice as it is related to voting and redistricting is reviewed. Finally, an assessment of potential gains and losses for African Americans and for the development of winning coalitions between African Americans and other groups in the 1990s redistricting process is made.

COUNTING THE PEOPLE: CONTROVERSIES AND METHODS

The most basic problem confronting the United States Census Bureau every ten years is obvious: how to count (and classify) the people. On the face of it, the answer to this problem appears to be straightforward; simply find the people and count them. But the history of the United States is filled with numerous debates about just who to count as people and how to classify the people counted. For example, the debate between slaveholding versus non-slaveholding states at the Constitutional Convention of 1787 demonstrates perhaps the earliest American debate over how to count the population. The clause of the early United States Constitution relegating African Americans to be counted as only "three-fifths of a man" in the first few censuses is a clear-cut example of a temporary resolution of how to count the population. Similarly, several paragraphs of the instructions for enumerating the population in the 1870 census were devoted to discussing the classification of "half-breeds" in reference to counting the aboriginal (Native American) population. The 1870 discussion posited: "Shall they be regarded as following the condition of their father or mother . . . superior or inferior blood . . . or white habits?" The enumerators chose the latter criterion, but the fact that the question arose at all demonstrates the controversial nature of census enumeration.

Controversies over how to count and classify the population are alive and well today. For example, the Asian community raised objections to the classification rules adopted in the 1990 census. With more than twenty Asian nationality groups in the nation, the limited number of subcategories provided by the Census Bureau in the 1990 enumeration was unacceptable to many Asian leaders.

Even if generally accepted categories for all groups could be adopted, other difficulties could arise. The Census Bureau's solution to the problem of classification is to accept a person's "self-identified" ethnicity as the proper classification, but even this solution presents problems for data users. For instance, Richard Rogers, looking at infant mortality data in California, noted that data on births tend to be supplied by the mother while data on deaths tend to be supplied by the father. He refers to this system as "biological and paternal" on the one hand and "social and maternal" on the other, and observes that the reported high levels of infant mortality reported for Latinos can be explained partially by different data supplied by the fathers and the mothers (confusion arises when the fathers' and mothers' reported races differ) and the relatively high mortality rate in interethnic births.[1] In short, even using self-identified ethnicity can lead to statistical artifacts instead of an accurate ethnic count.

The Undercount

No controversy over counting the population has been more volatile, however, than the controversy over the "undercount"; that is, missing or not counting some people. The Census Bureau typically claims that approximately 3 percent of the nation's population is not counted. Problems stemming from this undercount are multiplied because the undercount is not uniformly distributed across all subpopulations or all regions of the United States. Members of minority groups (especially African American males) are disproportionately undercounted. Given the importance of the census in commercial and governmental activities, the effects of the undercount ripple unevenly through the population.

The reasons the Census Bureau misses counting people are varied. They include the fear census takers might have of venturing into and closely investigating the population in some neighborhoods; the failure of census forms to reach transient or homeless people, the distrust some people have of government (including the United States Census Bureau) that leads them not to answer the census questionnaire; the fear undocumented aliens have that the census form will be used to deport them; the fear of those who share addresses that their answers on the census form will be used to evict them; and so forth.

The Census Bureau strongly argues that these fears are totally unjustified. No individual data are released to any governmental or private source, the Bureau proclaims; and census takers face relatively stiff penalties if they ever release individual data. To be sure, there is no evidence that the Census Bureau has ever released data for nonauthorized purposes such as the tracking of aliens or use by the Internal Revenue Service. Yet while the identity of individual respondents has never been revealed, it is nonetheless true that the release of group level data could be put to nefarious uses.

An interesting confirming case comes from World War II. The 1940 census reported the number of citizens by national origin in given districts. The figures were sufficiently accurate and Japanese Americans sufficiently concentrated that the United States government knew how to locate all Japanese Americans in a given district. Relocation of these Americans to concentration camps followed the outbreak of World War II and ensuing racial hysteria. While the Census Bureau did not release the name of any individual and deserves no direct blame for its role in this pathetic episode in American history, the Bureau's data did make it possible.

Today, however, there is more concern about being adequately counted among minority group leaders than there is about nefarious uses of an accurate count. In Baltimore, New York City, Detroit, Los Angeles, Atlanta, and other cities across the country, minority leaders have organized and unsuccessfully sued the government to mandate a full count. Meanwhile, many reports have surfaced since April 1990 about the inaccuracies of the 1990 count; for example, in California one whole zip code did not receive census forms. Statisticians typically like to "correct" for known errors in models and procedures, and many have joined minority and big-city leaders in demanding an accurate count. Toward this end, statisticians have proposed methods to correct the undercount. A past president of the American Statistical Association, for example, proposed an intense second survey of selected areas to measure the size of the undercount.[2] An avalanche of litigation on the question remains inevitable.

From the Census to Redistricting: The Impact of Computerization

Redistricting will be different in the 1990s than in earlier decades due to principal changes in law and technology. Since the end of World War II, computer speed and cost per operation have improved at an exponential rate. Tommaso Toffoli and Teuvo Kohonen looked at the density of microprocessors and estimated that computer speed increases by a factor of ten every five years.[3] Naomi Freundlich reports that TeraOps (trillion operations per second) machines are being developed.[4] At this point, both the software and the hardware have developed to such an extent that it clearly is feasible to draw district lines in the 1990s using even sophisticated personal computers.

To facilitate this development, the Census Bureau developed street-by-street computer maps of the entire nation. Anyone with this dataset is able to merge files containing maps with those containing demographic (and political) data. In effect, from census data alone, a researcher can create districts that optimize demographic characteristics. With other datasets, for example those containing data from previous elections, one can include those variables. Through this process, legislators are able to see instantly the effects of changing boundaries.[5]

This entire process has become possible in the past ten years due to the increased speed of modern small computers. Anyone able to buy into the technology can play. Products currently available can be found in *Byte* and other microcomputer magazines.

The critical factor here is that, due to changes in computer technology, many more individuals and groups than ever before can draw alternative district plans. As a result, redistricting in the 1990s is both more democratic and vastly more complicated. For blacks, Latinos, and other minorities to draw plans that play to their advantages, they need to understand and use the new technology, since one irony of the role of computers is that the growing number of players it makes possible also paves the way to potentially greater abuse in drawing districts and an explosion in litigation.

PUBLIC CHOICE THEORIES AND REDISTRICTING

While redistricting begins with demography, it is by and large a political affair—full of conflict and tensions. This section discusses two broad political dimensions (the two-party system and at-large versus district election systems) that influence the way demographic changes are reflected in drawing new district boundaries.

Political Parties, Blacks, and Redistricting

To begin, political parties influence the end products of redistricting. It is well known that despite the existence of minor parties, the United States is a two-party system. The two-party nature of the system roughly means that elections can be viewed as zero-sum games. Gains by one party result in losses by the other (although citizens do in fact have third options of not voting or voting for minor parties). Through redistricting, each of the two major parties tries to make gains. Thus, redistricting is usually a bitter partisan experience. Redistricting in the 1980s was overtly partisan in many states, where one party was firmly in control of the state legislature.[6] Indiana was perhaps the textbook case in 1980s redistricting. In Indiana, the district map passed by the Republican-controlled legislature in 1981 was a clear-cut model of partisan gerrymandering. Republicans drew the plan with the help of Market Opinion Research Corporation's sophisticated computer system at a cost of more than $250,000. The map's lines wove freely in and out of counties, concentrating Democratic voting strength into the districts of just three of the state's six Democratic incumbents and damaging the reelection prospects of the other three. The state's Republicans made no apologies for their plan. As it turned out, their elaborate schemes went for nought in the election of 1982, but it did strengthen their prospects for the future.

There is every reason to expect the redistricting process to be even more partisan in the 1990s and beyond. Both parties constantly boast about their efforts beginning earlier and earlier each decade and spending more and more.

Partisan and ethnic/racial concerns are intertwined in many places. Redistricting that places large blocs of minorities into some districts and takes them out of others will influence which party stands a better chance of winning those districts. This is so because the vast majority of blacks still identify with the Democratic party. Yet, blacks should not conclude that black aspirations for more black elected officials and the Democratic party's aspirations necessarily go hand in hand. Understandably, the Democrats' goal is to elect and reelect more Democrats—pure and simple. In some instances, this could mean alliances of conservative elements in both parties against more progressive elements. Moreover, numerous victories for the Democrats do not always or even often mean numerous advances for black candidates in public office. Take, for example, the 1986 mid-term elections. Democrats took control of an additional

189 new state legislative seats, but despite the heavy concentration of blacks among Democratic voters, blacks made a gain of only 14 additional state legislators. Thus, the Democratic party's redistricting plans and racial interests are linked, but not one and the same.

Meanwhile, Republican operatives are seeking to woo blacks into a redistricting coalition whose goal would be to create several new safe majority black districts in some southern states in order to make adjoining districts heavily white. The Republicans presumption is that these new heavily white districts would then fall into Republican coffers. To be sure, simple electoral arithmetic demonstrates that the higher the proportion of blacks in a congressional district, the greater the chances that the district will be represented by a Democrat.[7] Thus, amassing blacks heavily into a few districts and leaving many more districts heavily white would benefit Republicans as long as blacks vote overwhelmingly for the Democrats and whites vote disproportionately for the Republicans. In sum, the partisan nature of redistricting and its effects on political prospects for blacks are likely to generate a good deal of volatility and contentiousness.

Redistricting, Type of Electoral System, and Blacks

The first line of political battle in the redistricting process occurs over drawing the boundaries of United States House seats. It is at the state and local levels of redistricting, however, that the greatest controversies arise. This is in part a response to the wide range of voting rules that exist in state and local politics. This section scans the range of common electoral systems in state and local politics and discusses the ongoing debate over which type of electoral system is more advantageous to minorities, especially blacks.

At one end, there is the pure at-large electoral system. In such a system, all voters in a jurisdiction (for example, a city) can vote for or against any of the candidates running for a particular office.

Preference voting is a second type of electoral system. In preference voting, the voters rank their top choices from a list of candidates presented to them. Rules used for determining the victor(s) may be complex, but there are a number of criteria used to eliminate several classes of rules. For example, if candidate A is preferred by everyone over candidate B, the rules determining the outcome should maintain this preference order.

District systems make a third type of electoral system. Some district systems are modified at-large systems. In this type, a candidate for a given seat must reside in a given district, but voters from the entire jurisdiction vote on the slate of candidates from each district. Finally, there are pure district systems where the list of candidates for each district are voted upon only by citizens from the indicated district.

While there are other types of election systems, all are based on combinations of the systems listed above. For example, some systems might be based on the pure district type, but allow preference voting. Others might be based on the at-large type but might guarantee a minimum number of seats to both political parties.

These systems are not neutral in their impact on a minority candidate's chance of winning an election. The current conventional wisdom is that, as a rule, at-large elections tend to reduce the chances of minorities in winning political office. Jesse Jackson, for example, has argued that at-large elections are discriminatory and the Democratic party should work toward requiring district elections.

Historically, it is clear that at-large systems emerged in an attempt to weaken the power of members of the nonmajority population. Adopted by "reformers" in the early part of this century who opposed machine politics in the cities, the effect of at-large systems was to oppose nonmajority immigrants in urban centers. The argument typically advanced was that the best people could be elected to office in at-large systems, given the larger pool from which to draw applicants. As Edward Banfield and James Wilson concluded, the result was that the rich tended to benefit from at-large systems.[8]

Nevertheless, there is some debate on the effects of district elections. Leonard Cole looked at New Jersey elections and concluded that at-large systems were not discriminatory against blacks.[9] It is unclear whether his results would have held if he had controlled for a range of variables including income. Paul Jacob and Timothy O'Rourke, citing *Collins v. Norfolk*, have argued that the effects of district elections are unclear.[10] O'Rourke examined the legal requirement of intent to discriminate.[11] He observed that in some cases it is difficult to show intent, because some laws were established over a century ago. He cites a Mobile, Alabama, case where the districting law goes back to 1870, obviously before the participation of any current politicians. O'Rourke's argument, however, partially begs the question, since clearly the goal in Alabama politics in 1870 was to disenfranchise blacks and their Republican allies.

There are a number of works in game theory dealing with the power of voters. J. F. Banzhaf showed a surprising degree of unevenness in the power of voters across states,[12] while Irwin Mann and L. S. Shapley, using an index, showed nonuniformity in the power of groups.[13] In an interesting and highly theoretical piece, James Snyder argued that the voting power of an interest group is most powerful in an m district system when the members of that group are evenly spread across $(m + 1)/2$ districts.[14] An exception occurs when the interest group is small; in that case, the optimal condition for the group is to be spread over the m districts. The result goes against the desires of representatives, who tend to want groups that typically support them concentrated in their own districts rather than spread across many. In short, the interests of a particular representative in the redistricting process may differ significantly from the interests of an interest group. The results of Snyder's analysis indicate that minorities should prefer at-large over district elections and that they should prefer not to be concentrated in a single electoral district.

Empirical evidence, however, suggests the opposite of theoretical work. Albert Karnig and Susan Welch observed that multimember districts have tended to discriminate in the sense that minority populations tend to be underrepresented. However, they cite the Supreme Court decision of *Whitcomb v. Chavis* and a Marion County, Indiana, state legislative case to show that if there were no intent to discriminate, the election system is not illegal on that basis.[15] Welch and Timothy Bledsoe analyze several types of cities and conclude that at-large systems are in fact disadvantageous to blacks but advantageous to wealthy citizens. They conclude that district systems are better for minorities.[16]

Strong anecdotal evidence suggests that minority members of Congress, like other members, would rather have safe seats than have their most loyal supporters (minorities) spread over several districts. It is interesting that residential segregation patterns have been seen to a certain extent as providing benefits by creating safe seats for members of the segregated population.

REDISTRICTING, COALITION POLITICS, AND BLACKS: THE OUTLOOK

Two simple facts about black office-holding illustrate the importance of legislative redistricting to blacks' hopes and aspirations for full political empowerment. First, despite the substantial progress blacks have made in winning public office in the last twenty-five years, they remain grossly underrepresented in the nation's elective offices (see chapter 4). Undoubtedly, one important fact that partially accounts for this result is the way congressional, state, and local district boundaries have been drawn. Redistricting, then, or, more precisely, its most virulent form—racial gerrymandering—helps explain the underrepresentation of blacks in public office in various regions of the nation and levels of office-holding.

A second fact that illustrates the importance of redistricting to black American political empowerment is seen by examining developments ensuing from the redistricting process in the 1980s. In the year following the completion of the last nationwide redistricting process, black candidates experienced their largest annual gain in the decade of the 1980s in winning public office. In short, the effect of redistricting in the 1980s clearly was the big boost in the growth of black elected officials between 1982 and 1983. In order to experience more political progress as a result of redistricting in the 1990s, blacks and their allies are likely to pay careful attention to the census, reapportionment, and redistricting in the next few years.

Other factors will make blacks get more involved in the redistricting process in the 1990s. For example, as a result of the Supreme Court's decision in *Thornburgh v. Gingles* and other rulings (for example, *McNeill v. City of Springfield*), many more states and localities are now changing from at-large electoral arrangements to district plans. As a result, the redistricting process will be more political, more extensive, and have greater consequences for minorities than the redistricting process in the 1980s.

It is particularly significant that there are more blacks in state legislatures today than in the early 1980s. In 1982 when most plans were adopted, there were 330 black state legislators; by 1990 there were more than 100 additional black state legislators. Since state legislatures have an even greater impact on redistricting than governors, black state legislators are better positioned to play a significant role in the process in the 1990s. At the same time, the pattern of growth in the number of black state legislators since the 1980s redistricting demonstrates that redistricting can result in an immediate boost in the number. The number of black state legislators went up by 45 in one year alone immediately following the 1980s redistricting.

Another important development is the dramatic increase in the size of the Latino population. Latinos are heavily represented in half of the eight states gaining congressional districts in the 1990s (Arizona, California, Florida, and Texas). Moreover, much of the increase in the Latino population has occurred in close proximity to blacks, providing unprecedented opportunities for coalition-building between the two groups—for example, in Texas in the creation of a new Dallas-based district and in Florida in the creation of a new Miami-based district.

These are optimistic trends, but other factors also demonstrate pessimistic tendencies. Several dismal signs for blacks include: large declines in the composition of several districts that were majority black in 1980. Many of these districts are likely to find their boundaries changed. Two forms of migration account for this trend: migration from the Northeast and Midwest to the Sunbelt and migration within regions from central cities to suburbs. Guaranteeing that many of the majority black districts electing black representatives to the United States House will remain majority black requires political organization and, where necessary, litigation (especially under the clause of the Voting Rights Act that limits possibilities of retrogression where majority black districts have been created. Even in states not covered by the Voting Rights Act, black claimants have won some cases under this cause).

Gaining new or additional black majority districts will be more difficult. In general, blacks tend to be concentrated in several of the states losing congressional seats due to reapportionment (Illinois, Louisiana, Michigan, New Jersey, New York, Ohio, and Pennsylvania). And while the black population is large and/or growing in most of the states likely to gain seats due to reapportionment (California, Florida, Georgia, North Carolina, Texas, and Virginia), out-migration of blacks from central cities to suburbs reduced the concentration of blacks in ways that make carving out majority black districts more difficult.

Still, since redistricting is usually more about politics than demography, there are several places where politically organized blacks could encourage legislators to draw maps creating opportunities for black congressional candidates. Such places include the Tidewater region of Virginia (Newport News,

Norfolk, Portsmouth, and rural areas to the West), Durham, North Carolina, rural areas in southern Georgia, a "black belt" district between Birmingham and Montgomery, Alabama, as well as the black-Latino coalition possibilities in Texas and Florida.

The biggest gains for blacks and the greatest possibilities for coalitions with other racial/ethnic groups are likely to come at the state and local levels, however. Especially in the South and West, there are numerous places where heavily or majority Latino and black state, county, and city districts can be created.

CONCLUSION

Redistricting is always the politics of conflict. Redistricting is also always an opportunity. Those who are best organized will reap the rewards. Although population growth for Asians, Latinos, and blacks has been far greater than that for whites, gains derived through redistricting will depend more on political skill than mere population growth.

One thorny political issue that confronts racial minorities in the redistricting process is how far to go and with whom to ally in an effort to create new safe-haven constituencies so heavily laden with minority voters that they are nearly certain to elect a minority candidate. As Phil Duncan warned:

There is a downside to drawing safe-haven seats for minorities: In pulling together enough minority voters to guarantee that a newly created district will elect a minority member, surrounding districts often will be left almost lily-white. As a result, white members of the House who now represent districts with sizable minority populations— and who must take minorities' interests into consideration when they vote—will no longer be under direct political pressure to do so.[17]

Clearly to make gains, minorities will have to consider this trade-off. They will have to weigh offers coming from both major parties. While legal standards have never been more favorable, minorities still must be well organized to make progress through redistricting. A campaign designed around the redistricting process offers an opportunity for coalition-building among blacks, Latinos, other minorities, and progressive whites (especially white women and Labor). A campaign designed to maximize the districts where blacks and their progressive allies could be elected would change politics considerably. For example, in the South, legislation for more funding for public education, for the creation of jobs with decent wages and safe working conditions, for repeal of "right to work" laws, and so forth would have a stronger possibility of passing. In sum, where minorities are organized, redistricting in the 1990s could mean further movement toward realizing a truly equal or just society, but where minorities are unorganized and miss opportunities, redistricting in the 1990s could mean, in the words of Langston Hughes, "a dream deferred."

NOTES

1. Richard C. Rogers, "Ethnic Differences in Infant Mortality: Fact or Artifact," *Social Science Quarterly* 70 (September 1989): 642–49.

2. Barbara A. Bailar, "A Method for the Correction of the Undercount of the United States Census," *Journal of the American Statistical Association* 83 (March 1988): 150–64. For other methods of adjustment, see David W. Dunlap, "After the Census, a Second Survey to Guess at Who Was Missed," *The New York Times*, July 18, 1989, B4.

3. *Byte*, "Microbytes" November 1989, 17.

4. See Naomi Freundlich, "Developments to Watch: These Machines Would Make Supercomputers Look Slow," *Business Week*, December 18, 1989, 87.

5. William E. Schmidt, "New Age of Gerrymandering: Political Magic by Computer?" *The New York Times*, January 10, 1989, 1, 14. For examples of how to use software, see Stan Miastkowski, "Visually Map Your Data," *Byte*, October 1989, 211.

6. Linda Faye Williams, "What the Census Means in Money and Power," *Focus* (July 1989): 7.

7. For relevant data, see Linda Faye Williams, ed., *Congressional District Factbook: 1988* (Washington, D.C.: Joint Center for Political Studies, 1988), 41.

8. Edward Banfield and James Q. Wilson, *City Politics* (New York: Vantage Press, 1963).

9. Leonard Cole, "Electing Blacks to Municipal Office," *Urban Affairs Quarterly* 10 (September 1974): 17–35.

10. Paul Jacob and Timothy G. O'Rourke, "The Legal Basis of District Elections," *Journal of Law and Politics* 3 (Fall 1986): 295–353.

11. Timothy G. O'Rourke, "The Constitutionality of Electoral Reform," *University of Richmond Law Review* 17 (1989): 60–89.

12. J. F. Banzhaf, III, "One Man, 3,312 Votes: A Mathematical Analysis of the Electoral College," *Villanova Law Review* 13 (1968): 304–32.

13. Irwin Mann and L. S. Shapley, "The 'A priori' Voting Strength of the Electoral College," in *Game Theory and Related Approaches to Social Behavior*, ed. by Martin Shubik (New York: John Wiley and Sons, 1964), 151–64.

14. James Snyder, "Political Geography and Interest Group Power," *Social Choice and Welfare*, forthcoming.

15. *Whitcomb v. Chavis*, 403 U.S. 124, 1971.

16. Susan Welch and Timothy Bledsoe, *Urban Reform and Its Consequences: A Study in Representation* (Chicago: University of Chicago Press, 1988).

17. Phil Duncan, "Creating Black Districts May Segregate Voters," *Congressional Quarterly Weekly* (July 28, 1990): 2462.

9

African American Perspectives on Foreign Policy

Elliott P. Skinner

African Americans must develop the mechanisms and build the institutions with which to play a larger role in the foreign policy of the United States, if this nation is to compete and prosper in the twenty-first century. When in his inaugural address on March 4, 1933, Franklin Delano Roosevelt lamented that one-third of Americans were "ill-fed, ill-housed, and ill-clothed," he was talking about the commonality of Americans whose livelihood had been threatened by the Great Depression. He later pledged that he was "determined to make every American citizen the subject of his country's interest and concern; and we will never regard any faithful, and law-abiding group within our borders as superfluous."[1] More than thirty years later, another president, Lyndon Baines Johnson, aware that Roosevelt's pledge had not been fulfilled, launched his "War on Poverty." He wished to draw America's attention to the need for equality among the nation's poor—this time, primarily its minorities.[2] Johnson did not "overcome" as he had vowed, because this nation's tragic foreign policy led to disaster in Southeast Asia. The one-third of the nation that suffered most when the United States squandered lives and treasure in Vietnam must help to direct a foreign policy that will protect them and the nation in the future.

That continuing travail of "one-third of the nation," if not soon addressed, could endanger the future of the United States. The reason for this urgency is that there have been fundamental changes in the structure of the world system over the past decades. Thanks in part to Roosevelt, this nation recovered from the Depression to become the arsenal of democracy during World War II. Like a giant the United States bestrode the world, and using its diplomacy and economic might, it sponsored the United Nations, the Bretton Woods Agreement, and the Marshall Plan; treated relatively benignly the Germans and Japanese; and refused to support old-fashioned colonialism, thereby contributing greatly to the world as it is now known. The only cloud on the horizon was the messianism of the Soviet Union and the beginning of the Cold War.

Starting with the tragic diplomatic and military failure in Vietnam, an event that marked the retreat of the West from Asia, there arose a nagging sense that the United States has lost its *élan vital,* and like ancient empires is on the road to decline. This doom was recently spelled out by James Laxer in his book, *Decline of the Super-Powers,* and a number of incidents appear to have created concern in America and in the world. "Over the quarter-century from 1960 to 1984, the United States fell behind its major competitors in the rate of growth in every single significant category of economic life. In the quarter-century that followed, its lead was lost, or was slipping away in the major sectors of the economy."[3] To complicate the matter, during the 1980s, the Ronald Reagan administration felt more at ease "asserting American power against a host of sinister foes—the Libyans, the Sandanistas, the Angolans, and sometimes the Soviet Union—than against America's capitalist competitors."[4]

Alvin and Heidi Toffler concluded that "the major powers of the world are vigorously pursuing master plans for survival in the new century. There is one notable exception, however."[5] What attracted their attention was not only "Project Perestroika," but Europe's "Project 1992," "Project Deng," and the activities of the Tigers or dragons of East Asia—South Korea, Singapore, and Taiwan," which with Japan make up what used to be called "Asia's Co-prosperity Sphere." The Tofflers did not mention the recently created Magrebean Arab Union, nor SADCC (Southern African Development Coordinating Council) or ECOWAS (Economic Community of West African States) nor did they stress that Gorbachev's *glasnost* and *perestroika* threaten to change the very rationale of American post-WWII politics and diplomacy. The Tofflers did mourn that:

Americans, with good reason, are suspicious of master plans or industrial strategies but now face a world in which these are multiplying. Moreover, the absence of any American project, in turn, casts everyone else's project into high uncertainty. On the eve of the next century, outsiders increasingly see the United States as a "wild card" in the world system—a nation with immense muscle but little brain. . . . The 21st century has begun—everywhere but in Washington.[6]

ETHNICITY AND RACE IN THE U.S. RISE
TO WORLD DOMINATION

Linked to the perception of the danger to the United States' preeminence in the twenty-first century has been a series of statements about the possible cause for it. It has been said that the United States' success engendered the sense of security that prevented it from modernizing its technological infrastructure. It has also been alleged that the propensity of this country's capitalists for seeking greater profits by shipping industries abroad has ruined

America's ability to compete. American diplomacy has also been judged incapable of identifying or dealing with the course of tensions in the world system that even threaten the lives and safety of Americans. More serious have been statements about the weaknesses in American culture. And if Japanese leader Yasuhiro Nakasone is to be believed, America's decline is linked to the presence within its boundaries of a racial potpourri of African Americans and Latinos, and lesser breeds.

It is truly ironic that the racial mix that now characterizes the United States, and will increasingly do so in the near future, is being given as one of the reasons for its problems. It is doubly ironic that this charge has come not from Europeans, but from the leader of a nation that has been a victim of racism—Japan. After all, it was the United States' fear of a Japan that had defeated Russia in 1905, and thereby joined the ranks of the great imperialists, that raised the specter of the "yellow peril." Then during 1907–1908 in complicated diplomatic maneuvers, President Theodore Roosevelt was able to persuade the Californians to stop discriminating against American-born Japanese, if Japan would accept a "Gentleman's Agreement," and halt the emigration of its people to the United States. That the Japanese never forgot that humiliation was demonstrated at Pearl Harbor in 1941; and although defeated in World War II, Japan has risen, phoenix-like, from the infernos of Hiroshima and Nagasaki to challenge the world, not yet militarily, but economically and technologically.

Given the attempt of earlier generations of Americans to use diplomacy to control immigration to this country, Nakasone's brutal assertion that the United States is suffering the plight of being somewhat of a nation of mongrels leads to dealing with the question of why the United States became great and why it needs to chart a course that would ensure its future progress.

The English, who finally conquered the area that became the United States, were as interested as the contemporary Japanese in building a homogeneous nation. Ignoring the Africans who had been introduced among them as bond servants and who had been transformed into slaves, the English treated as contemptible "boers" those Dutch and German farmers who arrived in their midst. The Scot-Irish and the Irish received equally cold welcomes, and the Catholics, who, although of Western European origins, were subject to "Acts of Toleration."

In their efforts to build a new Jerusalem in America's green and fertile land, the English, like all the other Europeans in the Americas, felt that this was an impossible task without the labor of Africans. Black servants were brought to Jamestown, Virginia, in 1619, one year before the celebrated Pilgrim Fathers landed in Plymouth, Massachusetts. They proved so valuable that more than one hundred years later, in 1735, an agent of the colonists in Georgia, protesting an attempt to restrict the slave trade, declared: "In spite all Endeavors to disguise this Point, it is clear as Light itself, that Negroes are as essentially necessary to the Cultivation of Georgia, as Axes, Hoes, or any other Utensil of Agriculture."[7] Even though by this time most Africans in the British colonies were declared "slaves for life" and were increasingly being judged an unwelcome presence, southern planters still needed and wanted them. America had difficulty deciding whether to pay more for Negroes, who were held as important as axes and ploughs for their plantations, than for their more unfortunate cousins in Europe to come to this land.

Adhering to the dictates of Adam Smith, Ricardo, and the early theorists of capitalism, Americans permitted market forces to dictate their own behavior and railed at the mercantilism forced upon them by a cruel homeland. The War of Independence enabled the colonists to separate from England and to build a United States of America that hopefully would avoid the broils from embattled Europe. Paradoxically, however, a nation created in liberty permitted slavery to persist and the "unwelcome" presence of Africans led to a Civil War in which many thousands of newly arrived emigrants died, not to mention some of the flowers of North and South. That war preserved the Union but left the country with a legacy of racism and discrimination that has persisted to this day.

The United States, which sent its people West to conquer the lands of the Native peoples and crossed the Pacific to fulfill its manifest destiny, continued to welcome the huddled white masses of Europe yearning to breathe free, but it soon became clear that the elite groups in the nation feared for the very character of the nation. This was perhaps inevitable, given the changing demographic profile of the country. Initially a society of Englishmen whose values impregnated the emerging nation, the United States soon became a "nation of immigrants." Whereas between 1861 and 1870, 87.7 percent of the migrants came from northwestern Europe, by the turn of the century, a concentrated wave of some 70.8 percent of the migrants came from southeastern Europe. Moreover, this flood came as the United States was emerging as a world power; and at a time when liberal revolutionary movements were affecting Europe, and when racial theories asserting the superiority of Anglo-Saxon people were abroad in the land.

Concern for American values revived the anti-foreign feelings of the "Know-Nothing" movement of the 1850s, raising concern for future American homogeneity and culture. In reaction, the Congress passed an immigration law in 1924 with a "national origin" quota designed to favor white Anglo-Saxon and northern European immigrants. However, this was too late to change the demography of the country and its ethnic complexity. By 1976, the bicentennial year, nearly 50 million representatives of almost all nations of the world had settled in the United States.

ETHNICITY, RACE, AND U.S. FOREIGN POLICY

Despite America's success with immigrants, the nation's leaders have always been ambivalent about the role that ethnicity and race should play in national life, especially in foreign policy. A number of the founding fathers were deeply concerned that factionalism might hurt the emerging nation. In Federalist

Paper Number 10, James Madison warned against combinations of citizens who, "united and actuated by some common impulse of passion or of interest," might be adverse to the rights of other citizens, or to "the permanent and aggregated interests of the community."[8] George Washington in his farewell address cautioned that the primary allegiance of all Americans should be to the nation. He urged: "Citizens by birth or choice of a common country, that country has a right to concentrate your affections. The name of America, which belongs to you in your national capacity, must always exalt the just pride of patriotism more than any appellation derived from local discriminations."[9] Washington primarily feared the possibility of conflict due to ethnic concentrations within the United States. He felt that it was only in union that Americans could experience that "security from external danger, a less frequent interruption of their peace by foreign nations, and what is of inestimable value, they must derive from union an exemption from those broils and wars between themselves which so frequently afflict neighboring countries."[10]

President Theodore Roosevelt was particularly hostile to the attempts of ethnic groups (often referred to as "the hyphenates") to influence American foreign policy. In a speech in 1895 he inveighed against the particularisms of "the hyphenated Americans—the German-American, the Irish-American, or the native-American."[11] He warned that unless all of these groups considered themselves "American, pure and simple" then the future of the nation would be impaired. Woodrow Wilson attributed the propensity of many American ethnic groups to seek the interests of their ancestral lands to the fact that "only part of them has come over" from the old countries.[12]

Ethnicity was viewed as an important factor in American foreign policy in the years prior to, during, and after World War II. When the United States entered World War II, the editors of influential *Fortune* magazine warned that "There is dynamite on our shores." They thought that while some immigrant European groups unqualifiedly supported the war, others somewhat reluctantly supported it, and others submitted to the war effort with traces of subversive defiance. The editors wondered whether the United States could transform this melange into a "working model of political warfare."[13] There was apparently less question of the potential disloyalty of Japanese Americans; as noted in the preceding chapter, they were systematically rounded up and incarcerated in concentration camps.

Given the contemporary unraveling of the Soviet Bloc, it is instructive to note that Polish Americans exerted a great deal of pressure on President Franklin Roosevelt during his negotiations with the Soviet Union on the projected postwar boundaries between the USSR and Poland. They thought that the settlement at Yalta made a mockery of the Atlantic Charter, and urged representatives and senators not to ratify the agreement. When Dwight Eisenhower came to office, many citizens of central European origin wished the United States to "liberate" their ancestral lands. It is, however, generally admitted that while these groups failed in their effort "to force the government to do something it did not want to do, on occasion they have been able to sabotage steps that Washington would have liked to undertake."[14] George F. Kennan, America's brilliant ambassador to the Soviet Union, remarked bitterly in his *Memoirs* that Croatian-Americans "never failed to oppose any move to better American-Yugoslav relations or to take advantage of any opportunity to make trouble between the two countries."[15]

The most recent attack on the efforts of minorities in the United States to influence foreign policy was that of Senator Charles McC. Mathias, Jr. of Maryland. He lamented that "ethnic politics, carried as they often have been to excess, have proven harmful to the nation." Mathias updated George Washington's concern that factionalism, in this case ethnicity, can generate both unnecessary animosities among Americans and create among them illusions of common interests with outsiders, where in fact none exist. He expressed alarm at the attempts of U.S. ethnic groups to put pressure on both the domestic and foreign policy-making institutions of the United States to adopt measures in favor of their lands of origin. This included: Afro-Americans lobbying on behalf of Africa, Caribbean people on behalf of the people of the Caribbean basis; Greeks lobbying both the president and Congress against granting arms to Turkey, a NATO ally; Jewish groups promoting the cause of Israel; Mexican Americans and Italian Americans supporting immigration policies to benefit the areas from which their ancestors came; and Polish Americans and some central and northeastern Europeans attempting to enlist the aid of the United States against Soviet activities and presence in their ancestral homes. The senator did not suggest that the ethnic advocacy of Americans was unpatriotic. He did stress, however, that the administration's "resistance to the pressures of a particular group in itself signals neither a sellout nor even a lack of sympathy with a foreign country or case, but rather a sincere conviction about the national interest of the United States."[16]

Senator Mathias's concern that racial and ethnic advocacy on behalf of their ancestral lands might not be in the national interest should be examined theoretically and practically. Some scholars believe that it is true that ethnicity has played an important role in United States foreign policy, but there is less agreement about the effectiveness of it. Nathan Glazer and Daniel Moynihan believe that "without too much exaggeration it could be stated that the immigration process is the single most important determinant of American foreign policy." These two scholars admitted that United States foreign policy "responds to other things as well, but probably first of all to the primal facts of ethnicity."[17] But has this been as detrimental to the United States as some politicians have insisted? Gabriel Almond has argued that the attempts of ethnic and linguistic groups to influence U.S. foreign policy have historically been "mainly directed toward traditional national aims such as the preservation or return of national territory, the achievement of national independence, or the protection of minority ethnic or religious groups in foreign countries from persecution by the dominant groups."[18] This being the case, Almond concluded that the attempts of U.S. minorities to raise questions about U.S. foreign policy is not really a threat to the national interest. It might only be a threat to those people and groups who resent any challenge to their definition of what the national interest ought to be.

EUROCENTRICITY AND THE PROBLEMS OF THE MODERN WORLD

The problem with the question of what is in the national interest is difficult to define and changes over time. Historically, the answer for the query about the national interest has been, "What the public or the electorate wants." As Charles Evan Hughes once remarked, "Public opinion in a democracy wields the scepter;" and Abraham Lincoln declared, "With Public sentiment on its side, everything succeeds; with public sentiment against it, nothing succeeds."[19] The problem, of course, is that public opinion is often awkward to describe, elusive to define, difficult to measure, and impossible to see, even though it may be felt. A far greater conundrum for our country is that while equality is a basic political tenet, this has always been affected by the reality of socioeconomic ranking and stratification within the society. The White Anglo-Saxon Protestants have always believed that they have a better sense of what is in the national interest than do others among their fellow citizens.

So natural do the biases of the dominant American group appear that people do not often recognize their role in forming U.S. foreign policy and in determining what is in the national interest. For example, it has been remarked that the American Aid-to-Britain movement during the early stages of World War II was initiated, not because Germany posed a threat to the United States, but "simply because the vast masses of the dominant old-line American strain reacted instantly and passionately to England's sudden and extreme danger— England, the home of Magna Carta, of Shakespeare and of Milton and Keats and Shelley, of the King James version of the Bible; their imperishable home."[20] The special relationship of "old" Americans to England was no more clearly expressed than in February 1914, when New Hampshire Governor Robert O. Blood, an old-stock Yankee, presented the newly appointed U.S. ambassador to the Court of St. James to the state legislature as "the man who is going over to represent us in our fatherland." Seven members of the legislature, either conscious of their alien background, of the uproar caused by the activities of the German-Americans, or simply because they were "American-firsters," protested that "England was not our fatherland," that "we Americans cannot have two fatherlands." But the governor offered no correction. He probably considered his detractors to be not only boors but "anti-American" to boot.[21]

If Vietnam and other recent U.S. foreign policy initiatives suggest that those responsible for our foreign policy were not the brightest and best, it should be clear that these people are inadequate to deal with the more complex foreign policy issues of the twenty-first century. Roger Morris called attention to the danger posed to the United States by having its foreign policy under the control of "a small, ingrown elite of men clustered in New York and Washington." He writes that these men "awaited the call from the White House to determine America's role in the world, or to judge the fitness of one of their colleagues who would. The call usually came."[22] Schooled in selected private academies and colleges and later employed in prestigious old law firms, major banks, corporations, and foundations, these people, usually white males, have generally been considered to be among the best and the brightest. Yet their position in the U.S. social hierarchy has frequently made them oblivious to, or contemptuous of, the views of other Americans and of most of the country. They have also been largely contemptuous of Congress and they believe that the general American public knows, or needs to know, little about foreign policy.

The rapid changes taking place in the global system make it dangerous to leave foreign policy formulation and execution to the present actors. It is clear that many members of this establishment seldom recognize the role of institutionalized and habitual interactions—and often unarticulated ideologies—in the making of foreign policy. They remain largely unaware of the established patterns of nondisclosure and noninteraction that support largely unconscious and unarticulated patterns of interaction, custom, and manners. They are unable to make new decisions that are adaptable to a rapidly changing world in which past notions are clearly inadequate for our nation's future.[23]

AFRICAN AMERICANS CAN STRENGTHEN U.S. FOREIGN POLICY

African Americans and other racial/linguistic minorities who will compose one-third of the nation in the year 2000 can introduce new dimensions in the formulating and execution of U.S. foreign policy. By scrutinizing and raising questions about whether certain decisions are really in the national interest, this often-excluded one-third of the nation can raise the nation's level of consciousness and force the establishment to articulate the basis of its judgment before actions are taken that could jeopardize the nation's interest. It is surprising to note that when challenged, those responsible for our foreign policy often claim "privileged information," "gut-feelings," and "superior experience" as rationalizations for being unable to explain their positions. Often not sharing these unarticulable or plain wrong sentiments, African Americans and others like them, can see the negative implications of U.S. foreign policy in ways that the established practitioners do not. Thus, simply by raising questions about U.S. foreign policy, African Americans can force a reexamination of it. In many cases, racial/linguistic minorities are better informed about conditions in many parts of the world, including their ancestral lands, than the majority of Americans.

In the case of African Americans, it is unfortunate that until recently most Americans have either ignored or challenged their interest in U.S. foreign policy. Even the centuries-long interests of blacks in Africa were generally over-looked by most white Americans. Thomas Bailey, writing in *Man in the Street*—a criticism of the attempts of minority groups to shape American for-eign relations—declared quite openly: "No mention has been made of the most numerous hyphenate group of all, the Afro-Americans, who constitute about one-tenth of our population. They are racial hyphenates rather than national hyphenates, for they have since lost any foreign nationality."[24]

Bailey did note that when Benito Mussolini attacked Ethiopia in 1935, some American blacks reacted; Hubert Fauntleroy Julian ("Harlem's Black Eagle") went to fight in Ethiopia. But in Bailey's view, Julian "was an outstanding ex-ception." He asserted that as far as the Ethiopian war was concerned, "the sym-pathies of the American Negroes, in so far as they have any, were with their colored brethren."[25] Bailey was clearly convinced that blacks could have no possible interest in U.S. foreign policy. Their interest in the Ethiopian war was based not on the philosophically sophisticated notion of nationality, but on the more primordial sentiment of race.

Bailey is correct in suggesting that race is more primordial than the notion of nationality because this statement does reveal why African Americans have long been prevented from participating fully in American life, including its for-eign policy. A bloody civil war freed the slaves, but failed to transform them into people with full civil rights. After more than a century of protests and striving, the descendants of the Africans are still struggling to achieve full civil and economic equality with other Americans. And while it seemed—and still seems—quixotic to most white Americans (and even to some blacks) that Afro-Americans would seek to help anyone, including the Africans, many African American leaders have always realized that their fate was linked to those below the global color line, and that they had better involve themselves in foreign pol-icy. Bailey rightly observed: "To most Americans, God is Nordic, and the black and yellow do not fit into our color scheme."[26] African Americans have to help destroy this notion if they would have equality in this land.

The dramatic event that took place on Thanksgiving Eve, 1984, when prom-inent black Americans (a congressman, a member of the Commission on Civil Rights, and the leader of a black lobby known as TransAfrica) were arrested for "sitting-in" at the South African embassy in Washington, D.C., was a hallmark in the long and often ignored attempt of African Americans to influence U.S. policy, to the benefit of the nation and the world. These men and women de-cided to escalate black protest against South Africa's official policy of apartheid and the Reagan administration's policy of "constructive engagement," which was having detrimental effects in South Africa, in the rest of Africa, and in the world. They were determined to compel the United States to accept the almost worldwide consensus that it should cooperate with the rest of humanity in pressuring South Africa to abolish apartheid—a practice deemed repugnant to all civilized people.[27]

Despite increasing riots and civil disobedience in South Africa, the demonstrations and arrests of African Americans and their allies who created the Free South Africa Movement, the movement on university campuses and state and local institutions to secure divestment in companies doing business in South Africa, the hesitation of companies in South Africa to respect the Sullivan Principles, and the increasing activities in Congress to pass bills imposing sanctions against South Africa, the Reagan administration, claiming that it could not and should not take the side of the oppressed, stuck to its policy of "constructive engagement." When the Nobel Peace Prize Committee honored Bishop Desmond Tutu for his creative attempts to resolve the problems of his country peacefully, the president himself sought, but understandably failed, to convince Tutu that apartheid was not uncivilized and unchristian.[28]

Reluctant to change a mind-set that axiomatically placed the welfare of South African whites over that of the oppressed black majority, the United States refused to cooperate with those forces seeking peaceful resolution of the Southern African crisis. It took the callous attempt of South Africa to blow up American oil installations in Cabinda and to attack Botswana for Reagan to recall his ambassador. It took the deaths of almost 700 Africans, P. W. Botha's rejection of any but his own plans for political change, and the almost certain passage of relatively mild sanctions by the U.S. Congress for the president to issue an executive order applying even milder sanctions against South Africa. Nevertheless, on September 9, 1985, Reagan was forced to issue the following statement: "I, Ronald Reagan, President of the United States of America, find that the policies and actions of the Government of South Africa constitute an unusual and extraordinary threat to the foreign policy and economy of the United States and hereby declare a national emergency to deal with that threat."[29]

African Americans, using their political clout, were able to galvanize a process whose present activities may well bring majority rule in South Africa in the near future. Unfortunately, Reagan followed his announcement with remarks indicating that this order did not really represent his views and affirmed his support of the policy of constructive engagement by sending his ambassador back to Pretoria. An embarrassed White House staff and a saddened nation heard with disbelief the president's uninformed claim that Pretoria had abolished segregation and discrimination against blacks just as the United States had previously done. Whether it was cynicism or wisdom, Reagan did send Ambassador Edward Perkins as his representative to South Africa. This African American diplomat acquitted himself with distinction in that troubled land.

ENHANCING AFRICAN AMERICAN INFLUENCE IN FOREIGN POLICY

African Americans must support programs and create institutions or centers to enhance their ability to help the United States formulate and execute a successful policy. Institutions working in the foreign policy field (for example,

TransAfrica, Africare, and the Association of Black American Ambassadors) must be saluted and supported. It is also imperative that African American institutions of higher education assume a leadership position in the establishment of first-rate programs in foreign relations. African Americans, Asian Americans, and Latinos must attempt to make a difference, for they will comprise one of every three Americans by the year 2000.

As indicated above, the United States is uneasy in the context of multiple power centers and multiple competitors, but that is what tomorrow will be. African Americans have as yet not been fully involved in the debate about the position of this nation within the world system as many profound changes take place. While America's relative power might be decreasing as multipolar economic and political structures emerge, this country's power and impact will remain formidable and decisive in the affairs of this planet. The best recent example of this reality lay in the conduct and outcome of the Persian Gulf War in late 1990 and early 1991. The role played by blacks, from General Colin Powell to the 30 percent of all ground troops and 50 percent of all female troops, indicate that African Americans must and will play a meaningful role in America's future.

In preparing for the future, African Americans must accept axiomatically the reality of the cultural and linguistic diversity among the world's peoples. The assertion that to recognize the diversity of the world's populations means that the United States has lost power should be rejected; the United States can no longer force the world to be what it wants it to be. That was always an illusion. International affairs essentially involves dealing with foreigners, people with different cultural backgrounds and perceptions embodied in diverse languages and symbols. The cultures of people still largely provide them with necessary designs or models for living, indicating what is considered proper, or moral, or even sane; rules by which they relate to each other; a body of knowledge and tools by which they relate and adapt to their environments; and a veritable storehouse of knowledge, beliefs, and formulae through which they attempt to understand the universe and their place within it.[30]

The languages that people speak furnish their cognitive claim as to what is fact, or data, or reality, notions not readily available or easily explainable to outsiders who do not speak their languages.[31] If, as the history of the last two hundred years has shown, Americans have difficulties dealing with Westerners whose cultures have a common Judeo-Greco-Roman root and whose languages almost all stem from an Indo-European base, how much more difficult it is for Americans to deal with the peoples, cultures, and languages of Asia and Africa. Thus, there is not only the need to learn the cultures and languages but also the humanities and different historical backgrounds of other nations and peoples. Despite the arrogance or idiocy of Trevor Roper, Regis Professor of History at Oxford, who still believes that other peoples had no histories before the arrival of Europeans, this view is not challenged. But what is not challenged is the view of many non-Western peoples that their contact with the West was cata-

clysmic. Many firmly believe that having been conquered, colonized, or otherwise dominated by the West and by its successor-state, the United States, their
own development stopped or was impaired. Therefore, these people are deeply
disturbed by their economic dependence upon alien and remote powers that do
not appear to appreciate their problems. These people believe that there are
McLuan-like M factors (psychological features which treasure traditional life)
that cause them to remain underdeveloped. By knowing the histories of other
people, Americans would be better prepared to understand, if not always to accept, the views of other peoples.

African Americans also need a thorough grounding in the economics of international trade and development as well as the cultural-historical and technological factors that influence these issues. Multinational corporations, many of
which have sales that are larger than the GNP of all but the world's major powers, increasingly dominate this planet. Their statuses and their roles must be
understood. Even though the United States lost its position as the world's leading exporter in 1986, American corporations still earn 30 percent of their profits from international trade. American farmers depend upon foreign markets
for 40 percent of their income, and overseas credit contributes half of the combined incomes of this country's thirteen largest banks.

African Americans need to know how and why the United States shifted
from being the world's largest creditor to the world's largest debtor nation and
how to deal with this situation. Americans do have a *yen* for Japanese products,
and though Japan has replaced the United States as the largest provider of "foreign aid," (usually loans), it is important to know how to attempt to deal with
the increasing debt and development crises in the Third and Fourth Worlds.
Nixon and Kissinger rejected out of hand the Third World's proposal for a new
international economic order; and the Brandt Report's call for development
funds for the Third World was ignored. It is now, however, clear that economic problems are global. African Americans must be prepared to deal with
the difficult issues of protectionism, monetary stability and debt management,
and how to bring remaining communist and socialist countries into the global
economic system. This global economy will need to know how to distribute
the resources that should be available to all humankind: the mineral and fish resources of the sea, those from space, and so forth.

African Americans must clearly understand the processes that have enabled
this republic to survive for two hundred years and why some of its institutions
are still being borrowed by other nations. The political changes taking place in
Latin America, Asia, Africa, the Islands of the Sea, and Eastern Europe should
be studied carefully and not viewed simply as the result of imitating the United
States. American views about "human rights" are not shared by many of the
world's peoples. The United States will almost certainly object when in time
other nations attempt to impose certain universal rights on American society.
The United States did not sign the League of Nations treaty, and it only recently signed the treaty on genocide, which forbids nations to enact laws

whose purposes are to destroy ethnic groups or populations as took place in Nazi Germany. The United States government is also not convinced that one person, one vote is good for South Africa.

In summary, then, the time has come for African Americans to assert boldly that they have a perspective on foreign policy and international affairs that can help the United States deal with the problems of a new century that will affect the entire nation. Dr. W. E. B. DuBois prophesied at the end of the last century that the problem of the twentieth century was going to be the problem of the color line and the unequal relations between the darker and lighter peoples of this earth in Africa, Asia, America, and the Islands of the Seas. As weak and disenfranchised as blacks were then, DuBois was determined that they would help solve that problem. It is now clear that the problems of the twenty-first century will affect all of mankind, and that foreign policy is the key to dealing with them. African Americans have always attempted to help and have often pushed the United States to live up to ideals often only faintly glimpsed by its founders. More attention to, deeper understanding of, and greater participation in foreign policy-making on the part of African Americans should help the United States deal more effectively with all the world.

NOTES

1. Franklin Delano Roosevelt, cited in Henry W. Bragdon and Samuel P. McCutchen, *History of a Free People* (New York: Macmillan, 1967), 634.

2. U. S. Senate, *The War on Poverty: The Economic Equality Act of 1964*, 88th Cong. 2d sess., 1964, S. Rept. 2642.

3. James Laxer, *Decline of the Super-Powers* (New York: Paragon House, 1989), 9.

4. Ibid., 13.

5. Alvin Toffler and Heidi Toffler, "Grand Designs," *World Monitor*, October 1988, 48–50.

6. Ibid.

7. Winthrop D. Jordan, *White Over Black: American Attitudes Toward the Negro, 1550–1812* (Baltimore: Penguin Books, Inc., 1968), 260ff.

8. James Madison in *The Federalist*, no. 10 (New York: Modern Library, 1941), p. 55.

9. George Washington in Burton II Kaufman, ed., *Washington's Farewell Address: The View from the Twentieth Century* (Chicago: Quadrangle Books, 1969), p. 18.

10. Washington in Kaufman, *Washington's Farewell Address*, p. 18.

11. Quoted in Thomas A. Bailey, *Man in the Street: Impact of American Public Opinion on Foreign Policy* (New York: Macmillan, 1948), p. 16.

12. Quoted in Bailey, *Man in the Street*, p. 16.

13. Louis L. Gerson, "The Influence of Hyphenated Americans on U.S. Diplomacy," in *Ethnicity and U.S. Foreign Policy*, ed. Abdul Azez (New York: Praeger, 1981), 21ff.

14. Quoted in Stephen A. Garrett, "East European Ethnic Groups an American Foreign Policy," *Political Science Quarterly*, 93 (1978): 307.

15. George F. Kennan, *Memoirs, 1958-1963* (Boston: Little Brown, 1972), 286–87.

16.   Charles McC. Mathias, Jr., "Ethnic Groups and Foreign Policy," *Foreign Affairs* 59 (1981): 997; Jimmy Carter, whose presidency witnessed enormous pressures from America's ethnic groups to influence his foreign policy, complained in his farewell address: "We are increasingly drawn to single-issue groups and special interest organizations to ensure that whatever else happens, our own personal views and our own private interests are protected. This a disturbing factor in American political life." *Vital Speeches* 47 (February 1981): 226–28.

17.   Nathan Glazer and Daniel P. Moynihan, eds., *Ethnicity: Theory and Experience* (Cambridge, Mass.: Harvard University Press, 1975), 23–24.

18.   Gabriel A. Almond, *The American People and Foreign Policy* (New York: Harcourt & Brace and Co., 1950), 183.

19.   Quoted in Bailey, *Man in the Street*, 16.

20.   Louis Adamic, *Two-Way Passage* (New York: Harper & Row, 1941), 59–61.

21.   Ibid.

22.   Roger Morris, *Uncertain Greatness: Henry Kissinger and American Foreign Policy* (New York: Harper & Row, 1977), 23.

23.   Elliott P. Skinner, "Ethnicity and Race as Factors in American Foreign Policy," in *American Character and Foreign Policy*, edited by Michael P. Hamilton (Grand Rapids, Mich.: Wm. Eerdmans Publishing Co., 1986).

24.   Bailey, *Man in the Street*, 30.

25.   Ibid.

26.   Ibid.

27.   Study Commission on U. S. Policy Toward South Africa, *South Africa: Time Running Out* (Berkeley: University of California Press, 1981).

28.   See "Bush meets Tuto and vows to press Pretoria," *The New York Times*, May 19, 1989, p. A8.

29.   "Reagan Orders Sanctions on Pretoria," *The New York Times*, September 10, 1985, 1, 12.

30.   Edward B. Tylor, *Primitive Culture: Researches into the Development of Mythology, Philosophy, Religion, Languages, Art and Custom*, vol. 1 (New York: Morrow, 1889), 53; Margaret Mead, *New Lives for Old: Cultural Transformation-Manus* (New York: Morrow, 1956).

31.   The very discourse used by Westerners to "manage," and even to "produce" the non-West, culturally, politically, ideologically, and imaginatively has been the subject of criticism by Edward Said, *Orientalism* (New York: Pantheon Books, 1978), 3; Michel Foucault, *Power-Knowledge* (New York: Pantheon Books, 1980); Clifford Geertz, "Ritual and Social Change: A Japanese Example," *American Anthropologist* 59 (1957): 32–54; and Stephen A. Tyler, *Cognitive Anthropology* (New York: Holt, Rinehart, and Winston, 1969).

10

Toward the Future: What Is to Be Done?

Ralph C. Gomes and Linda Faye Williams

Black Americans have clearly made political progress in the United States, especially since 1965. This much each of the preceding chapters makes clear. Thus, chapter 1 points to the difficult two-century-long struggle for equal voting rights and the importance of its victory in securing the Voting Rights Act of 1965; chapter 2 analyzes the growing influence of black political organizations in mobilizing black voters; chapter 3 describes the election of an ever-increasing number of black officials; chapter 4 discusses the successful litigation strategy that lies behind many of these electoral victories; chapter 5 finds that black electoral success, albeit limited in helping the black poor, has been beneficial to creation of a black business, professional, and managerial class; chapter 6 posits that a consensus on civil rights (legal rights) is now in place and preservable even through conservative presidential administrations and strict constructionist courts; chapter 7 concludes that the consensus on civil rights has been a result of black participation in successful interest-oriented coalition politics; chapter 8 points out that blacks have tended to especially make progress when some of the rules of the game can be altered through redistricting; and chapter 9 discusses the long-term interest and growing influence of blacks not only in the domestic arena but in foreign policy making.

But just as each chapter has pointed to growing black political success, the emphasis has been, perhaps, more clearly focused on the limits of such progress. Thus, chapter 1 bemoans the continued low level of voter participation of blacks. The rapid gains in voter registration and turnout immediately after passage of the Voting Rights Act of 1965 have been replaced by a series of downturns to upturns to downturns in the last twenty-five years. Chapter 2 explains how the bewildering array of problems plaguing the black community has not allowed for the development of directly or solely black political organizations, but instead multi-issue organizations that perhaps are so diffuse in interests, aims, and goals that their influence is limited in any single sphere–including the political one. Chapter 3 describes the slower rate of progress of the election of blacks to public office in the 1980s compared to the 1970s. As blacks have filled many, if not most, of the offices in majority-black jurisdictions, they have found winning new positions difficult. Moreover, black elected officials still comprise fewer than two out of every one hundred officials in the United States.

Chapter 4 points out that many structural barriers, from at-large systems to gerrymandering to runoff primaries, still stymie black political candidates. The need to secure white votes in non-black-majority places may severely constrain successful black candidates from adequately representing blacks. Chapter 5 concludes that black electoral success has done little for the average black in the United States and even less for the poor black. As the number of black elected officials has grown, so too has the number and proportion of blacks in the so-called "underclass." Chapter 6 agrees that this is precisely the reality of the current situation. "Politics is *not* enough" to help the black poor. Indeed, this chapter indicates that there is a crisis in black political leadership—a leadership more and more committed to routine politics when it knows more fundamental changes are necessary to improve the social and economic status of the vast majority of blacks. Chapter 7 posits that class-based coalition-style politics is most likely the answer to going beyond this conundrum, but indicates that the more and more narrow constrictions of the two major parties are not addressing class- or even populist-style politics. So far, coalition politics remains exceptionally unstable, given that whether interest group or electoral coalitions, the only allies blacks have found are relatively affluent, upwardly mobile, generally younger whites who have the propensity to desert the coalition the more it is about economic justice. Poor and working-class whites, the natural allies of blacks, still are mystified by racial stereotypes rather than conscious of class realities.

Chapter 8 discusses how the round of redistricting in the 1990s presents some potential pitfalls for blacks. As long as whites (of any class) refuse to vote for blacks, the breakdown of segregation in housing ironically diffuses the black vote and thereby the chances of black political candidates. Finally, chapter 9 points out that blacks continue to be viewed as nonactors in foreign policy-making. They might carry out the policy on foreign soils whether as strategic leaders such as General Colin Powell or as soldiers, like a massive number and proportion of American troops in the Persian Gulf, but on the critical issue of war or peace, they are not serious players as decision makers.

Thus, black politics finds itself at a crossroads. After centuries of struggling for the vote, after making the vote almost a fetish in believing that it would not only be a symbol and reality of strictly "political" justice, but also a tool for social and economic redress, after believing that the election of black representatives would be everything required for blacks to gain political self-confidence and legislative policy influence, after thinking that black electoral success would mean the promotion of black representatives as spokespersons for equality, government intervention on behalf of the poor, and black "role-model" development, after promoting black electoral success to become a judicially manageable standard to enforce the Voting Rights Act, the only serious result of these actions has been the greatest bifurcation of the black population experienced in American history.

To be sure, the black middle class has benefited from "black politics" as currently defined and practiced. The greater voter participation of blacks has resulted in the greater election of blacks. The greater election of blacks has benefited the black middle class through minority business contracting, affirmative action in especially local government leading to the greater employment of skilled, professional, and managerial blacks, the inclusion of such middle-class blacks on commissions and committees, the appointment of such blacks to local, state, and federal office, and so forth. But while black electoral success produced black middle-class beneficiaries and might have romanticized black elected officials as empowerment role models for all blacks and legitimated the ideology "equality of opportunity," it has neither mobilized the black community nor realized the community-based reforms voter participation once promised. The position of disadvantaged socioeconomic conditions for poor blacks and social isolation of black voters has not visibly been altered.

What, then, can be done to increase the level of black voter participation, build more successful black political organizations, remove barriers to black representation and rapidly increase the election of black candidates of blacks' choice to public office, improve the outcomes for the black poor, and increase black influence in not only the domestic but foreign policy sphere?

Each of the authors of the preceding chapters were asked to provide answers to these questions. The recommendations that follow are drawn from their combined responses.[1]

RECOMMENDATIONS

In general, African Americans must not lose sight of the persistent influence of class exploitation, racism, and sexism in the nation's political economy. Class exploitation and racism are highly intertwined. Yet, an ironic development from the success of the Civil Rights Movement has been that while few of any race or ethnicity in the United States are proud to admit openly that, *in principle,* they are racially biased, many openly and without any shame admit that this or that act of discrimination is based on class "differences" or discrimination. The problem with such declarations is that (1) discrimination and exploitation on the basis of class is also a hideous basis in a country that has historically denied being a class-based society; and (2) blacks are disproportionately in the bottom class of this society and disproportionately out of the ruling class of this society—meaning that class-based exploitation and oppression is not only wrong in and of itself but also impacts most unfavorably upon blacks and other racial minorities. In short, the distinction that this or that act of discrimination is based on class rather than race often turns out to be "a distinction without a difference." Thus, the recommendations that follow begin with the need for political education about the nature of the American political economy per se.

Political Education

For the masses of black Americans, the following activities are recommended:

Black organizations from the NAACP and TransAfrica should develop educational and training programs geared toward grassroots organizations, high school students, community colleges, universities, women's organizations, and so forth in order to promote awareness of a full range of participatory activities (organizing, letter writing campaigns, lobbying, and so forth). Political education should be provided by these organizations on a steady basis, not just around elections. Political education should include a focus not only on narrowly defined political issues but about how the political economy is actually structured and works.

To provide information, a network for disseminating information about issues, policies, and political candidates should be developed. For example, a black political organization should produce and disseminate a monthly (at the very least) journal or magazine devoted to reporting on developments in the policy arena that have the potential of disproportionately affecting racial/linguistic minorities or the working class in general. Events and developments (especially successful ones) at the local levels should also be highlights of the journal because much that is innovative in solving problems is often first initiated in local and state contexts. Overall, a top-down strategy should be avoided; instead, a grass-roots decentralized leadership strategy (albeit guided by a national headquarter's ability to place developments in a national context) should be pursued. Regarding the journal, at least quarterly surveys should be taken to see whether it is meeting the needs of individuals and group partners. Changes should be instituted whenever coalition partners' views of the journal are justifiably unfavorable.

Black institutions of higher education should create excellent programs for the study of politics, including foreign affairs. These programs, centers, or institutes should provide multidisciplinary education in foreign policy and international affairs in particular with emphasis in the social sciences, humanities, foreign languages, and with options for studying the natural sciences and mastering technical skills. In addition to regular courses, such a facility should provide interdisciplinary seminars using specific case histories of international issues. Where possible, these should be conducted in foreign languages. Arrangements should be made to secure internships for students both in the private and public arenas of international affairs so that they could gain "hands on" experiences. The goal of this education should not only be to prepare its graduates for further academic or professional study and to pursue careers in the public and private dimensions of international affairs, but to foster a commitment to improving the lot of human beings and preserving the planet.

But not only the masses need education—so, too, do elected officials. To encourage or produce more and better African American candidates and candidates that are in general more knowledgeable about progressive policy directions, a candidates and elected officials school (similar to Harvard's Kennedy School of Government in organization, but different in policy prescriptions) should be established in a historically African American university.

Voting Rights

Despite limited gains in voting rights, as already indicated, much remains to be done. State registration procedures should be reformed to promote remedying continuing barriers, and national legislative proposals to remove restrictions and encourage uniformity and nondiscrimination should be supported.[2]

At-large election systems (since empirical studies demonstrate their potential for diluting the impact of minority voters) should be continuously opposed. Similarly, runoff requirements, since dual primaries tend also to dilute the impact of minority voters, should be opposed.

Moreover, alternatives to the single-member district electoral system must be explored. The single-member district system that prevails across the country rather automatically insures minority disadvantage as long as whites refuse or are reluctant to vote for black candidates. Not only should there be a focus on providing blacks a few single-member electoral districts in which they are a majority, but the bigger goal should be to challenge majority rule where it does not protect minorities. Blacks elected from single-member districts may enjoy minority legislative presence but not influence. Representing a geographically important but socially isolated constituency in a racially polarized environment, black representatives have little control over the policy choices made by majority white single-member district representatives. Thus, blacks need to encourage restructuring the electoral and legislative processes of representation based on a model of proportionate interest representation for self-identified communities of interest. By changing both the way representatives are elected and the rules under which legislative decisions are made, a model of proportionate interest representation would minimize the disadvantage in a majoritarian system of black voters' and black officeholders' minority members. This transformation would take blacks beyond electoral ratification to anchoring a broader theory of political empowerment, incorporating concepts of community-based representation, participation, and responsiveness.

Indeed, proportionate interest representation would pursue and integrate the twin elements of the Voting Rights Act definition of political equality: the right to (1) participate equally in the political process and (2) elect representatives of choice. Proportionate interest representation would thus more closely approximate the original civil rights movement goal of legislative accountability to black political interests.[3]

Other methods, such as limited voting, in which voters have fewer votes than the full slate of offices to be filled, cumulative voting, in which voters rank their preferences and top choice votes are transferred to lower ranked candidates once their first choices have received enough votes to get elected, should be explored.

In general, there must be a greater emphasis on accountable representation. The exclusive focus on election-day aspects of political control is incomplete. Whether an official is black, white, or other, they must be held to the standard of producing on their campaign promises.

Redistricting

The most immediate arena of political action is likely to be the battle over redistricting. How the nation is redistricted will play an important role in political configurations for at least a decade. The first demonstration of this product will be the 1992 elections—including that year's presidential contest. Thus, redistricting in the 1990s generates several recommendations. These recommendations include: first, supporting efforts, including lawsuits, to reduce the size of the census undercount, since population figures provide the necessary first step of redistricting; second, building a national coordinated effort to protect the existing majority black congressional and state and local legislative districts, particularly those that have lost population since 1980 or are substantially under 1990 population districting norms; and increasing the number of majority black districts where possible and where this action will not weaken minority influence in electing those (regardless of race) sympathetic to the interests of the black poor.

While there must be concern for what happens at the congressional level, gains in state legislative redistricting are especially important because state legislative redistricting provides more opportunities. Wherever necessary and possible, blacks and their allies must be prepared to use the Voting Rights Act to overturn reapportionment and redistricting plans designed to dilute the impact of the minority vote.

An additional aim must be to approach the redistricting process with the goal of making viable coalitions with other minority groups and progressive whites. A "divide and conquer" strategy must be avoided in redistricting in the 1990s.

Building Coalitions

In the process of joining coalitions in the 1990s redistricting process *and* beyond, the following activities are prescribed:

1. Join coalitions only with partners who agree to pursue common and clearly articulated goals. Develop strategies on the basis of these well-understood goals. Thus, the decision to coalesce should be based on a concrete analysis of whether the alliance will advance the long-term goals of the coalition rather than some temporary gain for the coalition.

2. Continue to seek winning coalitions for black candidates. On an ongoing basis, target groups (for example, other minorities and progressive whites of any class) more likely to support black candidates. Such allies, however, should be committed to helping the least fortunate among racial/linguistic minorities.

3. Encourage those with influence among poor whites to raise their consciousness regarding class interests. Issue-oriented coalitions rather than particular candidate-centered coalitions should be the goal. Issue-based coalitions should then choose to support a particular candidate because of the candidate's agreement with the coalition's positions. Such a coalition would antedate the politician's campaign and would be expected to outlive the candidacy—win or lose.

4. A high level of internal organization that uses all of the resources of the coalition must be established. Resources include money, numbers of participants, the climate of the larger environment, third party reference groups such as the media, governmental authorities, philanthropic foundations, and level of internal organization.

5. A political action committee (PAC) must be fully funded and as much as possible generate financial resources indigenous to groups in the coalition. From the start, agreements on the distribution of the payoff (benefits) received by coalition partners when obtaining the goals should be reached. Clearly, there must be give and take. Members of other racial and ethnic groups in the coalition who run for public office must be supported fully. Specific policy concerns of coalition partners, for example, bilingual education, immigration policy, and so forth must be part of the coalition's thrust. The coalition should include those leaders of various targeted groups who can influence their own constituencies.

6. The coalition should not rely on simply one strategy. Rather than endless debates about whether more can be achieved through economic boycotts, black capitalism, protest, legal strategies, or electoral politics within and without the two-party system, it should be understood that methods should be pursued in a well-organized, concerted effort. As for the two-party system, itself, there should constantly be kept in mind the ideological conclusion, "No permanent allies, only permanent interests." Thus, whichever party—Democrats or Republicans—pursues more closely ideological, interest, and issue positions that best represent those blacks not benefiting from the status quo, that party should be supported. Advice to split the black vote just to have some members

in each of the parties should be ignored. The lessons of supporting Woodrow Wilson in 1916 just to have some blacks in the Democratic party demonstrate the silliness of such a position. (Wilson's administration established Jim Crow on a more substantial foundation.) The major party that offers blacks more should be the one supported. When both parties closely approximate each other in issue stances, blacks have little or nothing to lose by pursuing a third party formation. At best, the third party would succeed, become a major party capable of winning elections (such as the present-day Republican party once did); at worst, items on the third party's progressive agenda that became popular would be coopted by one of the major parties. More likely than either of these two results, the third party supported by blacks would provide one of the most important contributions of third parties in American history—that is, the popularization of progressive legislation. For example, child labor laws, the minimum wage, and social security-like proposals—to name only three of many progressive policies—all got their start as third party programs. Finally, a progressive third party would provide the opportunity to teach and learn organizational skills, raise the consciousness of African Americans, and secure resources for the long struggle for social and economic justice that lies ahead.

7. In addition, cooperation between groups and strategies, not competition, must be the heart of the winning coalition. In cooperation, compromise in coalitions, like long-term and short-term planning, is an unavoidable reality.

International Arena

Blacks should endeavor to form coalitions not only for productive use in the domestic but also the international arena. Blacks and those they ally with must seek to play wider international roles in policy toward Africa, the black diaspora, and in major areas of traditional and emerging U.S. foreign policy concerns such as United States–Central European relations, United States–Middle East relations, and United States–Japan relations.

Blacks must struggle to halt the use of black ambassadors by the United States government as a substitute for effective, fair U.S. policies toward small, predominantly non-European populated, poor countries. Blacks need to effectively demand that black ambassadors should be assigned throughout the entire range of United States' postings.

The Free South Africa Movement (FSAM) example should be followed as a guide to building black American influence in the foreign policy arena. FSAM suggests a coalition strategy, and an inside (elected officials)-outside (protest) set of strategies.

CONCLUSION

By the turn of the century, blacks and other non-European-heritage Americans will compose one-third of the nation. Somewhere near the mid-twenty-first century, these groups are projected to become a majority of the nation's population. The term "minority," with its implication of a certain delegitimacy in a majoritarian system, will finally be extinct.

So far the "people of color" of the United States have not only experienced worse treatment but held more grievances against the American system, its structure, and process. No nation (at least without exceptionally massive repression) has survived for long with a majority of its people turned against it. No nation has survived with a majority of its people questioning its principles, legitimacy, and current activities. Hence, meeting the challenge of a non-European-dominated population base is ever and ever the challenge of the United States. The genuine viability of its Constitution, the genuine ability of the nation to incorporate nonwhite peoples, the genuine quest of those committed to the poor regardless of race are all items on the U.S. agenda that will be challenged, questioned, and tested in the next century.

Blacks, as a group, have made tremendous progress during the twentieth century, but the progress has been uneven. Middle-class blacks have benefited; working-class blacks have stagnated; poor blacks have deteriorated. Whether working class and poor blacks *and* other poor and working-class Americans in general can make progress in the American system as currently structured is the question of the next century. The problem of the twenty-first century is the problem of the *class* line. As long as blacks are disproportionately in the bottom classes, this class line remains also a color line. The central question of American politics is whether the system established by the founding fathers of the United States is even half as viable to meet the challenges of the "class line" as it was in the last decade of the "color line." With important and detrimental vestiges of the color line remaining not only influential but powerful after more than two hundred years of concerted struggle, it should be clear that the class struggle will not find easy going in the twenty-first century United States. It will be far, far more trying and full of potential for disparagement.

The most important development that the black experience in American politics demonstrates so far is that a people deprived will ultimately seek to right the wrongs, just the injustice, and fight as long as necessary to turn over the defeats.

Even limited African American victories only encourage blacks, other minorities, the poor in general, and all those who do not benefit from the status quo that change is possible; change should be struggled for; and ultimately change will be won.

NOTES

1. The recommendations that follow also owe a debt to Henry Richardson, professor of law at Temple Unversity; Ronald Walters, chairman of the Political Science Department at Howard University; Richard Hatcher, former mayor of Gary, Indiana; and Lani Guinier, professor of law at the University of Pennsylvania, among others.

2. On current voter registration restrictions and their impact, see Frances Fox Piven and Richard Cloward, *Why Americans Don't Vote* (New York: Pantheon Books, 1988).

3. Lani Guinier, "A Re-evaluation of Black Electoral Success Theory," unpublished paper, October 22, 1990, 10–11.

Selected Bibliography

Alkalimat, Abdul, and Doug Gills. "Chicago Black Power vs. Racism: Harold Washington Becomes Mayor." In *The New Black Vote*, edited by Rod Bush. San Francisco: Synthesis Publications, 1984.

Allen, Robert. *Reluctant Reformers*. Washington, D.C.: Howard University Press, 1983.

Almond, Gabriel A. *The American People and Foreign Policy*. New York: Harcourt & Brace and Co., 1950.

Axelrod, Robert. "Where the Votes Come From: An Analysis of Electoral Coalitions." *American Political Science Review* 66 (1972): 11-20.

Bailar, Barbara A. "A Method for the Correction of the Undercount of the United States Census." *Journal of the American Statistical Association* 83 (March 1988): 150-64.

Bailey, Thomas A. *Man in The Street: Impact of American Public Opinion on Foreign Policy*. New York: MacMillan, 1948.

Banfield, Edward, and James Q. Wilson. *City Politics*. New York: Vantage Press, 1963.

Banzhaf, J.F., III. "One Man, 3,312 Votes: A Mathematical Analysis of the Electoral College." *Villanova Law Review* 13 (1968): 304-32.

Barker, Lucius J., and Ronald W. Walters, eds. *Jesse Jackson's 1984 Presidential Campaign: Challenge and Change in American Politics*. Urbana: University of Illinois Press, 1988.

Barnes, Fred. "Invent A Negro, Inc." *The New Republic*, April 15, 1985, 9-10.

Bartley, Nunan V., and Hugh D. Graham. *Southern Politics and the Second Reconstruction*. Baltimore: John Hopkins University Press, 1975.

Bass, Jack, and Walter DeVries. *The Transformation of Southern Politics: Social Change and Political Consequence Since 1945*. New York: Basic Books, 1976.

Bell, Derrick. *Race, Racism and American Law*. Boston: Little Brown, 1980.

Berlin, Ira. *Slaves Without Masters: The Free Negro in the Antebellum South*. New York: Pantheon Books, 1974.

Berry, Mary Frances, and John W. Blassingame. *Long Memory: The Black Experience in America.* New York: Oxford University Press, 1982.

Bishop, C. F. *History of Elections in the American Colonies.* New York: Burt Franklin, 1893.

Black, Earl, and Merle Black. *Politics and Society in the South.* Cambridge, Mass.: Harvard University Press, 1987.

Black Elected Officials: National Roster. Washington, D.C.: Joint Center for Political Studies, 1989.

Brackett, Jeffrey R. *The Negro in Maryland: A Study of the Institution of Slavery.* New York: Negro Universities Press, a division of Greenwood Publishing, 1969 (originally published by John Hopkins Press, 1889).

Brown, Cynthia Stokes. *Ready from Within: Septima Clark and the Civil Rights Movement.* Navarro, Calif.: Wild Trees Press, 1986.

Brown, Elsa Barkley. "Womanist Consciousness: Maggie Lena Walker and the Independent Order of Saint Luke." *Signs: Journal of Women in Culture and Society* 14 (1989): 921-29.

Browne, Eric C. *Coalition Theories: A Logical and Empirical Critique.* Beverly Hills, Calif.: Sage, 1971.

Browning, Rufus, Dale Marshall, and David Tabb. *Protest Is Not Enough.* Berkeley: University of California Press, 1984.

Burk, Richard. *The Eisenhower Administration and Black Civil Rights.* Knoxville: University of Tennessee, 1985.

Carson, Claybourne. *In Struggle: SNCC and the Black Awakening of the 1960s.* Cambridge, Mass.: Harvard University Press, 1981.

Cavanagh, Thomas, ed. *Strategies for Mobilizing Black Voters: Four Case Studies.* Washington, D.C.: Joint Center for Political Studies, 1987.

Chute, Marchette. *The First Liberty.* New York: E.F. Dutton, 1969.

Cole, Leonard. "Electing Blacks to Municipal Office." *Urban Affairs Quarterly* 10 (September 1974): 17-35.

Cooper, Mathew. "A National Dividing, The Return of Segregation." *U.S. News and World Report,* November 6, 1989, 24.

Cruse, Harold. "Behind the Black Power Slogan." In *Rebellion or Revolution.* New York: William Morrow, 1988.

_____. *Plural but Equal: Blacks and Minorities in America's Plural Society.* New York: William Morrow, 1987.

Davidson, Chandler, ed. *Minority Vote Dilution.* Washington, D.C.: Howard University Press, 1984.

DeSwann, Abram. "Coalition Theory and Multi-Party Systems." In *Coalition Formation,* edited by H. A. M. Wilke. New York: Harcourt, 1985, 229-61.

Donovan, John. *The Politics of Poverty.* New York: Pegasus, 1967.

Duncan, Phil. "Creating Black Districts May Segregate Voters." *Congressional Quarterly Weekly* (July 28, 1990): 2462.

Farnam, Henry W. *Chapters in the History of Social Legislation in the United States to 1860.* Washington, D.C.: Carnegie Institute of Washington, 1938.

Feagin, Joel. "A Slavery Unwilling to Die." *Journal of Black Studies* 18 (1988): 451-69.

Fishel, Leslie, Jr. "Northern Prejudice and Negro Suffrage, 1865-1870." *The Journal of Negro History* 39 (1954): 12-15.

Flacks, Richard. "Who Protests: The Social Bases of the Student Movement." In *Protest: Student Activism in America,* edited by Julian Foster and Durward Long. New York: William Morrow, 1970, 137.

Foner, Philip S. *History of Black Americans: From the Emergence of the Cotton Kingdom to the Eve of the Compromise of 1850.* Westport, Conn.: Greenwood Press, 1983.

Franklin, John Hope. *From Slavery to Freedom.* New York: Alfred A. Knopf, Inc., 1974.

Gerson, Louis L. "The Influence of Hyphenated Americans on U.S. Diplomacy." In *Ethnicity and U.S. Foreign Policy,* edited by Abdul Azez Said. New York: Praeger, 1981.

Glazer, Nathan, and Daniel P. Moynihan, eds. *Ethnicity: Theory and Experience.* Cambridge, Mass.: Harvard University Press, 1975, 23-24.

Gomes, Ralph, Walda Fishman, Jerome Scott, and Robert Newby. "The Politics of Race and Class in City Hall: Race Politics and the Class Question." In *Research in Urban Sociology,* edited by Jerry Lembcke and Ray Hutchins. Greenwich, Conn.: JAI Press, Inc., 1989.

Gottschall, Jon. "Carter's Judicial Appointments: The Influence of Affirmative Action and Merit Selection on Voting on the U.S. Court of Appeals." *Judicature* 67 (1983): 165-73.

Gray, William. "Leadership in the Legislative Process." *Urban League Review* 9 (1985): 105.

Green, Charles, and Basil Wilson. *The Struggle for Black Empowerment in New York City: Beyond the Politics of Pigmentation.* New York: Praeger, 1989, 41.

Greenstein, Robert, and S. Barancik. *Drifting Apart.* Washington, D.C.: Center on Budget and Policy Priorities, 1990.

Grieder, William. *Secrets of the Temple: How the Federal Reserve Runs the Country.* New York: Simon and Schuster, 1987, 75–76.

Hamilton, Charles. *The Black Political Experience in America.* New York: Capricorn Books, 1973.

———. "Full Employment as a Viable Issue." In *When the Marching Stopped: An Analysis of Black Issues in the 70s,* edited by Hanes Walton. New York: National Urban League, 1973, 90-91.

Hanks, Lawrence T. *The Struggle for Black Political Empowerment in Three Georgia Counties.* Knoxville: University of Tennessee Press, 1987.

Harlan, Louis. *Booker T. Washington: The Making of a Black Leader, 1865-1910.* New York: Oxford, 1972.

Harris, John. *Registration of Voters in the United States.* Washington, D.C.: Brookings Institution, 1929.

Harvey, James. *Black Civil Rights During the Kennedy Administration.* Jackson: College and University Press of Mississippi, 1973.

Hill, Paul. *A Theory of Political Coalitions in Simple and Policymaking Situations.* Beverly Hills, Calif.: Sage, 1973.

Holden, Matthew, Jr. *The Politics of the Black "Nation."* New York: Chandler, 1973.

Jacob, Paul, and Timothy G. O'Rourke. "The Legal Basis of District Elections." *Journal of Law and Politics* (Fall 1986): 295–353.

Jaynes, Gerald, and R. Williams, Jr. *A Common Destiny: Blacks and American Society.* Washington, D.C.: National Academy of Sciences, 1985, 187.

Jordan, Winthrop. *White Over Black: American Attitudes Toward the Negro, 1550-1812.* Chapel Hill: University of North Carolina Press, 1968.

Kelley, E. W. "Techniques of Studying Coalition Formation." *Midwest Journal of Political Science* 12 (February 1968): 62-84.

Kellog, Charles. *NAACP—A History of the National Association for the Advancement of Colored People.* Baltimore: John Hopkins, 1957.

King, Martin Luther. "Where Do We Go From Here?" In *A Testament of Hope: The Essential Writings of Martin Luther King, Jr.,* edited by James Washington. New York: Harper and Row, 1986.

Kleppner, Paul. "Partisanship and Ethno Religious Conflict: The Third Electoral System, 1853-1892." *The Evolution of American Electoral Systems.* Westport, Conn.: Greenwood Press, 1981, 59.

Kluger, Richard. *Simple Justice: History of Brown v. Board of Education and Black America's Struggle for Racial Equality.* New York: Random House, 1975.

Lawson, Stephen R. *In Pursuit of Power: Southern Blacks and Electoral Politics, 1965-1982.* New York: Columbia University Press, 1985.

Mann, Irwin, and L. S. Shapley. "The 'A priori' Voting Strength of the Electoral College." In *Game Theory and Related Approaches to Social Behavior,* edited by Martin Shubik. New York: John Wiley and Sons, 1964, 151-64.

McAdams, Douglas. *Political Process and the Development of Black Insurgency, 1930-1970.* Chicago: University of Chicago Press, 1982.

McDonald, Laughlin. "The Quiet Revolution in Minority Voting Rights." *Vanderbilt Law Review* 42 (May 1989): 1249-97.

McKinley, Albert. *The Suffrage Franchise in the Thirteen English Colonies.* New York: Burt Franklin, 1905.

Mead, Margaret. *New Lives for Old: Cultural Transformation-Manus.* New York: Morrow, 1956.

Morris, Aldon. *The Origins of the Civil Rights Movement: Black Communities Organizing for Change.* New York: The Free Press, 1984.

Morris, Lorenzo, Charles Jarmon, and Arnold Taylor, eds. *The Social and Political Implications of the Jesse Jackson Presidential Campaign.* New York: Praeger, 1990.

Morris, Roger. *Uncertain Greatness: Henry Kissinger and American Foreign Policy.* New York: Harper & Row, 1977.

Noble, Jeanne. *Beautiful Also Are the Souls of My Black Sisters: A History of Black Women in America.* Edgewood Cliffs, N.J.: Prentice-Hall, 1978.

Norton, Eleanor Holmes. "The Role of Black Presidential Appointees." *Urban League Review* 9 (1985): 108-09.

O'Rourke, Timothy. "The Constitutionality of Electoral Reform." *University of Richmond Law Review* 17 (1989): 60-89.

Parker, Frank. *Black Votes Count: Political Empowerment in Mississippi After 1965.* Chapel Hill: University of North Carolina Press, 1990.

———. "Racial Gerrymandering and Legislative Reapportionment." In *Minority Vote Dilution,* edited by Chandler Davidson. Washington, D.C.: Howard University Press, 1989.

Phillips, Kevin. *The Politics of the Rich and the Poor: Wealth and the American Electorate in the Reagan Aftermath.* New York: Random House, 1990.

Pinderhughes, Dianne M. "Legal Strategies for Voting Rights: Political Science and the Law." *Howard Law Journal* 28, no. 1 (1985).

Piven, Frances F., and Richard A. Cloward. *Poor People's Movements: Why They Succeed, How They Fail.* New York: Pantheon, 1977.

———. *Why Americans Don't Vote.* New York: Pantheon, 1988.

Quarles, Benjamin. *The Negro in the Making of America.* New York: MacMillan, 1964.

Reed, Adolph L. *The Jesse Jackson Phenomenon: The Crisis of Purpose in Afro-American Politics.* New Haven, Conn.: Yale University Press, 1986.

Rice, Bradley. *Progressive Cities: The Commission Movement in America.* Austin: University of Texas Press, 1979.

Russ, William. "The Negro and White Disfranchisement During Radical Reconstruction." *The Journal of Negro History,* 19 (1934): 175.

Salisbury, Robert. "Political Movements in American Politics: An Essay on Concept and Analysis." *National Political Science Review* 1 (1989): 15-30.

Schmidt, William E. "New Age of Gerrymandering: Political Magic by Computer?" *The New York Times,* January 10, 1989, 1, 14.

Schwarz, Bernard. *Behind Bakke: Affirmative Action and the Supreme Court.* New York: New York University Press, 1988: 75-76.

Severn, Bill. *The Right to Vote.* New York: Ives Washburn, Inc., 1972, 6.

Sherif, Muzafer, O. J. Harvey, B. Jack White, William R. Wood, and Carolyn W. Sherif. *The Robbers Cave Experiment: Intergroup Conflict and Cooperation.* Middletown, Conn.: Wesleyan University Press, 1988.

Skinner, Elliott, R. "Ethnicity and Race as Factors in American Foreign Policy." In *American Character and Foreign Policy,* edited by Michael P. Hamilton, Grand Rapids, Mich.: Wm. Eerdmans Publishing Co., 1986.

Smith, Robert. "Black Appointed Officials: A Neglected Category of Political Participation Research." *Journal of Black Studies* 14 (1984): 369-88.

———. "Black Power and the Transformation from Protest to Politics." *Political Science Quarterly* 96 (1981): 431-43.

Taylor, Theodore. *The States and Their Indian Citizens.* Washington, D.C.: United States Government Printing Office, 1972.

Thernstrom, Abigail. *Whose Votes Count? Affirmative Action and Minority Voting Rights.* Cambridge, Mass.: Harvard University Press, 1987.

Thompson, Mildred. *Ida B. Wells-Barnett: An Exploratory Study of an American Black Woman, 1893-1934.* Brooklyn, N.Y.: Carlson Publishing, Inc., 1990.

Tushnet, Mark. *The NAACP's Legal Strategy Against Segregated Education, 1925-50.* Chapel Hill: University of North Carolina Press, 1987.

Walker, Thomas, and Deborah Barrow. "The Diversification of the Federal Bench: Policy and Process Ramifications." *Journal of Politics* 47 (1985): 596-616.

Walters, Ronald. "The Challenge of Black Leadership: An Analysis of the Problem of Strategy Shift." *Urban League Review* 4 (1981): 85-86.

Weiss, Nancy, J. *Farewell to the Party of Lincoln: Black Politics in the Age of FDR.* Princeton, N.J.: Princeton University Press, 1983.

Welch, Susan, and Timothy Bledsoe. *Urban Reform and Its Consequences: A Study in Representation.* Chicago: University of Chicago Press, 1988.

Wesley, Charles. "Negro Suffrage in the Period of Constitution-Making, 1787-1865." *The Journal of Negro History* 32 (April 1947): 143.

_____. "The Participation of Negroes in Anti-Slavery Parties." *The Journal of Negro History* 24, no. 1 (January 1944): 140-61.

Williams, Linda Faye, ed. *Congressional District Factbook: 1988*. Washington, D.C.: Joint Center for Political Studies, 1988, 41.

_____. *Focus* (June 1989): 4.

_____. "White Black Perceptions of the Electability of Black Political Candidates." *National Political Science Review* 2 (1990): 45-64.

Wolk, Alan. *The Presidency and Black Civil Rights: Eisenhower to Nixon*. East Brunswick, N.J.: Fairleigh Dickerson, 1971.

Wood, Forest. "On Revising Reconstruction History: Negro Suffrage, White Disfranchisement, and Common Sense." *The Journal of Negro History* 51 (1966): 99.

Woodson, Carter G. *The History of the Negro Church*. Washington, D.C.: The Associated Publishers, 1921.

_____. *The Negro in Our History*. New York: Associated Publishers, 1945.

Index

About the Contributors

THERESA CHAMBLISS, formerly a research analyst and the roster project director at the Joint Center for Political Studies, currently works as an analyst for the National Conference of Black State Legislators.

WALDA KATZ FISHMAN, Ph.D., is graduate associate professor and graduate program director of sociology at Howard University and was formerly editor of the *Humanity and Society* journal. Her most recent publications focus on race, class, and politics in the United States.

RALPH C. GOMES, Ph.D., has taught at a variety of universities, including Pennsylvania State University and Howard University. His most recent publications focus on race and class in the American political economy, the black family, and Caribbean political economy.

WALTER HILL, Ph.D., specializes in quantitative analysis of politics and has published in the areas of international politics, redistricting, and the public opinion of black college students. He is an assistant professor of political science at St. Mary's College in Maryland.

SONIA R. JARVIS worked for the National Council on Foundations. Currently, she is executive director of the National Coalition for Black Voter Participation (NCBVP), which grew out of Operation Big Vote and is an umbrella organization for more than 100 local black voter registration drives.

FRANK R. PARKER directs the Voting Rights Project of the Lawyers Committee for Civil Rights Under Law in Washington, D.C. He is one of the foremost voting rights litigators in the nation and is the author of *Black Votes Count* (a study of the impact of the Voting Rights Act in Mississippi). His articles in books such as *Minority Vote Dilution* have been cited in several Supreme Court decisions.

NELSON PEERY is chairman of the Central Committee of the Communist Labor Party and on-going contributor to the *People's Tribune*. He has a long history in the labor movement and was instrumental in establishing the Detroit Revolutionary Union Movement (DRUM) in the late 1960s. He is chief author of the monograph *The Negro National Colonial Question*.

DIANNE M. PINDERHUGHES, Ph.D., has taught at a variety of universities, including Dartmouth and Howard. Currently, she is Associate Professor of Political Science at the University of Illinois—Champaign-Urbana. She has published in the areas of black politics and urban politics and is the author of *Race and Ethnicity in Chicago Politics: A Reexamination of Pluralist Theory*.

JEROME SCOTT is a community organizer of Project South in Atlanta, Georgia. He is a long-time community activist and has published articles in *Humanity and Society* and contributed to several books on race, class, and politics.

ELLIOTT SKINNER, Ph.D., has taught at a wide variety of universities and is currently Franz Boas Professor of Anthropology at Columbia. He has published twelve books and many articles.

ROBERT C. SMITH, Ph.D., has published extensively in the areas of black politics, race and law, and urban politics. He has taught at a variety of universities, including the State University of New York (SUNY) at Purchase and Howard University. Currently, he is Professor of Political Science at San Francisco State University. He is the author of *Race, Class and Public Opinion*.

LINDA FAYE WILLIAMS, Ph.D., has taught at a number of universities, including Cornell, Howard, and Brandeis. Former Associate Director of Research at the Joint Center for Political Studies, she is currently Appleman Fellow at the Joan Shorenstein Barone Center at the John F. Kennedy School of Government of Harvard University. Her most recent articles focus on race, press and politics, black politics, urban politics, public opinion, and women in politics.